CRANMER
& THE REFORMATION
UNDER EDWARD VI

Der Puritanismus ist nichts anderes als der Versuch,
die Ideen und Praxis der schweizer Reformatoren auf
englischen Boden zu verpflanzen.

> MÖRIKOFER, *Geschichte der evangelischen
> Flüchtlinge in der Schweiz.*

Satisfacit piis *Eduardi Reformatio.* Melior haec est
multum Confess. August.

> *Heinrich Bullinger to Jan Utenhove,* Zurich,
> Aug. 24, 1559. (GERDES, *Scrinium Anti-*
> *quarium,* IV. 1. ii. L.)

CRANMER
& THE REFORMATION
UNDER EDWARD VI

BY

C. H. SMYTH

FELLOW OF CORPUS CHRISTI COLLEGE
CAMBRIDGE

THE THIRLWALL AND
GLADSTONE PRIZE ESSAY
FOR 1925

GREENWOOD PRESS, PUBLISHERS
WESTPORT, CONNECTICUT

Originally published in 1926
by Cambridge University Press

Reprinted from an original copy in the collections
of the University of Illinois Library

First Greenwood Reprinting 1970

Library of Congress Catalogue Card Number 75-100842

SBN 8371-4025-0

Printed in the United States of America

To

A. G. GRUNDY & G. B. SMITH

MASTERS AT REPTON SCHOOL

'Et ego in Arcadia vixi'

PREFACE

For purposes of publication, I have had to compress this Essay to less than half its original length. I cannot deny that it has gained rather than lost by abridgment: on the other hand, I have had to summarise many documents which I should have preferred to quote at length, and to put forward many conjectures and deductions with only the slightest indication of the evidence on which they are based. Under the circumstances, I feel that it would be unmannerly to remark the points on which I differ from the acknowledged authorities, except in a few cases.

What I have written clings very closely to documentary evidence, especially in the form of correspondence, some of it unpublished. In order to avoid an unmanageable profusion of footnotes, I have thought it best to indicate in this place the principal sources. First in importance are the *Epistolae Tigurinae*, or Zurich Letters (*Original Letters relative to the English Reformation, 1531–58*), published by the Parker Society (1846–8): though it must be admitted that the translation is not very satisfactory, that several of the letters are misdated, and that the transcript is occasionally at fault. Hardly less important are the manuscripts in the Simler Collection in the Stadtbibliothek at Zurich which the Parker Society did not publish. This collection consists of 200 massive folio volumes of manuscript copies of 18,000 original letters made by John Jacob Simler (a descendant of the Swiss historian Josias Simler), superintendent of schools in the Canton of Zurich, who died in 1788. Of these, 140 volumes are occupied by letters of the period 1530–1600, each volume covering six months. Other important sources are: the *Loci Communes D. P. M. Vermilii* (1583: English translation by A. Marten, *The Common Places of Peter Martyr*, of the same year): Bucer's *Scripta Anglicana* (1577), which contains disappointingly little correspondence: Gabbema's *Epistolarum ab Illustribus & Claris Viris scriptarum Centuriae Tres* (1663): Gerdes' *Scrinium Antiquarium* (1749–65): *Joannis a Lasco Opera tam edita quam inedita*, ed. A. Kuyper (1866): *Ecclesiae Londino-Bataviae Archivum*, tom. II. (1889), ed. J. H. Hessels: *Rogeri Aschami Epistolarum libri quatuor* (1703): the Collections of Strype and Burnet: Gorham's *Reformation Gleanings* (1857): *The Zurich Letters* (Parker Society, 1842, 1845: 2nd edtn, 1846): *The Remains and Letters of Archbishop Cranmer* (Parker Soc. 1846: based on Jenkyns' edition of 1833): Tytler's *England under the reigns of Edward VI and Mary* (1839): Ellis' *Original Letters illustrative of English History*, vol. II. (2nd edtn, 1825): and the *Calendar of State Papers (Domestic Series)*, 1547–80, ed. R. Lemon (1856). Some of Utenhove's correspondence is published at the end of Pijper's *Jan Utenhove: zijn Leven en zijne Werken* (1883), and Parker's correspondence with Gardiner concerning a tragedy acted in Christ's College in Lamb's *Collection of Letters, Statutes, and other documents, from the MS. Library of Corpus Christi College, Cambridge* (1838: also published, with modernised spelling, in Parker's *Correspondence*, Parker Soc. 1853). Individual letters are to be found elsewhere: two letters by Cheke (to Bucer, May 11, 1550: to Parker, March 9, 1551) in *The Gospel according*

to *Saint Matthew, translated by Sir John Cheke,* ed. J.
Goodwin (1843): the Latin original of Cranmer's letter to
Bucer, December 2, 1550, in Pocock's *Troubles connected
with the Prayer Book of* 1549 (Camden Soc. 1884):
Cranmer's letter to the Lords of the Council, October 7,
1552, in Lorimer's *John Knox and the Church of England*
(1875), or in Tomlinson's *The Prayer Book, Articles and
Homilies* (1897): a letter from the Duke of Northumberland
to the Council, April 26, 1552, in Haynes' *Collection of
State Papers at Hatfield House* (1740): a letter from Martyr
to Bullinger, June 14, 1552, in Goode's *An unpublished
Letter of Peter Martyr* (pamphlet, 1850), or in Bradford's
Writings, vol. ii. (Parker Soc. 1853): and a letter from
Protector Somerset to Calvin, April 7, 1551, in Baron de
Schickler's *Églises du Refuge en Angleterre,* tom. iii. (1892).
I am aware of the existence of other sources, but lacked
either the time or the opportunity to explore them.

It is only since this book was in proof that I have been
able to procure a copy of a work of which I could wish to
have availed myself in writing this essay: Mr A. E. Harvey's
Martin Bucer in England (*Inaugural-Dissertation zur
Erlangung der Doktorwürde der Hohen Philosophischen
Fakultät der Universität Marburg*), published at Marburg
in 1906. Quite apart from its value as a survey of Bucer's
work in England, this thesis also contains, in an Appendix,
copies of the following letters: Fagius to his wife, July 22,
1549; Bucer to his wife, Aug. 1549; Bucer to Ulrich Geiger
(Chelius), [Aug. 1549]; Bucer to the Princess Elisabeth,
Aug. 27, 1549 (clearly on behalf of Ascham: see p. 160);
Bucer to Dr Johann Echt, May 13, 1550 (partially translated by Gorham, *R.G.,* pp. 145–6); Bucer to Cheke,

Aug. 29, 1550; Bucer's letter on the Demolition of Altars, [Nov.–Dec. 1550], (summarised and quoted by Gasquet and Bishop, p. 267 *note*: translated by Gorham, *R.G.*, pp. 209–12); Bucer to the Marquis of Dorset, Dec. 26, 1550; William Bill to Bucer, Nov. 5, 1550 (extracts); Bucer to Bill, Nov. 17, 1550; Bucer to Edward VI, Oct. 21, 1550, enclosing a copy of the *De Regno Christi*: and also the text of Bucer's will, drawn up at Strassburg, Jan. 23, 1548, with a codicil dated Cambridge, Feb. 22, 1551. Mr Harvey also gives a very useful Bibliography, and a valuable list of the letters referred to in the text.

Finally, I wish to express my gratitude to Professor J. P. Whitney, of Emmanuel College, to Professor W. R. Sorley and to Mr W. F. Reddaway, of King's College, to Mr Will Spens and to the Rev. Sir Edwyn Hoskyns, of my own College, and to the Rev. Dr H. J. Wilkins, for many valuable suggestions; to my father, for advice on medical questions; and to Dr B. Hirtzel, of the Stadtbibliothek at Zurich, and Mr A. I. Ellis, of the British Museum Library, for their very courteous assistance.

I desire it to be understood that throughout this Essay I have used the words 'Papist,' 'Puritan,' and 'Protestant' in no derogatory or offensive sense, but merely for convenience.

C.H.S.

1926

CONTENTS

CHAPTER ONE

INTRODUCTION

Deinde comperit satis S.M.T. quot &
quantorum malorum causam dederit,
quòd non praemissa sufficienti doctrina,
facto et edictis tantùm populis tuis
extorti sunt falsi cultus, & impietatis
erepta instrumenta, veraeque religionis
administratio ex imperio iniuncta.

BUCER, *De Regno Christi*, II. v.

M. Morgan.... For this proposition,
which we haue in hand, is doubtfull,
wherein it is said; *This is my bodie.* For
hereof some do gather transubstantiation; others, a bodilie presence with the
bread; others impanation, whereby the
bodie of Christ and the bread doo ioine
together into one person: others appoint
a bare signe, and others an effectuall
signe.

*Disputation on the Eucharist held at
Oxford*, May 28–June 1, 1549.
(*The Common Places of Peter Martyr*,
pp. 210 *b*–211 *a*.)

CHAPTER ONE

INTRODUCTION

THE most striking, indeed almost an unique feature of the Reformation under Edward VI, is the portentous fact that it was not governed by considerations of foreign policy. The considerations that determined its course were primarily social and domestic.

This was certainly unusual in sixteenth-century Europe: but in England it was the more remarkable, for few religious movements have been more influenced by the exigencies of foreign policy than the Reformation under Henry VIII and under Elizabeth, or the Counter-Reformation under Mary. The best explanation of the policy of Henry VIII and of Elizabeth is that both, while Catholics at heart, found it impossible to continue anti-papal without taking help from foreign Protestants. The key to the reign of Mary is the Spanish Match: which is also, by reaction, the key to the reign of Elizabeth. But England under Edward VI was curiously withdrawn from the whirlpool of foreign politics: it lay for six years in a diplomatic backwater. Even under Protector Somerset foreign policy was of secondary importance: under Northumberland its influence was negligible. The editor of the *Acts of the Privy Council* has noted the absence of the usual memoranda from the Council Book: 'There is little mention of foreign relations in the period between the final fall of Somerset and the accession of Mary': and there was much truth in the peroration of Bale's Epistle Dedicatory to the young King, prefixed to his edition of *The Laboryouse Journey of Iohan Leylande*:

Salomon is commended of Jesus the sonne of Syrach, Eccle. xlvij. for that the Lorde had hym replenyshed wyth all wysdome, and for hys sake had dryuen the enemyes awaye farre of, that he myghte buylde an howse in hys name, and prepare vnto hym a sanctuary for euer, whych al to this daye we behold in youre kyngelye persone fulfylled, prayeng vnto God that it may so styl endure.

But the building of that Temple was entrusted to fraudulent contractors, men more eager to pull down the old fabric and use its stones for their own princely mansions than to erect a new one to the glory of God. The progress of the Reformation in England was no longer subordinated to the commodity of an alliance with the Lutheran princes, nor yet subordinated to the necessity of a counter-offensive against Spain: but it was subordinated to the ambitions of the New Nobility for their own financial aggrandisement. The tragedy of the Edwardine Reformation is that these men found a certain section of the Reformers sufficiently bigoted to play blindly into their hands.

One thing made this subordination possible: the fact that the English Reformation in the first half of this century was not in any sense a popular movement. England was not even predominantly Protestant under Edward VI. Outside London and the two Universities the Reformation made very little headway, except in Kent and Essex, where, under alien influences, it progressed at such a violent pace that the death of Edward VI left the whole country seething with Anabaptists, Arians, Marcionists, Davigeorgians, heretics and sectaries of every description. It may be a comforting reflection for a Roman Catholic that at least two-thirds of the martyrs who were burnt by Queen Mary would almost undoubtedly, had Edward VI survived, have been burnt in the normal course by the Church of England. Joan Bocher—commonly known as Joan of Kent—had been the first, she would not have been the only victim. It is particularly noticeable that most of the martyrs under Mary came from the eastern counties: and although, unfortunately, Fox (for the purposes of his great monument of invective) and the other Protestant martyrologists were more concerned with the sufferings

than with the opinions of the martyrs, there are strong
grounds for Crosby's presumption[1] that most of the
victims belonged to those extreme sects of Protestantism
against whom the Church of England showed the same
relentless, uncompromising opposition as the Church of
Rome. The trouble was local, but the fear of it was
universal. Münster was the Moscow of the period: the
propaganda, the adherents of Anabaptism were suspected
to be everywhere: Barnes even at the stake was careful to
clear himself from the charge of being an Anabaptist:
Bale, under happier circumstances, found it necessary to
repudiate them equally clearly—'The very name of thē is
so odious to yᵉ faithfull yᵗ they thinke their bokes unworthy to be had among christē mē'[2]: while Calvin's first
letter to Somerset (Oct. 22, 1548) opened with a solemn
exhortation to restrain all seditious Anabaptists—and
Papists—with the sword. The suggestion was practical,
for the persistence of these extremists gravely endangered
the whole Protestant cause: the odium incurred by these
'men of fierce and barbarous tempers' who 'denied almost
all the principles of the Christian doctrine'[3] was inevitably
reflected upon the more moderate supporters of the
Reformation.

This was particularly true of the remoter districts of
the north, west, and south of England, where Protestantism
as yet had hardly penetrated. The Reformation under
Henry VIII had been purely destructive. That, on the
whole, was popular. The shaking-off of the Pope's

---

[1] *The History of the English Baptists, from the Reformation to the
Beginning of the Reign of King George I*, by Tho. Crosby (1738);
p. 63; cf. p. 59.

[2] *A bryefe and plaine declaracion of certayne sentēces in this litle
boke folowing* [i.e. *A brife and faythfull declaration of the true fayth of
Christ*], *to satisfie the consciences of them that haue iudged me therby to
be a fauourer of the Anabaptistes* (1547).

[3] Burnet (ed. Pocock), II. 202.

imperium meant the abolition of his taxes: and in an age when England was still regarded as 'the milch-cow of the Papacy,' '*regnum sacrosanctae Romanae ecclesiae specialiter devotum*'[1], it was with a good grace that Parliament hurried through the Acts of Annates (1532, 1534) and the abolition of Peter's Pence (1534). The Dissolution of the monasteries was not unjustified: certainly it evoked no national protest. That the reports of the Commissioners were exaggerated and distortive no one denies: they were men who knew what was required of them. But it would appear that most of their charges were exaggerations and not inventions[2]. Dr Creighton has noted that the great epidemic of morbus Gallicus (syphilis) at the beginning of the century was used as one of the strongest arguments for Suppression[3]: and the obscene prayer of *Infidelity* in Bishop Bale's *Comedy concernyng thre lawes* indicates, no doubt, a great deal of the popular hostility to the monks, wherever it existed:

Post cantionem, *Infidelitas* alta voce dicet. *Oremus.*
Omnipotens sempiterne Deus, qui ad imaginem & similitudinem nostram formasti laicos, da quaesumus, ut sicut eorum sudoribus vivimus, ita eorum uxoribus, filiabus & domicellis perpetuo frui mereamur. Per dominum nostrum Papam.

But beyond the expulsion of the Pope and the expulsion of the monks neither the King nor the country had any wish to go. There were no popular risings against the Six Articles of 1539, as there had been against Crumwell's Injunctions and the Ten Articles of 1536, and as there were to be against the English Prayer Book of 1549. The country as a whole remained loyal to the old faith, the

[1] Matthew Paris.
[2] This was less true of the north of England. Mr J. S. Fletcher's *The Reformation in Northern England* (1925), though in other respects not very useful, makes this point very well.
[3] *A History of Epidemics in Britain*, I. 414–15, 421.

clergy as a whole still preached the old doctrine: the only fundamental change that had occurred was the submission of the clergy to the Supplication against the Ordinaries (May 1532), confirmed (November 1534) by the Act of Supremacy: by it the governance of the Church of England, *potestas ordinis* as well as *potestas jurisdictionis*, was transferred from the Pope to the King, this time without even the reservation, 'so far as the law of Christ allows.' This change was fundamental: for if it did not introduce, at least it firmly imprinted the principle of erastianism upon the minds of the educated and the half-educated of that generation: erastianism was as much an orthodoxy in the sixteenth century as evolution was in the nineteenth, and its practical consequences are far more clearly evident. But England remained Catholic, though no longer Roman Catholic: that was the sum of the Henrican Reformation: beyond that point it would be impossible to go without arousing popular resistance[1]. In the end it was not Protestantism that converted England from Catholicism, but the Spanish Match.

The Edwardine Reformation was a dangerous and an unpopular experiment. 'I do not yet see,' wrote John à Lasco to Dryander (Sept. 21, 1548), 'what I can promise

[1] 'As to true religion, nowhere in the world is idolatry in greater strength: our king has destroyed the Pope, but not popery; he has expelled all the monks and nuns, he has pulled down their monasteries, he has ordered all their goods to be transferred into his treasury; yet they themselves are bound by the king's command to perpetual chastity, even the frail sex of women: England has at least ten thousand nuns, not one of whom is allowed to marry. The impious mass, the most shameful celibacy of the clergy, invocation of saints, auricular confession, superstitious abstinence from meats, purgatory, were never held in greater esteem by the people, than at this time.' (*Hooper to Bullinger*, Jan. 26, 1546.)—'What helpyth the deposyng of the pety membres of the Pope, and to leaue his whole body behynd...? Surely it helpyth as moch as to say, I wyl go kyll all the foxes in .S. Iohans Wodde, because I would haue no more foxes bred in all England!' (*The Complaynt of Roderyck Mors*, p. 55.)

myself about the restoration of the Church here.' 'The disturbance of the kingdom,' wrote Bucer to Dryander (Oct. 11, 1549), 'was certainly very grave, but it is reported, thank God, that everything is quiet again. *Satan rages and we provoke his fury by not plainly and purely receiving the kingdom of Christ.*' This idea occurs very frequently in contemporary letters and sermons of the Reformers, and in such pamphlets as Bishop Ponet's *A shorte Treatise of politike pouuer*, Becon's *Supplicacyon to the Quenes maiestie*, and Goodman's *How svperior powers oght to be obeyd of their subiects*, written during the Marian Counter-Reformation. These allegations of popular hostility to the Protestant cause can be checked, not only by the history of the reign of King Edward, but also by the evidence of the risings in the reign of Queen Mary. Admitted that the ignominious failure of Northumberland's rebellion is no evidence of the weakness of Protestantism in England, it is yet highly significant that the motive of Lord Thomas Stafford's insurrection in 1557 was purely political—his proclamation '*exciting the English to deliver themselves from the Spaniards*' is given in Strype's *Memorials*—while Sir Thomas Wyat, in 1554, whether or not the Queen and the Council were right in their opinion 'that the matter of the mariage seemed to bee but as a Spanish cloak to couer their pretensed purpose against our religion,' equally 'determined to speake no worde of religion, but to make the colour of hys commotion, only to withstande straungers, and to aduaunce libertie.'

...There came to hym [Wyat] one...of good wealthe, saiyng: 'Syr,' quod he, 'they saye I loue potage well, I wyll sell all my spones, and al the plate in my house, rather than your purpose shall quayle, and suppe my potage with my mouthe. I truste,' quod he, 'you wyll restore the ryght religion agayne.' 'Whiste,' quod Wyat, 'you maye not so much as name religion, for that wil withdraw from vs the heartes of manye: you must only make your quarel for ouerrunninge by straungers. And yet to thee be it sayd in counsell, as vnto my frende, we minde only the restitution of God's word.'

Whether this last were true or not—and certainly that understanding brought Wyat a great measure of Protestant support—the fact that it could not be openly proclaimed is a strong testimony to the failure of the Edwardine Reformation. John Proctor, the contemporary chronicler of the rebellion, clearly states that 'the restoring or continuaunce of the new and newelye forged religion' was not a cause 'apte to further hys wycked purpose, being not a case so general as to allure al sortes to take part with him'[1].

In effect, then, the work of the Edwardine Reformation was—except, of course, in individual cases—entirely superficial. It was a State-made Reformation. Throughout, the clergy were supported by political patronage or hampered by political control. The people submitted, in general, from deference to Tudor despotism, and England was called a Protestant country: but it remained profoundly Catholic.

> Ses évêques bénissent l'eau
> Et conduisent les païens au baptistère.
> S'il en est un qui contredise Charles,
> Il le fait pendre, ou brûler, ou occire.
> On en baptise plus de cent mille
> Qui deviennent vrais chrétiens.

Between the writing of the *Chanson de Roland* and the work of Reformation in the sixteenth century, the difference in time was greater than the difference in manners. And even the verdict of the Thirty Years' War, pronounced a century later in Westphalia, was still *cujus regio, ejus religio*—though with a recommendation to mercy.

[1] John Proctor's *History of Wyat's Rebellion: with the order and manner of resisting the same* is reprinted in *Tudor Tracts* (1532–1588), ed. A. F. Pollard (a revised edition of part of Arber's *English Garner*).

But this fact—that the Reformation under Edward VI was a State-made Reformation—was, in a double manner, the cause of its utter failure. 'Here things are as yet in a very feeble state,' wrote Bucer to Brentius (May 15, 1550). '...The work is carried on for the most part by edicts, which the majority obey very grudgingly.' Sweeping doctrinal changes cannot be carried through by a series of royal proclamations. This Cæsaro-Papalism was the fatal heritage of Henry VIII: fatal, that is, in the hands of men who did not appreciate the people's will as wisely as the deceased Defender of the Faith. That the Reformation should be identified with the Government, a fact dangerous at any time, was at this time disastrous, because the Government was singularly unpopular. So was the Reformation: and the unpopularity of each increased the unpopularity of the other. The Government was now, in the mind of the people, identified with the New Nobility, men who had carved ministerial estates out of the monastic lands, and were already stretching out greedy hands towards the episcopal and collegiate[1] revenues. Somerset was to their minds the one honourable exception, but they hated his Calvinist opinions, while his desecration of various City churches and churchyards for the building of Somerset House made him unpopular in London. It was probably for this reason that they let him fall without striking a blow to save him. But when the cloak of Counter-Reformation was torn off from the intrigue that had displaced him, and Warwick appeared as lord of the event, the legend of Somerset's democratic sympathies spread rapidly: and after his execution he was everywhere compared with Humphrey, the good Duke of Gloucester. No doubt, had he been a Catholic instead of a Calvinist, miracles would have been wrought at his tomb, as at Duke

[1] Lamb's *Documents*, pp. 59–60: 'Matthew Parker,' by Dr E. C. Pearce, in *Theology* (July 1925), p. 35.

Humphrey's. Now all this increased the popular hatred against Warwick and his associates: and, because Warwick, with a view to his own profit, favoured the extreme Zwinglian or puritan party in the Reformed Church of England, the Reformation, as it fell increasingly into the hands of the puritans, became increasingly detested.

The second fatal consequence was the shortage of reforming clergy. The Upper House of Convocation was half sincerely erastian, half intractably and outspokenly papist: the Lower House was outwardly submissive, but inwardly sullen and disloyal. Outside Convocation were Protestants indeed, but fanatical extremists, more dangerous to the Reformation by their impassioned advocacy than the old clergy by their tacit resistance. It was against these almost as much as against the Papists that the frequent inhibitions of preaching were directed. Thus at this crisis in our Church history the leaders of the Reformation, and especially the leaders of the moderate party, had few ministers whom they could trust. 'The harvest is plenteous, but the labourers are very few' is a phrase that recurs frequently in the letters of the foreign Reformers in England to their friends abroad. 'It is fallow ground here, such as the devastation of antichrist is wont to leave,' wrote Bucer to Hardenberg (Aug. 14, 1549): 'for, as in Italy, very few sermons have been preached here, nor are they frequent yet, nor is there [any] catechising. For the parish priests are for the most part neither learned nor zealous for the kingdom of Christ.' (Of the truth of this observation, the record of Bishop Hooper's Visitation of the Diocese of Gloucester, 1551–2, affords melancholy but conclusive evidence[1].)

---

[1] See 'Bishop Hooper's Visitation of Gloucester,' by James Gairdner (*English Historical Review*, 1904, XIX. 98–121). Of 311 clergy examined, 171 were unable to repeat the Ten Commandments, 31 of that number being further unable to tell in what part of the Bible they were to be

'There is much that we have already effected in this business of religion,' wrote Martyr to Gualter (June 1, 1550), 'but up to the present little or nothing, believe me, has been completed. The pertinacity of [our] opponents is very great, and of those who are either able or willing to instruct the people, how small is the supply; nor can an inconvenience of this sort be remedied by aid from foreigners, inasmuch as they are ignorant of the English language. There is no lack of preachers in London, but throughout the whole kingdom they are very rare....The sheep of the divine pasture, the sheep of God's hand, the sheep redeemed by the blood of Christ, are defrauded of their proper nourishment of the divine word; and certainly, unless the people be taught, the change of religion will avail them little.'

What could be done to remedy the shortage was immediately set in hand. Shortly after their arrival in England, Bucer and Fagius, writing to the Ministers of Strassburg (April 26, 1549), noted that 'they have numerous and liberal scholarships for students of theology: for which reason also very many apply themselves from youth to sacred learning.' But such a remedy must inevitably be slow of operation. Before this new supply of pastors was available, the Counter-Reformation under Mary had already begun. 'While I taught in that countrie,' wrote Peter Martyr (from Strassburg, Nov. 3, 1553), 'there were verie manie learners of the holie scriptures, and verie toward scholers in Diuinitie, whose haruest was welneere ripe, whom now against their willes I see either miserablie wandering in uncertaine habitations, or else most unhappilie subuerted if they tarie.'

Moreover the attitude of the nobles added another difficulty. 'It may perhaps seem strange,' wrote Burnet (II. 44–5), 'that the earl of Hertford had six good prebends promised him; two of these being afterwards converted

found: 10 were unable to repeat the Lord's Prayer, 30 did not know where to find it, and 27 could not tell who was its author.

into a deanery and a treasurership. But it was ordinary at the time. The lord Cromwell had been dean of Wells; and many other secular men had these ecclesiastical benefices without cure conferred upon them.' They were not all, moreover, benefices without cure that were used for the enrichment of the New Nobility. 'Roderyck Mors,' in the xiiij. Chapter of his *Complaynt*, treats thus '*Of lordes that are parsons and vicars*':

...Your pretence of putting down abbeys was to amēd that was amysse in them. It was far amys, that a gret part of the lādes of the abbeys (which were geuyn to bring vp lernyd men, that myght be preachers afterward, to kepe hospitalyte, & to gyue almesse to the poore) shuld be spent vpon a fewe supersticyos monkes, which gaue not .xl. pownd in almesse, whan thei shuld haue geuen .ij. hundreth. It was amysse, that the monkes shuld haue personages in their handys, and deale but the .xx. part therof to the poore, & preached but ones in a yere to them that payd the tythes of the personages. It was amysse, that thei scarsely among .xx. set not one sufficyent vicare to preach for the tythes that thei receyued. But see now how it that was amysse is amended, for all the goodly pretense. It is amended, euen as the deuel mēdyd his damys legg (as it is in the prouerbe): whan he shuld haue set it right, he bracke it quyte in pecys! The monkes gave to lytle almesse, and set vnable parsons many tymes in their benyfyces. But now, where .xx. pownd was geuen yearly to the poore, in moo than an .C. places in Ingland, is not one meales meate geuen. This is a fayre amendmēt. Where thei had alweys one or other vicar, that eyther preached or hyred some to preach; now is there no vicar at all, but the fermer is vicar and person all to gether, and onely an old cast away monke or fryre, which can scarsely say his mattens, is hyred for .xx. or .xxx. shillings, meat and drinck; yea, in some place, for meate and drinck alone withowt any wages.

I knowe, and not I alone, but .xx.M. moo knowe, more than .v.C. vycarages and personages, thus well and gospelly serued,

after the newe gospel of Ingland....My lord personys, howe
can ye defend yourselvys, if a man shuld bring this argument
agaynst you, and proue you all theuys, that haue personages
and vycarages in your handes and cannot preach?...Wherfor
gyue ouer your personages to learned men, & enter not in to
other mennys vocacyōs, to robbe the ministers both of their
office & of their liuyng, that ye be not punisshed of God. But
yf ye will nedys be parsons and vicars styll, and haue all the
profightes of the personages, and will haue all, euen to the
tythe eg of a pore woman that hath but .ij. hennys, ye must
haue the paynes that belong to such parsons as yow be....Loke
well vpon this matter, and byld thy conscyence vpon Godds
word[1].

But the greatest obstacle to the progress of the Reformation lay in the stubborn passive resistance of the old
parish priests who continued to hold their livings, and
who, though outwardly submissive, yet remained at heart
loyal to the old faith which they had formerly taught, and
disloyal to the new faith which they now professed[2].
'All the sacred [offices],' wrote Bucer to Hooper (Nov.
1550), 'are so frigidly, slovenly and mumblingly recited by
several Pseudo-parish-priests or vicars, that they are as
well understood by the people as if they were recited in
the Punic [i.e. African] or Indian tongue....The Lord's

---

[1] 'For as yet sacrilegious persons hold and plunder the chief
parishes, and often one, four, or six, or more: and it is said that there
are not a few who bestow two or three benefices on their Stewards
or Huntsmen, yet on condition that they themselves retain a good
part of the ecclesiastical revenues; and they present to livings vicars,
not whom they know to be best fitted for this office, but whom they
can hire most cheaply.' (*Bucer to Hooper*, [Nov. 4,] 1550.)
[2] '"Out with them," said Latimer to the King, "I require it in
God's behalf. Make them *quondams*, all the pack of them."' (Strype,
Mem. III. 319.) He suggested that the King's chaplains should be put
in their livings: 'and in case they were not enough to fill all the
vacancies,' he wished the many 'laymen well learned in the Scripture,
and of a virtuous and godly conversation...to be placed in the
Church.

Supper is in very many places celebrated as the Mass, from which indeed the people do not know that it differs, beyond that the vernacular tongue is used[1]. There is no proper care for Christ's sheep: the more ignorant are not instructed in the Catechism.' Again, Bucer's *De Regno Christi* indicates how little effective had been the Royal Visitation of 1549:

Others turn the prescribed form of the sacred [offices] altogether into a popish abuse: since the sacrificers, although they recite the sacred [words] of Christ in the vernacular tongue, yet take pains to recite them so indistinctly and so confusingly that they cannot be understood: and entirely prevent the common people from understanding or hearing them.

And not a few of the sacrificers exhibit Christ's holy communion as the popish Mass, nor are the common people present with any other intention. Hence in several places, just as they used to celebrate three Masses a day, so they celebrate three communions: and they distinguish them by the names of Saints and of the mother of the Lord, calling them the Mass of St. Nicholas, of the Blessed Virgin, or of other Saints: and hardly anyone receives the sacraments from the Lord's table, except the sacrificer alone, or the verger, and he unwillingly. But by such horrid mockeries of the religion of Christ, the wrath of God is very gravely provoked.... [2]

Open rebellion, in whatever form, was easier to deal with than that incessant, stubborn, covert resistance. The Council Book contains not infrequent mention of priests imprisoned for speaking 'lewd [i.e. disloyal] words,' and there is one case of a priest arrested for spreading seditious pamphlets: moreover in most of the rebellions during this

[1] 'And lest popery should perish: the mass-priests, although they are compelled to give up the Latin idiom, yet most diligently observe the same tone and chants, to which they were accustomed hitherto under the papacy.' (*Hooper to Bullinger*, Dec. 27, 1549.)

[2] *De Regno Christi*, II. v. Cf. Bucer's letter to Hooper on the Vestiarian Controversy, [Nov. 4], 1550.

reign, priests were implicated. In the summer of 1549, for example, after the suppression of the rising in Oxfordshire, Fagius wrote to Ulstetter (Aug. 15), 'About two hundred popish priests, the originators of all the disturbances, have been killed, besides those who here and there have been hanged.'

The greatest Traitors and rebells that godly Kinge Edwarde had in the weste partes / were priests / and such as had subscribed to the booke [of Common Prayer] or what so euer bylawe was then in force / but for all their subscribings / there was no skirmishe / where some off those subscribers left not their karkaises in the filde againste god and their prince. Plumtree and his fellowe priests off the northe / I dowte not but they were conformable and applyable to all orders and neuer staggered at subscriptions. But for all that / time tried their traiterous hartes[1].

Such overt treason the State was always able to repress: but covert treachery to the Church was far more difficult to detect and punish. Those who practised this most effective form of sabotage must for the most part have done so (like the Puritans of the next generation) from the highest motives and with no consciousness of the dishonesty of their position. Against them the discipline of the Church, which royal policy had robbed of much of its force and the internal divisions of Protestantism of its direction, proved generally unavailing.

In the internal divisions of Protestantism and in the union of its opponents lay the fatal weakness of the Reformation party during this period, in England as on the Continent. But those divisions were not yet so sharp, nor that unity so solid, as they shortly became: in 1548, when the foreign Reformers began to arrive in England,

---

[1] *A Brieff discours off the troubles begonne at Franckford in Germany Anno Domini* 1554. *Abowte the Booke off off* [sic] *common prayer and Ceremonies*. [By William Whittingham?] (1575), p. cxcv.

it would have been impossible to foresee the *débâcle* of Protestantism in 1618: a reconciliation was still possible with all but the Anabaptists and the extreme sectaries, whom every one agreed in regarding as outside the pale of Christian charity. Bucer, the 'dear *politicus* and *fanaticus* of union,' had failed, it is true, to effect this reconciliation, and wore himself out in the attempt: but his failure did not necessarily mean that reconciliation was impossible, while the Council of Trent made it imperative. So Cranmer saw, and strove to call a Protestant General Council, which should arrive at an 'unanimity of godly doctrine': but he was baffled by the reluctance of Melanchthon, as Bucer had been by the pig-headed obstinacy of Luther.

It was, naturally, the Sacramental Controversy upon which the Protestants most bitterly disagreed. 'It is truly grievous,' wrote Cranmer to Melanchthon (March 27, 1552), 'that the sacrament of unity is by the malice of the devil made food for disagreement, and like $\mu\hat{\eta}\lambda o\nu$ $\check{\epsilon}\rho\iota\delta o\varsigma$ [an apple of contention].' Yet it was inevitable. Hallam, in an unimaginative moment, thought the importance attached to what he regarded as a matter of comparative indifference was quite excessive, since 'no errors on this point could have had any influence on men's moral conduct, nor indeed much upon the general nature of their faith'[1]: but only his own generation could accept that view. Orthodoxy—right judgment—upon the significance of the mystery of Communion was, indeed, a fundamental. In England under Edward VI the Sacramental Controversy never actually came to a crisis: the only clearly marked division that then obtained was the broad line of demarcation between those who rejected transubstantiation and those who retained it. But the two outstanding controversies of the reign were symptomatic of the subdivisions

[1] *Constitutional History of England* (7th edtn, 1854), ι. 88.

that existed, though unproclaimed as yet, within the Protestant camp. The first was the controversy upon vestments, that controversy which has since recurred at irregular but frequent intervals in the history of the Established Church, like an ancestral ghost prophesying disaster: the second was the controversy upon kneeling at Communion. The battle-ground was, in each case, a question of external observance: but far more fundamental conceptions were at stake, and for that reason the ground was stubbornly contested. For the underlying struggle was between those who maintained the Real Presence in the Eucharist, and those who maintained the Real Absence.

The various sacramental doctrines current at this period fall naturally into four main groups: the Roman doctrine of Transubstantiation, the Lutheran doctrine of Consubstantiation, the Sacramentarianism of Zwingli and the Swiss theologians, and the Suvermerian (or Bucerian) doctrine of the Strassburg School.

The Roman doctrine of Transubstantiation is comparatively simple. It is based on the Scholastic distinction between the *substance*, or imperceptible essential nature of every material object, and its *accidents*, or sensible qualities (as shape, touch, appearance, taste, and so forth). Transubstantiation implies a mutation of substance, but not of accidents: for at the moment of consecration the accidents of the bread and wine remain unaltered, but their substances are changed into those of the body and blood of Christ. Thus this doctrine contains nothing repugnant to the evidence of our senses, since substance is imperceptible: but similarly the senses can afford no evidence of its truth, and therefore to accept it is an act of faith. In fact, the ultimate condition of acceptance or rejection must consist in individual prejudice for or against the implications of this doctrine.

It is hardly necessary to add that the above summary refers to the doctrine as properly taught and not as commonly received in the pre-Reformation period.

A passage from Cranmer's *Avnsvver vnto a craftie and Sophisticall cauillation*[1] may make this exposition clearer:

First, the papists say, that in the supper of the Lord, after the words of consecration (as they call it), there is none other substance remaining, but the substance of Christ's flesh and blood, so that there remaineth neither bread to be eaten, nor wine to be drunken. And although there be the colour of bread and wine, the savour, the smell, the bigness, the fashion, and all other (as they call them) accidents, or qualities and quantities of bread and wine, yet, say they, there is no very bread nor wine, but they be turned into the flesh and blood of Christ. And this conversion they call 'transubstantiation,' that is to say, 'turning of one substance into another substance.' And although all the accidents, both of the bread and wine, remain still, yet, say they, the same accidents be in no manner of thing, but hang alone in the air, without anything to stay them upon....And so there remaineth whiteness, but nothing is white: there remaineth colours, but nothing is coloured therewith: there remaineth roundness, but nothing is round: and there is bigness, and yet nothing is big: there is sweetness, without any sweet thing; softness, without any soft thing: breaking, without anything broken: division, without anything divided: and so other qualities and quantities, without anything to receive them. And this doctrine they teach as a necessary article of our faith.

But it is not the doctrine of Christ, but the subtle invention of antichrist, first decreed by Innocent the third, and after more at large set forth by school [i.e. Scholastic] authors, whose study was ever to defend and set abroad to the world all such matters as the bishop of Rome had once decreed....

The principal objection to this theory, as Cranmer indicated, lay in this hypothetical separation of substance

---

[1] I. *Cranmer* [Parker Society], p. 45.

from accidents: for how could the accidents of a material object exist apart from its substance? And it was further objected that the simultaneous existence of a body in many places—and, moreover, of a body that was declared by Scripture to be enthroned in Heaven—was inconceivable, and even contradictory.

The first of these objections Luther attempted to remove. By his doctrine of Consubstantiation, the substances as well as the accidents of bread and wine remain unchanged by the act of consecration, but to the substances of bread and wine are joined those of the body and blood of Christ, existing side by side with them under the accidents of bread and wine, not mingled with them to form one substance. '*Nostra sententia est corpus ita cum pane, seu in pane esse, ut revera cum pane manducetur, et quemcunque motum vel actionem panis habet, eundem et corpus Christi.*' But this is a complication rather than a simplification of the Roman doctrine: if it removes one objection, it invites others: how, for example, can two different substances exist under the accidents of one? Moreover it presents no answer to the second objection, the charge of ubiquitarianism. Thirdly—and this was particularly repellent to the radical temper of the English revolt from Rome—

They because they se that upon this so nere a coniunction or couplyng together of Christe with the sacramente, it foloweth that the same sacramente maye bee wurshypped: (For yf the lorde be ther conteined realy & corporalli, what his he that woulde not wurshyp hym? (they teache that we maie indifferently at our pleasures either doe it, or leaue it undoē[1].

It is not surprising that the Lutheran doctrine never obtained much currency in this country, in spite of a slight initial success during the reign of Henry VIII.

[1] *A discourse or traictise of Peter Martyr Vermill concernynge the Sacrament of the Lordes Supper* (Nich. Udall's translation of Martyr's *Tractatio de sacramento Eucharistiae*).

Under Edward VI no theologian in England of any influence subscribed to it, with the rather insignificant exception of Dryander.

The Sacramentarian, or Zwinglian, doctrine had, on the other hand, the supreme attraction of simplicity. It repudiated Scholastic abstractions and the refinements of mediæval metaphysics. It was impatient of Luther's tinkering reformation. It was the creed of men so determined to lop the dead branches of sacramental worship that in their destructive enthusiasm they hacked at the roots as well.

It will be necessary to examine this doctrine further when the theology of Hooper comes to be studied. For the present, it may be said that, regarding the sacraments, the Zwinglian theologians denied all but their efficacy for salvation: yet even this lies not in the sacraments themselves, nor in the administration, but in the worthy reception of them. The celebration of the Lord's Supper is a commemorative rite, in which, moreover, the pledge of our redemption is renewed, and the communicants confirmed and strengthened in their faith by their public confession of it and by their participation in an act of corporate worship. Christ is not present, except in the sense of the prayer of St Chrysostom: the consecrated elements are sacred symbols merely; not *signa exhibitiva*, signs which exhibit what is present, but *signa representativa*, signs representative or commemorative of what is absent; bare signs, although, by the nature of what is therein commemorated, of peculiar importance.

The dominance of the commemorative aspect has not been sufficiently recognised. It is notable that those of the Reformers who were good Hebrew scholars were almost without exception impressed with the analogy between the two sacraments of the Old Law—Circumcision and the Passover—and the two sacraments of the New Testament

—Baptism and the Supper of the Lord. Between the Passover and the Eucharist they drew a parallel so close as to make them practically identical. This, it might have been anticipated, should have led them to stress the sacrificial element: but it did not. The point that impressed them was that the Passover, whatever its origin, had long since come to be regarded as a purely commemorative ritual: and so, naturally, this purely commemorative aspect became transferred from the Passover to the Eucharist. Now this conveys an important implication. The body and blood of Christ, they argued, could not have been in the sacraments of the Old Law, because he had not yet been born: but Christ is in no other way present in the sacraments of the Church than he was present in the sacraments of the Mosaic Law: therefore the sacraments of the Church and the sacraments of the Law are both merely symbolic of his body and blood offered upon the Cross for man's redemption, the former in a commemorative, the latter in a prophetic sense, and Christ is in no other way present in the Eucharist than he is present in Baptism, or was present in the Passover. It was a matter of profound consequence that the Church of Zurich at this period came partly under the guiding influence of such learned Hebraists as Leo Judae, Pellican, and Bibliander.

Zwingli himself had been killed in the second battle of Kappel (October 1531), but in the hands of his successor, Heinrich Bullinger[1], his doctrines, though given a wider

---

[1] Heinrich Bullinger (1504–74) succeeded Zwingli as Antistes, or chief pastor, of Zurich at the age of twenty-seven. He was a man of vigorous and commanding personality: at the age of nineteen he had converted his own Abbot (Pestalozzi, p. 22). In 1549 he joined forces with Calvin by the *Consensus Tigurinus* (summarised by Dr H. C. G. Moule, App. III to his edition of Ridley's *Brief Declaration of the Lord's Supper*, pp. 268–9): but although this led ultimately to the absorption of Zwinglianism by Calvinism, it was many years before Geneva became the dominant partner in the alliance.

currency, remained substantially unchanged. His last pamphlet, a letter to Francis I of France written in the summer of 1531, was translated from the Latin after his death by Leo Judae and published, under the title, *Eyn kurtze klare sū̄m und erklarung des Christenen gloubēs | von Huldrychen Zwinglin gepredigt | und unlang vor synem tod zů eynem Christenen Künig geschriben*, as his testament to the Church of Zurich. As such it is recognised by Bullinger, in his preface:

> Man lisst von dem Schwanen das er | so er dem tod nach | ein lieblich håll gesang usslasse: also auch diser held hat vor synem tod etwas lieblichen hållen gschrifft gedichtet | und zů bereytung synes todes vorgesungen. In disem bůchlin erklårt er gar håll und kurtz | was der recht gloub und gotsdienst sye....

Since the book bears this imprimatur, those chapters in it which treat of the Lord's Supper demand a fuller examination. The most important for our purpose is the chapter, *Von krafft und vermôgen der Sacramenten*. Having rehearsed his conception of the Eucharist, Zwingli adds (with some justice), 'Now might some one say, How is this? have then the sacraments no power at all?' In reply, he gives seven examples of their power and efficacy: they are sacred and precious, because ordained and used by Christ himself: they testify to the thing signified, the death of the Lord: they stand in the stead of the things they signify: they signify precious things, and therefore are themselves precious: there is a certain resemblance between the signs and the things they signify (*a*. Christ is the Bread of Life, the food and drink of the soul; *b*. as bread is made of many grains of corn, and wine of many grapes, so the body of the Church, of which Christ is the head, is made up of innumerable believers): the sacraments strengthen our faith somewhat (through the recitation, in the service, of the Comfortable Words and the other passages of Scripture; through the symbolism of the sacred elements, reminding the participant of the death of the Lord): the sacraments betoken and convey God's promise (*eydspflicht*) to mankind (*sacramentum*=an oath). 'From all this it follows that the words of the Lord, This is my body, must be understood *nit natürlicher wyss ...sund' bedütlicher wyss* [not literally, but figuratively]': 'This is my body' means 'This is a symbolic sacred sign and sacrament of my body,' or 'This is the symbolic and sacramental body,' or 'This symbolises my body which was given for you in death.'

This explanation may well seem to carry simplicity to the verge of annihilation: and at the time it was naturally intolerable to those who retained any reverence for Catholic tradition. Even Calvin, in his *De Coena Domini* (1540), which Coverdale translated, showed that he was more shocked by Zwingli's theology than by Luther's: and Peter Martyr charitably suggested that both Luther and Zwingli were driven to say more than they intended by their mutual exasperation, Luther 'because he supposed that zwynglius and others mynded to stablishe the sacramentes to bee naked & vain signes,' Zwingli because he feared lest by Luther's teaching 'supersticion myght yet stil bee more and morere (*sic*) nourished.' What men desired was a *via media* between Luther's doctrine, which retained too much, and Zwingli's, which retained too little. That *via media* Suvermerianism might claim to supply.

Suvermerianism was the name given by the Lutherans in derision to the doctrine of Martin Bucer and the Strassburg school. This doctrine may most conveniently be explained by means of a simple analogy. Now it is a commonplace of our physical life that if, for example, something is thrown at a person's face, he instinctively closes his eyes, while, in the same instant, he experiences the emotion of fear: as, indeed, the occurrence of other emotions—pleasure, pain, surprise, amusement, love, and so forth—is almost invariably accompanied, simultaneously, by some physical gesture. Then what can be predicated of the body and the mind can also, surely, be predicated of the body and the soul: a similar relation may occur in the life of the spirit, the physical sequence may have its concomitant in a changed condition of the soul. In this way, the reception of the bread and wine may be accompanied by a special kind of experience on the part of the soul: yet only where the soul is qualified or adapted therefor by its own condition. For even as, in unconsciousness, the living body may react to a physical stimulus in the same way that it would react if fully conscious, although the mind has not the experience which it would have when conscious of the stimulus, so also the soul that is dead through lack of faith, or perverted and deformed by sin, will be insensitive to the experience of the normal or healthy soul in normal circumstances. In fine, upon this hypothesis, the presence of Christ in the sacrament of the Eucharist may thus be explained: while the mouth receives the bread and wine, the worthy soul receives and feeds upon the very body and blood of Christ. But in the case of unworthy receivers of the sacrament— and here this theory stands in accord with Zwinglianism, and in antithesis to the Roman and Lutheran doctrines— only the bread and wine are received, because the soul from lack of faith cannot receive the body and blood of Christ.

This is, naturally, an over-simplification of a complicated metaphysical theory by means of a physical analogy of which its sixteenth-century exponents were not aware: but it sufficiently indicates in what that theory consisted. Without that analogy, the theory is far more baffling:

moreover in the sixteenth century it was peculiarly unfortunate in its exponents. Bucer had no gift for lucid
exposition, and the language in which he enveloped his
formula was further complicated by the endeavour to
make it such that both Luther and Zwingli could subscribe
to it. Cranmer's style was overweighted with his learning,
and what he wrote upon this question is usually prosy,
laboured, and apparently confused. Martyr, tormented
by the Oxford Papists, was rapidly driven into Zwinglianism, dragging Bucer with him. This change of doctrine
on their part led to endless confusion: contemporaries, not
understanding that Suvermerianism was a distinct and
separate theory, tried to include its exponents under some
other theological group; an error in which they have been
largely followed by subsequent historians, who have
generally played for safety by calling Bucer 'a moderate
Lutheran'[1]. Moreover it is misunderstanding of this
doctrine that has caused Cranmer to be charged with a
degree of inconsistency inconceivable in an intelligent
layman. Historians, while generally agreed that Cranmer
was a Zwinglian in the last years of Edward VI, are still
divided as to whether he did or did not pass through a
Lutheran phase between his conversion from Catholicism
and his conversion to Zwinglianism, and if he did, how
long it lasted. That Cranmer after his initial conversion
from the Roman doctrine embraced, consistently maintained, and never abandoned the Suvermerian theory of
the Eucharist, it is one of the principal objects of this essay
to prove.

[1] E.g. Canon Dixon, *History of the Church of England*, II. 522.

CHAPTER TWO

CRANMER

I cannot deny in the abstract the real and
substantial presence.
Hierome Zanchius to Bishop Grindal.
[Strassburg, *before* Aug. 23, 1563.]

CHAPTER TWO

CRANMER

FEW Reformers have been so contemptuously regarded as the first Protestant Archbishop of the
Church of England. 'Mehr klug als charaktervoll'[1],
'ingenio quod habebat magis blandum quam acutum'[2],
'a weak man' who 'trusted to his suppleness for security
in opposition'[3], a man of 'compliant temper'[4]—these
charges have been so frequently repeated that they have
almost ceased to be challenged. Other authorities have
presumed even further upon this treacherous foundation.
'Saintly in his professions, unscrupulous in his dealings,
zealous for nothing, bold in speculation, a coward and a
timeserver in action, a placable enemy and a lukewarm
friend, he was in every way qualified to arrange the terms
of the coalition between the religious and the worldly
enemies of Popery'[5]: this tirade affords a better sample
of Macaulay's instinct for invective than of his sense of
justice. 'This large, timorous, and unwieldy nature,'
wrote Canon Dixon[6], 'was needful to the men of violence
and craft who now held in their hands the destinies of the
country and the Church. He became their scribe, their
tool, their voice. It is the misfortune of a nation when such
a character is discovered and so used...' Canon Dixon is
not the only author to regret that Thomas Cranmer was
not Thomas à Becket, or to exhibit a marked preference
for Gardiner. But then follows a sentence that improves
on the customary estimate of Cranmer's theological
opinions: 'In doctrine he ran from one position to another'

---

[1] Anrich's *Martin Bucer*, p. 112.
[2] *Bishop Cranmers Recantacyons* (Philobiblon Society), p. 3.
[3] Gasquet and Bishop, p. 277.
[4] Pocock's preface to *Troubles Connected with the Prayer Book of
1549* (Camden Soc.), p. v.
[5] Macaulay's *History of England* (3rd edtn, 1849), p. 52.
[6] Dixon, I. 155–6.

—'ran' is good—'with the whole rabble of innovators at his heels, until at last he seemed ready to surrender the Catholicity of the Church to the Sacramentarians.' Yet not content with this, Dr Leighton Pullan in his Bampton Lectures (1922) tacitly passed a further amendment to the charge by his contemptuous reference to 'the vacillations of Cranmer, blown about by every wind of doctrine from the Rhine'[1]: a remark of which the general purport is evident, though the precise application must remain, to anyone who has studied the history of the period, somewhat obscure.

But the main charge of inconsistency cannot be shirked, because it involves the validity of the entire Edwardine Reformation. If the charge be proven, only the last part of that Reformation, centring round the Prayer Book of 1552, can be accepted as doctrinally sound, unless we are prepared to preserve what Cranmer rejected, and to reject what Cranmer, in the maturity of his experience, came to maintain. The mass of Cranmer's Reformation work must be dismissed as worthless unless the whole body of it can be regarded as coherent.

In the first place Cranmer was, of course, an erastian, and erastianism has been in very bad odour since the Oxford Movement. But in his time the Church was not ripe for autonomy: it would have been paralysed by an Enabling Act. Royal Supremacy was, indeed, the only alternative to Roman obedience. A hundred years later Germany, after a period of anarchy followed by an armed truce and thirty years of devastating war, arrived at the same conclusion. Royal Supremacy had established the Church of England, and was a necessary condition of its survival: somewhat paradoxically, it was only by submitting to the authority of the Crown that the Church could

[1] *Religion since the Reformation*, by Leighton Pullan (Bampton Lectures, 1922), p. 36 (1924).

maintain its independence. The English Reformation had not been initiated for the reform of doctrine, and its original leaders were not Lollards, but loyalists: the movement was part of an universal protest against alien domination: it was designed to abolish an *imperium in imperio*, and to achieve the independence less of the Church than of the State[1]. It was an essentially patriotic movement: and in that age politics and religion were less clearly distinguished than they are to-day, and the clergy were, for the most part, as good patriots as the laity. Now the first article in the nationalist creed in the age of the New Monarchy was, *Le nouveau Messie est le Roi*: and this was binding upon all citizens. National patriotism identified itself with personal loyalty, and was justified by expediency. From the point of view of the clergy, the Establishment was grounded in patriotism, and therefore in loyalty: the Reformation was a *translatio imperii*: the only legitimate defence of the abolition of the Pope's jurisdiction was that it usurped the King's, and therefore erastianism and anti-papalism were complementary and inseparable. From the point of view of the Crown, there was no use in abolishing one *dominium in dominio* in order merely to erect another: the Majestic Lord intended to have no further trifling. And so the clergy were, of double necessity, erastians all: and to blame Cranmer for being an erastian is as reasonable as to blame him for living in the first half of the sixteenth century[2].

[1] Even the leaders of the Pilgrimage of Grace (1536) had no wish to restore the Papal Supremacy, and actually suggested that such functions as it entailed should be delegated to the Archbishops of Canterbury and York, 'so that the said Bishop of Rome have no further meddling.' (Pollard's *Cranmer*, p. 107.)

[2] Cf. Tyndale's *Practice of Prelates* (*Expositions &c.* [P.S.] pp. 294, 296), or the disgusting passages in Becon's *Pleasante newe Nosegay, ful of many godly & swete floures* (*Early Writings* [P.S.], pp. 216–17), or, in another connection, Strype's *Parker*, 1. 85–6. Oddly enough, Edward VI in his *Petit Traité a lencontre de la primauté du pape* (1549)

There is nothing either shameful or illogical in his own statements of his attitude, two of which merit quotation. The first is taken from a Memorial on General Councils (1537), signed by Cranmer and seven bishops, including Tunstall, Stokesley, Goodrich and Latimer, and by four other clerics.

...Other places of scripture declare the highness and excellency of christian princes' authority and power; the which of a truth is most high, for he hath power and charge generally over all, as well bishops, priests, as other. The bishops and priests have charge of souls within their own cures, power to minister sacraments, and to teach the word of God, to the which word of God christian princes [ac]knowledge themselves subject; and in case the bishops be negligent, it is the christian princes' office to see them do their duty.

The second occurs in Cranmer's Examination before Brokes, September 1555. It is remarkable for its restraint.

Cranmer. I will never consent that the bishop of Rome shall have any jurisdiction within this realm.

Story. Take a note thereof.

Cranmer. I will never consent to the bishop of Rome; for then should I give myself to the devil: for I have made an oath to the king, and I must obey the king by God's laws. By the scripture the king is chief, and no foreign person in his own realm over him. There is no subject but to a king. I am a subject, I owe my fidelity to the crown. The pope is contrary to the crown. I cannot obey both: for no man can serve two masters at once....The king is head in his own realm: but the pope claimeth all bishops, priests, curates, &c. So the pope in every realm hath a realm.

Christ biddeth us to obey the king, *etiam dyscolo* [δυσκόλῳ] :

makes use of every argument except the erastian one: he is eager enough to show that the Pope and Mahomet are the two eyes of the little horn of the Beast in Daniel vii, and that the Pope is 'the man of sin' of II Thess. ii, but the idea of an *imperium in imperio* does not seem to have crossed his mind. (*King Edward the Sixth on the Supremacy*, ed. R. Potts, 1874.) But this was exceptional.

the bishop of Rome biddeth us to obey him. Therefore, unless
he be antichrist, I cannot tell what to make of him. Wherefore
if I should obey him, I cannot obey Christ.

...I say therefore, the bishop of Rome treadeth under foot
God's laws and the king's....

Martin. As you understand then, if they [the clergy]
maintain the supremacy of Rome, they cannot maintain
England too.

If it could be proved that Cranmer's erastianism ever
deflected his policy as Primate of all England, or led him
to profess doctrines which he did not believe, the censure
would carry more weight. He accepted the Royal Supremacy, but only because he believed in it (he had been
praying for the abolition of the Pope's authority in England
since 1525): and in this his conduct compares favourably
with that of his predecessor, 'the saintly and venerable
Warham,' who assented to the Supremacy when he
privately believed it to be evil, or that of his antagonist,
Gardiner, who was equally conspicuous as an erastian
under Henry, a malcontent under Edward, and a papalist
under Mary; in fact, in the days when he was playing a
leading part in the restoration of the Pope's supremacy, he
was seriously embarrassed by Bale's republication, in an
English translation, of his *De Vera Obedientia*, written in
1535. The proof of Cranmer's sincerity lies in his re-
cantations, which he faced with far more hesitation than
his martyrdom: he was logically committed to repudiate
the Royal Supremacy by his unwavering belief in it. The
argument by which he had confuted More's reasoning,
though without breaking his resolution, had become
fatally applicable to his own case.

...But then (said my Lord [of Canterbury]) you know for
a certainty, and a thing without doubt, that you be bounden to
obey your sovereign lord your King. And therefore are ye
bounden to leave of the doubt of your unsure conscience in

refusing the oath, and take the sure way in obeying of your prince, and swear it.... This argument seemed me suddenly so subtle, and namely with such authority coming out of so noble a prelate's mouth, that I could again answer nothing thereto but only that I thought myself I might not well do so....[1]

If the Crown had the right to enforce the Act of Supremacy, had it not also the right to repeal it? It was not until Cranmer had determined that he had been commanded 'to do against God,' and was therefore released from his obedience, that he felt himself able to defy the royal architect of Counter-Reformation, and so died for the Royal Supremacy in defiance of the Crown.

Pocock declared his contempt for Cranmer for being 'content to celebrate the office of the mass at the very time when he believed it to be idolatrous and blasphemous[2].' Cranmer was not content: but he was Primate of the Church of England, and not an irresponsible individual. He could not abolish the Mass and substitute the Communion by a stroke of the pen upon the instant that he himself had ceased to believe in it. Precipitate action would merely provoke mutiny, if not anarchy, within the Church. But as soon as he came to disapprove of such superstitious ceremonies as creeping to the Cross, covering images in Lent, and ringing the church bells all night on All Hallows, he applied to the King to sanction their abolition—the permission was first given, but soon afterwards withdrawn—and himself omitted all marks of veneration of the Cross in the liturgy that he was then drafting: and in the same year (1546), upon his conversion to Suvermerianism, began to work for the abolition of the Mass, urging the King (who was diffident, being then preoccupied with the project of an alliance with the Emperor and the French king) to agree provisionally to the drafting of an English Order of the Communion, and

[1] Roper's *Life of More*.　　[2] Pocock, *Troubles*, p. v.

eventually, in August 1547, obtaining the royal assent. To have acted without that assent would have been futile and dangerous.

Cranmer was no time-server: but he possessed the statesmanlike quality of patience, and gained his ends by persuasion, not by defiance, of his Prince. He was accommodating, but not subservient: he never yielded on fundamentals, nor allowed Henry to manipulate his conscience or juggle with his convictions. But he was accommodating, if that were indeed a fault: and of this we have a curious, and neglected, instance.

There is extant a MS. notebook, containing two separate drafts for a revised liturgy, which has been published by the Henry Bradshaw Society under the title, *Cranmer's Liturgical Projects*. Part I, which bears a strong resemblance to the Lutheran *Kirchenordnungen*, supplied the groundwork of the offices of Matins and Evensong in the Prayer Book of 1549: Part II, which was obviously composed under the influence of the Reformed Breviary of Cardinal Quignoñ, did not, apparently, lead to any practical result. But, contrary to the opinion generally received, Part I is the earlier in date. It may be stated with confidence that the date of this draft is 1538. Part II may be dated roughly between 1543 and 1546[1]. These dates are significant. In 1538 the period of Lutheran influence upon the English Reformation was indeed drawing to a close: but for the time that influence was again paramount. Henry, yielding for the last time to Crumwell's foreign policy, had resumed negotiations, more or less seriously, for an alliance with the Lutheran Princes, who had sent to England three ambassadors—Burckhardt, the Chancellor of Saxony, supported by a lawyer and a theologian—to conclude a treaty and to advise the Church. Melanchthon sincerely desired, and confidently expected a religious concordat on

---

[1] See the Appendix at the end of this chapter.

the basis of the Augsburg Confession, which would bring
England into line with Wittenberg. The King seemed to
approve, and a commission of four prelates and four
doctors was appointed to confer with the German orators.
Cranmer, like his master, favoured the project, although
his colleagues did not: he drew up Thirteen Articles,
closely modelled on the Confession of Augsburg, to serve
as a basis of negotiation: and was privately engaged with
Crumwell's chaplain, Malet, in drafting a revised liturgy
on the Lutheran pattern, as a gesture of goodwill. The
preface is derived from Quignon, but the offices (Matins
and Evensong) are clearly inspired by Bugenhagen's *Pia
et vere Catholica et consentiens veteri Ecclesiae ordinatio*
(1537), a copy of which had been presented to Henry by
the author.

The conference proved abortive. What Henry wanted
was not a religious, but a political alliance with the
Lutherans: and he was outgrowing his desire even for
that. Negotiations were broken off, and never resumed
under as favourable circumstances, though the Germans
returned to England in the following spring and lingered
for some months in the hope of a successful issue. The
arrival of Anne of Cleves furnished the last goad to
Henry's impatience: in June, 1539, the Act of Six Articles
had already initiated the Catholic Reaction, and in the
following year Crumwell, too deeply committed to the
Lutheran alliance to escape the consequences of its
failure, went to the block. Cranmer's second draft of a
liturgy is based exclusively on the Sarum Use ·and the
Reformed Breviary of Cardinal Quignon.

Superficially, this change of policy seems entirely discreditable: Cranmer's accommodating disposition appears
to have overstepped the bounds of decency. But the
explanation is simple. Cranmer was always afraid of the
isolation of his Church. In the Confession of Augsburg

he saw the potential basis of an alliance with the Lutherans, whose moderation and conservatism he found extremely sympathetic, in sharp contrast to the radicalism of the Sacramentarians. The Article on the Eucharist, which he copied verbatim into his Thirteen Articles, had been deliberately left ambiguous: both Catholics and Lutherans could subscribe to it with a good conscience. It seemed possible to build upon this basis a Centre Party, composed of the Catholic Party of Reform and the Moderate Party of Reformation: a coalition strong enough to secure reform and to stem the tide of revolution. But the conference of 1538 revealed that this was merely a pious aspiration, for upon the fundamental question of the Eucharist the parties could come to no agreement. Cranmer, who throughout had conceded no point of doctrine to the Lutheran envoys, regretfully abandoned the project, and shelved his unfinished liturgy: in the resumed negotiations of 1539 he seems to have had no part: instead, he set himself to strengthen his position with the Catholic Party of Reform, who were now in power. The doctrine that he maintained in both cases was the same.

In 1546, when he was converted to the Suvermerian doctrine, the situation was profoundly modified. Upon this altered basis an alliance with the Lutherans seemed to come once more within the range of possibility. Alike in their theology, Cranmer and Martin Bucer were alike also in their belief in conferences. It was an echo of the Conciliar Movement. To convene a General Council of Protestantism that should establish 'one sound, pure, evangelical doctrine, agreeable to the discipline of the primitive church,' to discover a formula that could unite all the divergent forces of Reformation against the common foe while leaving ample room for differences of interpretation: this was the dominant aim of Cranmer's statesmanship, and one that frequently seemed upon the threshold of success. In 1538 the basis of agreement appeared to be provided by the Confession of Augsburg: in 1547 by the *Consultation of Archbishop Hermann of Cologne*: then by the English Prayer Book of 1549: and finally, in 1552, by the *Consensus Tigurinus*. Had Cranmer succeeded in destroying the isolation of the English Church, the reign of Mary might have run a different course: had he succeeded in uniting Continental Protestantism, the history of the Counter-Reformation would certainly not have been the same.

The Consultation of Hermann of Cologne, the charter of Reformation in that diocese, was the work of Bucer and Melanchthon in collaboration. Following on the Wittenberg Concordat of 1536, it consummated the alliance between the two great schools of Strassburg and Wittenberg. The articles on the three Natures, on creation, original sin, justification by faith and by works, the Church, and penance, are by Melanchthon: those on baptism and the Lord's Supper are by Bucer. It is not surprising that the vagueness and ambiguity of the latter made Luther indignant: 'von der Substanz mummelt es, dass man nicht soll vernehmen, was er davon halte in aller Masse.' But the popularity of this work was remarkable. It was first published, under the title *Einfältiges Bedenken*, in 1543: a Latin version (*Simplex ac pia Deliberatio*), which Cranmer used[1], appeared in 1545, and two English editions in 1547 and 1548. From the *Consultation*, the *Order of the Communion* of 1548 derived its inspiration. Here was a more definite overture to the Lutherans than that of 1538, for in Cranmer's draft of a liturgy the question of the sacramental Presence had not been involved. And it was followed by an amazing offer. The need for a complete revision of the liturgy was now

[1] His own copy is still preserved in the library of Chichester Cathedral.

imperative: and so Cranmer invited the leading foreign Reformers to come to England, and, in effect, to compile the English Prayer Book.

The project was ambitious, but under the circumstances there was no reason why it should not have succeeded. The disaster of Mühlberg made the dominions of the Emperor unsafe for Protestants. The Interim had not yet been promulgated, it is true: but a far more stringent measure might have been anticipated. Melanchthon was meditating flight to Magdeburg. Strassburg was a doomed city: the return of the exiled Bishop was a question of days. East Friesland, where John à Lasco laboured, could no longer defy the Emperor with impunity. For most of the Reformers in Germany sentence of banishment at least seemed the inevitable penalty of defeat: while the generous hospitality of Lambeth offered sanctuary to them all. Some had already come to England; notably Peter Martyr, from Strassburg; Ochino, from Augsburg; Peter Alexander, late Chaplain to Mary of Burgundy, Regent of the Netherlands; Dryander, a Spanish Lutheran; Tremellio, a learned Italian Jew; Valérand Poullain, who had succeeded Calvin as pastor to the French Church at Strassburg; among others. Some of these were exiles; others merely travellers; not a few had come in the hope of obtaining more lucrative employment than they could find abroad. But here was already the nucleus of a 'godly synod': if Melanchthon, Bucer, and à Lasco could also be induced to come and to join with these other foreigners in a Conference with the leaders of the Church of England, they might draw up a formulary of faith that would command general obedience, and a liturgy that would be adopted by all the Protestant Churches of Europe. The Lutheran and Suvermerian Churches, and the Catholic Party of Reform, would be strongly represented: while à Lasco would hold a watching brief for more radical and

Sacramentarian interests. The Conference was, in fact, to effect a coalition of the moderate parties, and to found a Centre Party upon the basis of uniformity of creed and ritual: the leading rôle was, inevitably, allotted to Melanchthon. The Swiss were not represented, partly because Cranmer had no sympathy for their theology, and partly because they had already wrecked too many conferences by their uncompromising temper: but it was vaguely hoped that they would accept the findings of this council, if unanimous.

The first essential was to persuade Melanchthon to come. He ought to have leapt at the opportunity, since the Conference was, after all, his own idea; he had urged upon King Henry, in his letter of March 26, 1539, the necessity of a *consensus piae doctrinae*, and had attached the greatest importance to the visit of the three Lutheran orators for that purpose. But now he showed an unaccountable reluctance. Cranmer wrote to him at least three times, urging him to come: he made Justus Jonas, the younger, who was then in England, write to him to the same purpose: he wrote to à Lasco and to Hardenberg, begging them to persuade him to come at all costs. Melanchthon sent two replies, conveying his warm approval of the proposed Conference, but made a childish pretence of not observing that he had been invited to it. In his first letter he 'did not desire to do anything more than to express his grief' [at the bitterness of the Sacramental Controversy]—'which is so great that it could not be exhausted, though I were to shed a flood of tears as large as our Elbe or your Thames': he had to be brief, as the messengers were waiting: but he begged Cranmer 'to deliberate with the good and truly learned men both as to what should be determined, and as to what moderation may be expedient at first in teaching,' and reminded him that he had always wished (as he had written in a former letter) 'that a summary of necessary doctrine might be publicly set forth,' without ambiguities, such as the Council of Trent employed. His second letter is written in the same strain:

The longer I think about your conference, than which nothing more weighty and necessary can be set on foot among mankind, the more I hope, and think you should be exhorted, that you will publish a true and perspicuous confession on the whole body of doctrine, having compared the judgments of learned men, whose names should be subscribed to it, in order that there may be extant among all nations an illustrious testimony concerning doctrine, delivered with grave authority, and that posterity may have a rule to follow. Nor, indeed, will that confession be very different from ours, but I could wish a few articles to be introduced more clearly explained to posterity, lest ambiguities should subsequently furnish new dissensions.... In the Church it is more proper to call a spade a spade, than to throw ambiguous expressions before posterity. ...If you really press me for my opinion and vote also, I will gladly listen to the other learned men, and declare my own opinion in my turn and offer the reasons for my opinion, both persuading and being persuaded, as is fitting in a conference of pious men....

This was very vague and indefinite, and it made no direct reference to coming to England: but it was rather more encouraging, and Cranmer promptly wrote his third invitation, and sent it with a covering letter to à Lasco, begging him to add his own suasions to this appeal. Three weeks later Cranmer wrote to Hardenberg, the pastor of Bremen, asking him to add his voice also to the chorus of invitation. All was useless. If Melanchthon replied to Cranmer's third letter, his reply has not survived. The truth was, he preferred the ignominy of submitting to the Interim to the inconvenience and possible danger of a

journey to London: and nothing could persuade him to
move. As to the others, Bucer with characteristic courage,
and to the anxiety of his friends, refused to desert his flock
until the last moment consistent with his safety: while
à Lasco was delayed 'by the sudden intervention of some
other business,' and did not arrive in England until
September, and then, finding his presence not so urgently
required, returned to his duty in East Friesland.

In the absence of Melanchthon, the idea of a Conference
had to be abandoned. But the reformation of the liturgy
had to proceed. It is, certainly, to Cranmer's credit that
he did not lose all patience with the men who had failed
him: though the foreign Reformers were not present, they
were not forgotten: but the Catholic Party of Reform
received more generous concessions than they might have
had if the Conference had met. The First Prayer Book
of King Edward VI is characterised by conservatism and
moderation. It was designed to open the door to the
New Learning without closing it to the Old. 'I hear,'
wrote Bucer and Fagius to their old colleagues in Strassburg, 'that certain concessions have been made both to a
respect for the past and to the infirmity of the present.'
The Communion Office, though it was taken over, almost
unaltered, from the *Order of the Communion* of 1548,
which derived from the *Consultation of Hermann of
Cologne*, was entitled *The Supper of the Lorde and the Holy
Communion commonly called the masse*: while the liturgy
as a whole was called *The Booke of the Common Prayer and
Administracion of the Sacramentes, and other Rites and
Ceremonies of the Churche after the use of the Churche of
England*: guarded phrases to which a Catholic could hardly
take exception. Much, too, was borrowed from Quignon:
particularly the increased use of the Scriptures in divine
service. And much was left optional: as 'kneeling,
crossing, holding up of handes, knocking upon the brest,

and other gestures,' and auricular confession, a paragraph
being inserted at the end of the second Exhortation to the
Communion

requiryng suche as shalbe satisfied with a generall confession,
not to be offended with them that doe use, to their further
satisfiyng, the auriculer and secret confession to the Priest:
nor those also whiche thinke nedefull or conuenient, for the
quietnes of their awne cōsciences, particuliarly to open their
sinnes to the Priest: to bee offended with them that are
satisfied, with their humble confession to GOD, and the
generall confession to the churche. But in all thinges to folowe
and kepe the rule of charitie, and euery man to be satisfied
with his owne conscience, not iudging other mennes myndes
or consciences; where as he hath no warrant of Goddes word
to the same.

This passage perfectly expresses the spirit of the compilation. It was intended to be sufficiently comprehensive to
include the Catholic Party of Reform, the Lutherans, and
the Suvermerians. It was a liturgy for a Centre Party.
Later Cranmer had reason to regret his generosity when
Gardiner, with laboured ingenuity, contrived to read even
transubstantiation into it.

On the other hand, there were no concessions to the
papalists. The petition, 'from the tyranny of the Bysshop
of Rome and al hys detestable enormities....*Good lord,
deliuer us,*' was retained from the Litany of 1544, and the
name of St Thomas of Canterbury vanished from the
Calendar. Moreover the old ritual was purged of 'things
standing against true religion and godliness,' of various
ceremonies and uses not warrantable by the practice of
the Primitive Church but interpolated by mediæval popes,
such as the elevation of the host, the reservation of the
sacraments for adoration, the use of holy bread and holy
water, the doctrine of Purgatory, the veneration of images,

and of 'vncertein stories[1], Legendes, Respondes, Verses, vaine repeticions, Commemoracions and Synodalles.'

But, above all, free rein was given to Cranmer's democratic sympathies. He came of yeoman stock, and in an age of social snobbery, boasted of it: 'I take it,' he said upon a later occasion, 'that none of us all here, being gentlemen born, but had our beginnings that way from a low and base parentage.' Throughout, his sympathies lay with the people. He fought the New Landlordism, at considerable personal risk; he advocated democratic education, to the almost lyrical admiration of Professor Pollard. Now the Roman Church, as Cranmer saw it, was an essentially undemocratic organisation. It is true that it drew its priests from among the people, but it also withdrew them from among the people. They formed a caste apart, exalted above the laity and segregated from them by an entirely different rule of life. The Church of Rome, while it raised a small proportion of the people into the sacred ministry itself, held the vast majority of them apart from God, permitting only indirect communication through the mediation of the priests on earth and of the saints in heaven: the offices were celebrated in mumbled Latin: the Bible itself was for the laity a sealed book. It was against this undemocratic system that

---

[1] Of what sort these 'vncertein stories' were Cranmer set forth in very plain English in his *Answer to the Fifteen Articles of the Rebels* (1549). 'But forasmuch as you understood not the old Latin service, I shall rehearse some things in English that were wont to be read in Latin, that when you read them, you may judge them whether they seem to be true tales, or fables....' *The devil entered into a certain person, in whose mouth St Martin put his finger; and because the devil could not get out at his mouth, the man blew him...out behind.* This is one of the tales that were wont to be read in the Latin service....Yet more foolish, erroneous and superstitious things be read in the feasts of St Blaise, St Valentine, St Margaret, St Peter, of the Visitation of Our Lady, and the Conception, of the Transfiguration of Christ, and in the feast of Corpus Christi, and a great number mo....'

Cranmer revolted: for what it led to was not religion, but superstition.

In 1537 he had successfully importuned Crumwell and the King to sanction the publication of the Bible in English[1]. In 1544 he translated the Litany, with various alterations. In 1545 he induced the King to issue an authorised English Primer, and his hand is surely evident in the Preface:

...We have thought good to bestow our earnest labour in this part also, being a thing as fruitful as the best, that men may know both what they pray, and also with what words, lest things good and principal, being inwrapped in ignorance of the words, should not perfectly come to the mind and the intelligence of men....

In consideration whereof we have set out and given to our subjects a determinate form of praying in their own mother tongue, to the intent that such as are ignorant of any strange or foreign speech may have what to pray in their own acquainted and familiar language with fruit and understanding; and to the end that they shall not offer unto God (being the searcher of the reins and hearts) neither things standing against true religion and godliness, nor yet words far out of their intelligence and understanding.

This declaration foreshadows the liturgy of 1549. But in that the use of the vernacular in all the offices was accompanied by other democratic reforms: the services, especially the Communion, were made more congregational: private Masses were discouraged, and the sacraments were administered in both kinds.

The Prayer Book of 1549 was a monument to Cranmer's tolerance and discrimination. But it was immediately followed by a serious rebellion in Cornwall and Devon

---

[1] Gardiner opposed it, submitting a list of 'venerable words' which, he alleged, lost all their virtue by translation: such words as *Ecclesia, Penitentia, Baptizare, Martyr, Adorare, Sacramentum, Mysterium, Spiritus, Peccatum, Concupiscentia, Christus.*

and by risings, partly agrarian (as in Norfolk), partly
religious (as in Oxfordshire), all over the country. Conditions in the south-west were, however, peculiar. The
harm had been done some years earlier by the extortions
of an Irish adventurer and of a son of Cardinal Wolsey—
respectively holding the offices of Royal Commissioner
and of Archdeacon of Cornwall—through whose work
Reformation had become confused with rapacity in the
minds of the people. The embers of discontent had been
fanned by disaffected priests and also, perhaps, by agents
of the French Ambassador[1]. Naturally prejudiced against
change, the Cornish peasantry gained nothing from the
new liturgy: for if they did not understand Latin, many
of them did not understand English either, and the Latin
offices had the advantage of familiarity. It is to Cranmer's
credit that the Peasants' Revolt did not stampede him, as
it stampeded Luther, into a subservient reliance upon
authority. After the rising had been suppressed, he
published a vindication of his Prayer Book in the form of
an Answer to the Articles of the Rebels, but clearly
addressed to a wider audience. This pamphlet is both
learned and popular, written in 'the accustomed speech
of the homely people,' but giving proof of Cranmer's
remarkable knowledge of ecclesiastical history. The most
valuable part of it is that in which he defends the innova-
tions which made for more congregational worship. '*Item*,'
wrote the rebels, '*we will have the sacrament of the Altar
but at Estur delivered to the lai people, and then but in one
kind.*' Cranmer replied:

[1] So Prof. Pollard conjectures (*Thomas Cranmer*, p. 248, *n*. 1), from
the publication of a pamphlet entitled *La Responce du Peuple Anglois
à leur Roy Edouarde* at Paris in 1550. But Pocock regarded this
pamphlet as a translation from an English original, now lost: and Miss
Rose Troup, the latest historian of this Rebellion, brings forward some
weighty objections to Prof. Pollard's theory (*The Western Rebellion of
1549*, 1913).

Be you assured that there never was such law nor such request made among Christian people to this day....In the apostles' time the people at Jerusalem received it every day, as it appears by the manifest word of the scripture. And after they received it in some places every day;...commonly everywhere at least once in the week....But when the Spirit of God began to be more cold in men's hearts, and they waxed more worldly than godly, then...the more the people withdrew themselves from the holy communion....

What enemies ye be to yourselves also, to refuse to drink of Christ's cup, which he commanded all men to drink, saying: 'Take and divide this among you'; and, 'Drink ye all of it'!

Item, we will have the Mass in Latin as was before....Item, we will not receive the new service because it is but like a Christmas game, but we will have our old service of matins, mass, evensong, and procession [i.e. litany] *in Latin, not in English, as it was before. And so we Cornishmen (whereof certain of us understand no English) utterly refuse this new English....Item, we will have the Bible and all the other books of Scripture in English to be called in again; for we be informed that otherwise the clergy shall not of long time confound the heretics.*

The priest prayeth to God for you [in the Mass], and you answer *Amen*, you wot not whereto. Is there any reason herein?...Had you rather be like [mag]pies or parrots, that be taught to speak, and yet understand not a word they say, than be true christian men, that pray unto God in heart and faith? The priest is your proctor and attorney, to plead your cause, and to speak for you all; and had you rather not know than know what he saith for you?...The heart is not moved with words that be not understand....St Paul, in the first epistle to the Corinthians, saith,...'I had rather have five words spoken in the church to the instruction and edifying of the people, than ten thousand in a language unknown, that edifieth not.'...

Can you name me any Christians in the world, but they

have, and ever had, God's word in their own tongue?...And
will you have God farther from us than from all other countries;
that he shall speak to every man in his own language that he
understandeth and was born in, and to us shall speak a strange
language that we understand not? And will you that all other
nations shall laud God in their own speech, and we shall say
to him we know not what?

To bring God to the people—to reassure the English
Catholics, without re-admitting the Pope—to keep open
the road to union with the moderate Continental Protestants: these were the three main objects that directed
the compilation of what proved, quite incidentally, to be
the most beautiful of Christian liturgies. But as regards
doctrinal controversy, the Prayer Book decided nothing.
It offered a truce, and not a settlement. Dryander was
right when, communicating to Bullinger the rumours
about the character of the new liturgy, he observed that
the activity of the English Reformers was apparently
directed, not 'to form a complete body of christian
doctrine and to deliver a fixed and positive opinion
without ambiguity upon particular articles; but...to the
right institution of public worship.'

But Cranmer had other plans. Though thwarted at the
first attempt, he never abandoned hope of establishing
a *consensus piae doctrinae* with the collaboration of the
German theologians. Now he had secured a second
opportunity to achieve his object. In February, 1549, the
Prayer Book was finished. He had reason to believe that
it would commend itself to moderate men, and supply a
basis for further deliberation. To induce the Continental
Reformers to approve, perhaps even to adopt it, and to
secure their assistance in drawing up the Articles by which
it had to be supplemented and explained, was now his
hope. Since the repeal of the Six Articles in 1547, there
had existed no general criterion of orthodoxy: the Ten

Articles of 1536 were obsolete, the Thirteen Articles of 1539 had never had any legal force: and now the somewhat neutral colour of the new liturgy, coupled with the danger that its generosity would be abused, pointed the necessity for definition. Torn between hope and doubt, Cranmer wrote a last desperate invitation to Melanchthon, and entrusted it to à Lasco to deliver personally into his hands. No answer was returned. 'Cranmer and the Lord Protector sought to be aided with counsel; this counsel Wittenberg refused in the most decisive hour. We cannot then wonder that the doctrine of the Church of England has received an impress which does not originate in the school of Luther'[1].

In each of its three objects, then, the Prayer Book of 1549 was an immediate failure. Designed to bring God to the people, it produced an epidemic of popular rebellion. Designed to conciliate the English Catholics, it was rendered useless by Gardiner's sophistry. Designed to keep open the road to union with the moderate Continental Protestants, it revealed that that road was blocked at the other end by the indolence, or cowardice, of Melanchthon. It seemed to have failed utterly. It is only after this length of time that we are able to appreciate the measure of its success.

The fact that the main doctrinal issues were left unsettled by the Prayer Book of 1549 does not imply that they were unsettled in Cranmer's mind. Hitherto we have proceeded on the assumption that Cranmer had been a Suvermerian in his sacramental theology since 1546. This runs counter to the generally received opinion, expressed for example by Pocock, who refers to Cranmer at the end of 1549 as 'having passed through the phase of Lutheranism, and settled down into the Zwinglianism which is

---

[1] Dalton (tr. Evans), p. 364.

represented in the second Prayer Book of 1552.' It is therefore necessary to justify it.

Now the general opinion is based mainly on the evidence, not of Cranmer's own writings, but of the so-called Zurich Letters, addressed, for the most part, to Bullinger by the Zwinglians in England. Unfortunately this evidence is not trustworthy. The information of three of the writers— ab Ulmis, Burcher, and Micronius—is second-hand, and, like that of Hooper and Traheron, is coloured by the Zwinglian bias of the writers and, above all, by their desire to persuade Bullinger that Zwinglianism in England was carrying all before it. A man who could write, like Traheron (in August 1548), that he knew none of the nobility on the Reformation side who did not hold the Zwinglian doctrine; or, like Hooper (in December 1549), that 'all the English who are free from popish tyranny and Roman guile hold correct [i.e. Zwinglian] opinions about the Supper'; cannot be regarded as an honest and impartial witness. Moreover, read *in their chronological sequence*, the references to Cranmer are not perfectly consistent with each other: and in many cases they are still less consistent with such facts and documents as we have to check them by. Certainly, the evidence of the Zurich Letters cannot be ignored: but it must not be read without suspicion.

These letters contain thirty-five leading references to Cranmer, which may be analysed as follows:

1548. Upon the publication (in July) of Cranmer's translation of Justus Jonas' Lutheran Catechism, the Zwinglians in England promptly assumed that he was a Lutheran. Then they believed him to be converted to Zwinglianism by à Lasco on his arrival in England in September: and Traheron affirmed that he maintained the Zwinglian doctrine of the Eucharist in the debate of December 14–18.

1549. The Zwinglians were apprehensive of Bucer's

influence over Cranmer. The Archbishop began to be more friendly to Hooper—according to Hooper. But the coolness with which he still received Bullinger's advances could not be concealed.

1550. Hooper still maintained that Cranmer was friendly towards him, though somewhat more dubiously during the Vestiarian Controversy. He expressed some doubts as to the extent of Cranmer's conversion from Lutheranism.

From the summer of this year, references to Cranmer become progressively fewer, while references to the nobility, especially to Warwick and Dorset, become increasingly frequent, although the Zwinglians would never directly admit that they had been wrong in their appreciation of Cranmer's doctrine. This tendency is very significant.

1551. A Lasco was perturbed by Cranmer's resolution to invite the Lutheran Brentius to succeed Bucer at Cambridge. Hooper assured Bullinger three times in one letter that Cranmer 'loved him dearly.'

1552. Cranmer wrote to Bullinger, as well as to Calvin and to Melanchthon (but rather more distantly), inviting him to a Conference. Not one of the Zwinglians mentioned Cranmer in his letters this year.

1553. No references to Cranmer until after the death of Edward VI, when Martyr expressed a certain anxiety on his behalf.

Now these letters point to three important conclusions: (1) Cranmer was at some time a Lutheran, (2) he was converted from Lutheranism by à Lasco, and (3) remained a Zwinglian till his death. To what extent are these conclusions true?

1. *Was Cranmer ever a Lutheran?* Fox, Burnet, and Strype all held the view that Cranmer's first change in sacramental doctrine was from the tenets of Rome to those of Luther. Then, at the beginning of the nineteenth century, Wordsworth and Todd challenged this theory: but were refuted by Jenkyns, who brought forward evidence that they had overlooked.

But it is a material point that the first occasion upon which this theory was advanced was that of the publication of Cranmer's translation of Justus Jonas' Catechism, in July 1548.

'This Θωμᾶς,' wrote John ab Ulmis to Bullinger (London, Aug. 18), 'is fallen into so heavy a slumber, that we entertained but a cold hope that he would be aroused even by your most learned letter: for a few days ago he published a catechism, in which he has not only approved that filthy and sacrilegious metamorphosis of the papists in the sacred supper of our Saviour; but also all the dreams of Luther seem to him to be sufficiently sound, perspicuous, and lucid. O how lamentable a thing it is, and worthy to be deplored in the discourse, letters and monuments of all peoples, that the sheep of Christ are to-day surrounded by certain persons with new error, nor do any of those who are most influential by learning and by authority, boldly oppose these ploughmen, *das ist holzböcken*, and drive them into exile!'

'Canterbury, no doubt moved by the advice of Peter Martyr and other Lutherans,' wrote Burcher to Bullinger (Strassburg, Oct. 29), 'has ordered a catechism of some Lutheran opinion to be translated and published in our language. This little book has occasioned no little discord; so that the common people have often fought on account of the diversity of their opinions, even during sermons.'

Evidently neither of these correspondents had read the book in question. Ab Ulmis did not understand English, and Burcher lived in Strassburg: both merely passed on to Bullinger the common gossip. Now, although it is perfectly true that the original was Lutheran, the translation certainly was not: in fact, it actually led Gasquet and Bishop to conclude that Cranmer had abandoned the Real Presence, and now held the Real Absence[1]. For the original read:

God is almighty. Therefore He can do all things as He will....

---

[1] Gasquet and Bishop, pp. 130-1.

When He calls and names a thing which was not before, then at once the very thing comes into being as He names it. Therefore when He takes bread and says: 'this is my body,' then immediately there is the body of our Lord. And when He takes the chalice and says: 'this is my blood,' then immediately His blood is present.

But Cranmer left out of his translation the words given in italics, and rendered the rest as follows:

...wherefore when Christ takes bread and saith: 'Take, eat, this is my body,' we ought not to doubt but we eat His very body; and when He takes the cup and saith: 'Take, drink, this is my blood,' we ought to think assuredly that we drink His very blood.

This striking alteration suggests not Lutheran, but rather Suvermerian doctrine. And this impression is confirmed by Cranmer's explanation of the passage in his *Defence* (1550) and in his *Answer* (1551):

And in that Catechism I teach not, as you do, that the body and blood of Christ is contained in the sacrament, being reserved, but that in the ministration thereof we receive the body and blood of Christ; whereunto if it may please you to add or understand this word '*spiritually*,' then is the doctrine of my Catechism sound and good in all men's ears, which know the true doctrine of the sacraments.

Again, in his *Answer to Smyth's Preface*, he wrote, 'I confess of myself, that not long *before* I wrote the said catechism, I was in that error of the real [i.e. corporeal] presence': which proves that he was not in that error *when* he wrote it.

It may be objected that all these explanations were made some time after the publication of this Catechism, and that Cranmer was consciously or unconsciously reading into what he wrote in 1548 the views he held in 1550. Compare, then, the Exhortation in the *Order of the Communion* of the same year (1548):

...wherfore our dutie is, to come to these holy misteries with most harty thākes to be geuen to almightye God, for his infinite mercy and benefites, geuen & bestowed upon us, his unworthye seruauntes, for whome he hath not only geuen his body to death and shed his bloud, but also doth vouchesaufe in a Sacrament and misterye, to geue us his sayd body and bloud spiritually, to fede and drynke upon.

In view of this passage, was it entirely unreasonable in Cranmer to assume that the word 'spiritually' would be understood? Yet it was not only the Zwinglians who judged Cranmer to be a Lutheran upon the evidence of this Catechism, for the Romanist Dr Martin accused him in 1555 of having taught consubstantiation in it, on the same evidence as that on which Cardinal Gasquet calls him a sacramentarian. Here is another instance of the degree of misconstruction to which Suvermerian theology was liable. Even as late as June 1550, when Cranmer had already been triumphantly hailed as a Zwinglian by Traheron, ab Ulmis, and Hooper himself, we find Hooper wondering how much of his 'Lutheranism' he had really put away, and Gardiner putting upon the second book of the *Defence* a Lutheran construction, which Cranmer scornfully denied.

It is necessary, then, to conclude with Jenkyns that 'so far as it [the charge of Lutheranism] rested on the translation of Justus Jonas' Catechism it must be admitted without foundation.' But this does not exclude the possibility that Cranmer was a Lutheran before this date. He admitted himself, in his *Answer to Smyth's Preface*, that it was 'by little and little' that he put away his 'former ignorance': may not one of these preliminary stages have been Lutheranism? Those historians who wish to prove that it was, bring forward two important pieces of evidence in support of their contention. The first is the following passage from the *Answer to Smyth's Preface* (1551), appended to the *Answer to a Crafty and Sophistical Cavillation devised by Stephen Gardiner*:

> I confess of myself, that not long before I wrote the said catechism, I was in that error of the real presence, as I was many years past in divers other errors: as of transubstantiation, of the sacrifice propitiatory of the priests in the mass, of pilgrimages, purgatory, pardons, and many other superstitions and errors that came from Rome; being brought up from youth in them, and nousled therein for lack of good instruction from my youth, the outrageous floods of papistical errors at that time overflowing the world....
>
> But after it had pleased God to shew unto me, by his holy word, a more perfect knowledge of his Son Jesus Christ, from time to time as I grew in knowledge of him, by little and little I put away my former ignorance. And as God of his mercy gave me light, so through his grace I opened mine eyes to receive it....

Here it is necessary to insert a *caveat*, which will be explained later: wherever Cranmer alludes to the real (or corporeal) presence, either in the *Defence* or in the *Answer*, he invariably speaks of it as a *Roman* doctrine, implied by transubstantiation, though distinct from it: for, although it is impossible to believe in transubstantiation without believing in the presence of Christ's body in the consecrated elements, it is possible to believe in this real presence without believing in transubstantiation, or even in consubstantiation, for that matter. Therefore to read in place of the words 'real presence' the word 'consubstantiation' is a serious error. The passage should, in fact, be read as follows:

> I confess...that not long before I wrote the said catechism [i.e. 1548], I was in that error of the real presence, as I was many years past in divers other errors...that [also] came from Rome....But...by little and little I put away my former ignorance.

The truth is that Cranmer retained the Roman doctrine of the real presence for some time after he had discarded the Roman doctrine of transubstantiation: but this does not necessarily imply that he held the Lutheran doctrine of consubstantiation with it.

This point is brought out more clearly by the second piece of evidence: the Case of George Bucker, of Calais, *alias* Adam Damplip.

The whole story is somewhat confused, and Fox, in telling it, makes two mistakes, dating the case 1539, instead of 1538, and confusing the proceedings against Damplip with the trial of Lambert. The gist of the story is this: Damplip, lately chaplain to Fisher, Bishop of Rochester, had gone to Rome on pilgrimage and returned utterly disillusioned. On his way home he preached in Calais, and met with such success that he remained for three weeks, preaching daily and inveighing against transubstantiation and the doctrine of a propitiatory sacrifice in the Mass. He appears to have been 'well lyked by the [Lord] Deputye & the Counsayle of Calice': but he became involved in a dangerous controversy with the Prior of the Black Friars, and, since his position was irregular, prudently hastened to Lambeth, armed with a letter of commendation from John Butler, the Archbishop's commissary at Calais, and applied to Cranmer for a curacy at 'our lady's church at Cales.' He arrived at Lambeth on July 24, and was examined by Cranmer, who found him 'of right good knowledge and judgment,' and sent him on to Crumwell with a letter of introduction, requesting Crumwell to give him the curacy and to furnish him with letters commendatory to the Council of Calais. Damplip also seems to have informed against his enemy, the Prior, who was sent for by Cranmer, and on his arrival was kept in safe custody, according to Crumwell's instructions, and subsequently (it seems) deprived. But meanwhile two

friars arrived from Calais, and laid information against
Damplip as having denied the real presence. Damplip
seems to have lost his nerve and fled, 'suspecting the
rigour of the law [rather] than the defence of his own
cause.' He was not pursued, and seems to have returned
afterwards to Calais: where (according to Fox) after the
passing of the Six Articles he was arrested and martyred
on a trumped-up charge of treason.

All this is not very material. What is material is the
following sentence in Cranmer's second letter to Crumwell
on behalf of Damplip (Aug. 15, 1538):

As concerning Adam Damplip of Calice, he utterly denieth
that ever he taught or said that the very body and blood of
Christ was not presently in the sacrament of the altar, and
confesseth the same to be there really; but he saith, that the
controversy between him and the prior was, by cause he
confuted the opinion of the transubstantiation, and therein
I think he taught but the truth.

This statement corroborates the *Answer to Smyth's
Preface*: together they present conclusive proof that
Cranmer continued to believe in the real presence after
he had ceased to believe in transubstantiation. But they
give no indication that Cranmer had come to believe in
consubstantiation. It is manifest from all his writings that
he regarded the real presence as a Roman, and not a
Lutheran doctrine: 'for although these men [the Lutherans]
...agree with the papists in part of this matter, yet they
agree not in the whole.' In the *Answer* he speaks of
Innocent III as 'the chief author of your doctrine both of
transubstantiation and of the real presence': and again of
'the whole papistical doctrine in the matter of the sacrament, as well touching transubstantiation, as also the
carnal presence.' Then in the *Defence*, in a passage which
enumerates the 'four principal errors of the papists,' the

first error is 'transubstantiation, that is to say, the turning of one substance into another substance'; the second, regarded as similar but distinct, is the doctrine 'that the very natural flesh and blood of Christ, which suffered for us upon the cross, and sitteth at the right hand of the Father in heaven, is also really, substantially, corporally, in or under the accidents of the sacramental bread and wine, which they call the forms of bread and wine.' This, and not consubstantiation, is what Cranmer means when he alludes to the real presence: nor, for that matter, can consubstantiation very easily be fathered upon Pope Innocent III. Moreover he afterwards maintained that the real presence is easier to defend than transubstantiation: for when Gardiner in his reply to Cranmer's *Defence* changed the order of it, confuting Book III (*Of the Presence of Christ*) before Book II (*Against Transubstantiation*), Cranmer accused him of having done so for this very reason:

For he saw the matter of transubstantiation so flat and plain against him, that it was hard for him to devise an answer in that matter, that should have any appearance of truth, but all the world should evidently see him overthrown at the first onset. Wherefore he thought, that although the matter of the real presence hath no truth in it at all, yet forasmuch as it seemed to him to have some more appearance of truth than the matter of transubstantiation hath, he thought best to begin with the first, trusting so to juggle in the matter, and to dazzle the eyes of the simple and ignorant, and specially of such as were already persuaded in the matter, that they should not well see nor perceive his legerdemain.

Evidently what Cranmer held was the Scholastic doctrine of Impanation, which teaches that the very body and blood of Christ are *in* or *under* the accidents of bread and wine, but without either mutation or conjunction of substances, that is, without either transubstantiation or consubstantiation. To adapt Luther's definition, Christ's body is not *cum pane, seu in pane*, but *in pane* alone[1].

This statement of Cranmer's doctrine at this period may seem a doubtful supposition: and it may be objected that his belief in the real presence would fit consubstantiation as well. But, happily, we hold final and conclusive proof that Cranmer was not a Lutheran in 1538. Indeed, the date of this letter about Adam Damplip could not have fallen less opportunely for those who wish to claim Cranmer as a Lutheran than on August 15, 1538. For on June 21 of the same year he refused the urgent request of Franz Burckhardt, Chancellor of Saxony and head of the Lutheran embassy then in England, that a recanted Lutheran named Atkinson might be permitted to do his penance more privately in his own parish church instead of in the publicity of St Paul's:

whereunto we made him this answer, that forasmuch as the error of the sacrament of the altar was so greatly spread abroad in this realm, and daily increasing more and more, we thought it needful, for the suppressing thereof, most specially to have him do his penance at Paul's, when the most people might be present, and thereby, in seeing him punished, to be ware of like offence.

And besides this, in the Examination before Brokes in 1555, when Martin asked, 'What doctrine taught you when you condemned Lambert the sacramentary in the king's presence in Whitehall?' Cranmer replied, 'I maintained then the papists' doctrine.' Now the date of Lambert's trial and condemnation was November 16, 1538. If Cranmer was relentless in his opposition to the doctrine

---

[1] There is some indication, though by no means certain, that Cranmer also held that evil men do not receive the body and blood of Christ, but only the bread and wine. Even Gardiner admitted this theory in two passages of his *Explication*, though he denied it in two others (*Ridley* [P.S.], p. 313). Such a belief was repugnant to Lutheranism.

of consubstantiation on June 21, and 'maintained the papists' doctrine' on November 16, it becomes extremely difficult to maintain that he was a Lutheran on the 15th of August.

Cranmer was never a Lutheran. Whenever he was taxed with it, he always, by implication at least, denied the charge. He was sympathetic to the temper of Lutheranism: but he never subscribed to its doctrines. Nor did Latimer, whose mind was profoundly under Cranmer's influence[1]. 'You, master Cranmer,' said Martin, at the same Examination, 'taught in this high sacrament of the altar three contrary doctrines, and yet you pretended in every one *verbum Domini*': meaning Catholicism, Lutheranism, and Zwinglianism. 'Nay,' said Cranmer, 'I taught but two contrary doctrines in the same.' We have established that his second doctrine was not Lutheranism: but what it was, and who converted him to it, it is now our business to discover.

2. *Was Cranmer converted by à Lasco?* The only direct evidence in support of this theory is ab Ulmis' letter to Bullinger of November 27, 1548:

England is flourishing in all the glory of the gospel....Right and excellent decisions concerning the sacred supper of Jesus Christ have been declared by the primates [i.e. the bishops?]: that base and crass opinion of a feigned σαρκοφαγια [flesh-eating] has long since been banished, and sent to Jericho [εἰς κόρακας *delegata*]. Even that Θωμᾶς (about whom I wrote to you when I was at London), by the goodness of God and the instrumentality of Dr John à Lasco, a man of most upright character and sound judgment, has been much delivered from his dangerous disease of lethargy.

This, however, is supported by the general testimony of

---

[1] At Latimer's trial in 1555, when Weston put to him the question, 'You were once a Lutheran,' he replied, 'No. I was once a papist: for I never could perceive how Luther could defend his opinion without transubstantiation.'

the Zwinglians (especially Traheron) that Cranmer came over to their opinion during the period of à Lasco's first visit to England (Sept. 21, 1548—Feb. 1549): a conversion that was evident to them from Cranmer's speeches in the great debate on eucharistic doctrine in the House of Lords, December 14–18.

Upon this evidence Dr Hermann Dalton, à Lasco's biographer, ascribed the credit of Cranmer's conversion to à Lasco: he admitted that the English historians prefer the claims of Ridley, but attributed this to modern nationalist prejudice (p. 330). But a few pages farther on— farther, unfortunately, than the English translation runs— he more or less retracted this in a footnote, admitting that it was probably Ridley who first shook Cranmer's faith in Roman doctrine, shortly before the arrival of à Lasco (*Note*, p. 364).

Cranmer himself stated quite unequivocally in his Examination before Brokes that it was Ridley who had converted him:

> I grant that then [1538] I believed otherwise than I do now; and so I did, until my lord of London, doctor Ridley, did confer with me, and by sundry persuasions and authorities of doctors drew me quite from my opinion.

This statement leaves only the date in doubt: and that is supplied by Cheke (who had been so intimate with Cranmer that his statement can be taken as entirely trustworthy), in his preface to the Emden (Latin) edition of Cranmer's *Defence*, published in 1557:

> ...this man [Cranmer], after much searching of the scriptures, by the instruction of one blessed martyr, Ridley, bishop of London, at long last (in the year '46, to be precise) was led into that opinion, which he here defends.

Inevitably this raises the question, to what did Ridley convert him? what doctrine did Ridley himself maintain?

By his own admission, Ridley had been converted (apparently in 1545, when he was vicar of Herne) by reading the ninth-century treatise *De Corpore et Sanguine Domini*, written at the request of Charles the Bald by the Benedictine Ratramnus (commonly called 'Bertram' in Ridley's day), and recently printed at Cologne (1532) and at Geneva (1541).

This Bertram was the first that pulled me by the ear, and that first brought me from the common error of the Romish church, and caused me to search more diligently and exactly both the Scriptures and the writings of the old ecclesiastical fathers in this matter[1].

References to Ratramnus' book, and quotations from it, are frequent in Ridley's writings and disputations: and the English translation of it, published in 1548, was probably due to his interest. Now to Ratramnus' doctrine that of Bucer approximates very closely. Ratramnus' doctrine is based on the distinction between Verity (actuality, *rei manifestae demonstratio*) and Mystery (*mysterium*). In every sacrament exist both its verity and its mystery. In the sacrament of the Lord's Supper, the verity is bread and wine: the mystery is the Body and Blood of Christ. The one is outwardly taken, refreshing the body: further, it signifies, or is a figure of (1) Christ's body crucified for our redemption, and (2) Christ's mystical body, the Church, by way of pledge and image. The other, feeding invisibly the soul, is taken by faith, not by the senses: it is the very substance of life eternal. The consecrated element is one thing in nature (*species*, verity), another in significance: in nature bread, in sacrament the body of the Lord. In its outward verity it is the

---

[1] Disputation at Oxford, April 17, 1555. (*Ridley* [P.S.], p. 206.) After his degradation, before his judges could leave the Divinity School, he urged Bishop Brokes to read Bertram's book 'with an indifferent judgment.' For an abridged rendering of this treatise, see Moule, App. II, pp. 223-48.

perishable food of the perishable body: in its inward
mystery—its inward reality—it is the immortal food of the
immortal soul. The body of the recipient receives and
feeds on the symbolic bread and wine: his soul by faith
receives and feeds on the very body and blood of Christ.
There is little difference between this and the Suvermerian
doctrine. And this, be it remembered, was the doctrine
that Ridley maintained consistently to the end: it is to be
found in his answers to the *Queries put concerning some
abuses of the mass* addressed to the bishops at the end of
1547, in his speeches in the great debate in the House of
Lords, December 14–18, 1548, or in his defence at the
Oxford Disputation of April 1554—there perhaps best of
all, for his repudiation of Zwinglianism was as clear and
as candid as his repudiation of Roman or of Lutheran
doctrine.

Weston. Ye say, Christ gave not his body, but a figure of
his body.

Ridley. I say not so: I say, he gave his own body verily;
but he gave it by a real, effectual, and spiritual communication.
...I understand...the very flesh of Christ to be eaten, but
spiritually: and further I say, that the sacrament also pertaineth
unto the spiritual manducation: for without the spirit to eat
the sacrament is to eat it unprofitably; for whoso eateth not
spiritually, he eateth his own condemnation.

Cranmer had arrived at this position, abandoning the
corporeal for the spiritual presence, long before the visit
of à Lasco. This is indicated by the Exhortation in the
Order of the Communion of 1548, previously quoted[1], or by
his alteration of Justus Jonas' Catechism: it is clearly
apparent from his answers to the *Queries concerning abuses
of the mass*. Moreover—though this may be a small point—
it was on September 28, 1548, that Traheron wrote to
Bullinger, 'But that you may add more to the praises of

[1] p. 53, *supra*.

God, know that Latimer has, respecting the truth of the eucharist, come over to our opinion together with Canterbury and the rest of the bishops, who previously seemed Lutherans.' Now, it is true that à Lasco was at Lambeth on September 21: but Cranmer was not, for à Lasco, writing on that date, mentioned that the Archbishop was not expected for a week. Even allowing that Cranmer arrived a day or two earlier, Traheron's letter would imply that that conversion was phenomenally rapid, if à Lasco were indeed its author.

We have, then, sufficient evidence to deny that it was à Lasco who converted Cranmer from his belief in the real presence (in the strict sense of the term). But did à Lasco either permanently or temporarily modify Cranmer's conception of the spiritual presence? This leads on to the third question—

3. *Did Cranmer become a Zwinglian?* The answer to this question, as to the other two, is in the negative. Those who would seek to prove an affirmative from the Zurich Letters may well be oppressed by the ominous silence in which Cranmer's policy is shrouded after the summer of 1550. From December 1548 to June 1550—that is, before the Vestiarian Controversy—the letters of the Zwinglians to Bullinger contain many such references as this: 'The bishop of Canterbury understands correctly the business about Christ's supper.' But why do the references to Cranmer become less frequent and less friendly (for Hooper's letter of August 1, 1551, protesting repeatedly to Bullinger that 'my lord of Canterbury loves you indeed dearly.... You have no one, I know, of all your dearest friends, who loves [you] in Christ with greater solicitude or more lovingly than he. I know and am certain that he loves you from his heart,' is an isolated instance, and transparently incredible) after the Vestiarian Controversy: and why do they cease altogether after August 1551, during

the very period when the characteristically Zwinglian
Prayer Book of 1552 was being compiled—that Prayer
Book which is commonly held to embody Cranmer's
altered doctrinal views? Why was Cranmer's attitude to
Bullinger so consistently unfriendly (for example, he never
answered Bullinger's letters, and only wrote to him once,
and then somewhat stiffly, when he had need of him for
a conference) that even the Zwinglians, excepting only
Hooper, made no attempt to conceal it? And why were
Cranmer and Ridley constantly found allied against à Lasco
and the Zwinglian leaders in such disputed matters as the
independence of the Strangers' Church in London, the use
of vestments, or the custom of kneeling at Communion?

It may be worth while to test the veracity of one or two
of the statements made by Bullinger's correspondents
during the phase of their enthusiasm for the Archbishop,
as a sample of the rest. Allusion has previously been made
to the motive underlying most of their correspondence:
the desire to give Bullinger the most favourable impression
possible of the progress of Zwinglianism in England.
Thus, for example, on August 28, 1550, Micronius writes
to Bullinger, 'The bishop of Canterbury...has just published an enormous volume about the Lord's supper, in
which he stoutly attacks every [opinion of the] presence of
the body of Christ.' It may be stated with assurance that,
but for the date, it would be impossible to recognise this
for a description of Cranmer's *Defence of the true and
Catholic Doctrine of the Sacrament of the Body and Blood
of our Saviour Christ.* Or again, take these two statements
from Hooper's letters to Bullinger:

The bishop of Canterbury...has some articles of religion,
to which all preachers and lecturers in divinity are compelled
to subscribe, (or else a license for teaching is not allowed them,)
in which he holds the pure and religious and Swiss opinion
concerning the eucharist. (*Dec.* 27, 1549.)

Canterbury, who is head of the king's councils (*sic*), is making a supply of suitable lectures and sermons for lecturers and preachers: first, however, they all subscribe to certain articles, which I will send you some time (if I can), among which one is about the eucharist, and it is manifestly true and Swiss. (*Feb.* 5, 1550.)

Historians have found some difficulty in identifying these 'articles.' But surely they can be none other than the *Articles to be followed and observed according to the king's majesty's injunctions and proceedings*, which, as Cardwell notes[1], are evidently later than the Act of Uniformity of January 21, 1549, though of the same year. And the 'one about the eucharist,' so 'manifestly true and Swiss,' is merely—

§ 2. Item, For an uniformity, that no minister do counterfeit the popish mass, as to kiss the Lord's table; washing his fingers at every time in the communion; blessing his eyes with the paten, or sudary; or crossing his head with the paten; shifting of the book from one place to another; laying down and licking the chalice of the communion; holding up his fingers, hands, or thumbs, joined towards his temples; breathing upon the bread or the chalice; shewing the sacrament openly before the distribution of the communion; ringing of sacrying bells; or setting any light upon the Lord's board at any time; and finally to use no other ceremonies than are appointed in the king's book of common prayers, or kneeling, otherwise than is in the said book.

It does not appear that Hooper ever found himself able to send Bullinger a copy.

So much for the veracity of these reports that Cranmer had become a Zwinglian. Nevertheless, other and more reliable evidence makes it impossible to deny that Cranmer's opinions were modified, and even deflected, by his intimacy with à Lasco in the winter of 1548-9.

[1] *Documentary Annals,* p. 75 *n.*

The doctrine that Cranmer maintained consistently (with this slight modification, due to à Lasco's influence) from his conversion in 1546 to his martyrdom ten years later, may be identified with that of Bucer, but also distinguished from it. Cranmer had been led to Suvermerianism by reading Ratramnus, Bucer by a very different process. Yet their doctrines were built upon the same conception. The doctrine that Cranmer maintained in the Disputation of April 1555, to the incomprehension of his opponents, can only be described as Suvermerian:

The soul is fed with the body of Christ, the body with the sacrament....So one thing is done outwardly, another inwardly: like as in baptism the external element, whereby the body is washed, is one; so the internal element, whereby the soul is cleansed, is another....The sacrament is one thing; the matter of the sacrament is another. Outwardly we eat the sacrament; inwardly we eat the body of Christ....

Tertullian also saith: *Nutritur corpus pane symbolico, anima corpore Christi*: that is, ' Our flesh is nourished with symbolical or sacramental bread, but our soul is nourished with the body of Christ.'...

But in one point he varied from Bucer. Bucer held that Christ's body is present spiritually in the sacraments, and is spiritually received with the soul by all who receive him worthily. Cranmer after 1548 maintained that Christ's body is present, not in the sacraments, but in the administration of the sacraments, and is spiritually received by all who receive him worthily, that is, by those in whom Christ is already spiritually present. The difference is not very considerable, and seems to reflect the influence of à Lasco's doctrine as expressed in the *Epistola ad amicum quendam*[1].

Certainly, for a short period, à Lasco's exposition of his Sacramentarian doctrine seems to have shaken Cranmer's

---

[1] See p. 184.

confidence. By its simplicity and directness it avoided all those obstacles that a less radical theology had laboriously to circumvent. The Archbishop was evidently puzzled. As a theologian or as a debater, he never appeared to worse advantage than in the famous Debate on the Sacrament in the House of Lords, December 14–18, 1548. Traheron was not far from the truth when he said that Cranmer maintained the Zwinglian doctrine: but that was not the only doctrine which he maintained. His interventions during the first three days of the debate show him to have been confused and unhappy. Holbeach of Lincoln put his finger on the root of Cranmer's difficulties when he asked, 'Whether the body is in the Sacrament or in the receiver?' It seems that à Lasco had provided Cranmer with arguments and quotations which did not fit in very well with his own doctrine. But it is not surprising that Traheron jumped to the conclusion that the Archbishop had become a Zwinglian when he heard that he had made use of such arguments as these:

There be two things, to eat the Sacrament and to eat the body of Christ.

The eating of the body is to dwell in Christ, and this may be though a man never taste the Sacrament. All men eat not the body in the Sacrament. *Hoc est corpus meum.* He that maketh a will bequeaths certain legacies, and this our legacy, remission of sins, which those only receive that are members of his body.

And the Sacrament is the remembrance of this death which made the will good....

Our faith is not to believe him to be in bread and wine, but that he is in heaven; this is proved by Scripture and Doctors, till the Bishop of Rome's usurped power came in....

I believe that Christ is eaten with the heart....

Eating with his mouth giveth nothing to no man, nor the body being in the bread....

The good man hath the word within him....

AUGUSTINE. *Quid paras ventrem et dentes? Crede et man-ducasti....*

TERTULLIAN. *Appellavit panem suum Corpus....*

Hoc est Corpus meum, id est figura Corporis. Thus sayeth the old fathers....

For Christ when he bids us eat his body it is *figurativè*; for we cannot eat his body indeed....

It is significant that on the second day Cranmer intervened but once, leaving his cause to Ridley, in whose hands it was safer. But on the last day of the debate he recovered his balance. Probably it was Ridley's argument that saved him:

No man sayeth instead of *Hoc* put in *Panis*, but we say that *Hoc* meaneth *Panis....*

How the body is present.

And in what manner.

Quia divinitas infundit se elemento.

Then Cranmer clutched at St Paul's words: '1 CORIN. 10. Saint Paul saith: *Panis quem frangimus est communicatio Corporis.* Even so Christ when he said: *This is my body* he meant *communionem corporis.*' And so dragged himself into safety: his last argument in the debate was this:

It was natural bread, but now no common bread, for it is separated to another use. Because of the use it may be called the bread of life.

That which you see is bread and wine. But that which you believe is the body of Christ.

AUGUSTINE. We must believe that there is bread and the body.

The triumph of the Zwinglians—of Traheron, who wrote to Bullinger, 'Canterbury beyond all men's expectation most openly, most resolutely, and most learnedly defended your opinion about this business....The truth never obtained a more brilliant victory among us. I see plainly that it is all over with Lutheranism, since those who were

formerly regarded as its principal and almost only supporters have become entirely ours,' or of ab Ulmis, who
added his postscript, 'There has been a marvellous
recantation of the foolish bishops at London'—was premature. Traheron, although a Member of the Lower
House, does not appear to have been present at this
debate: and evidently the course of the last day of it had
not been reported to him.

However, Cranmer was not yet free from à Lasco's
influence. The *Defence*, written in the following year,
shows traces of his uncertainty: for in Book I (except in
the last chapter) there are several characteristically
Zwinglian expressions, although in the four other books
there are practically none. The natural inference is that
the former was written under the influence of à Lasco,
who had only just left England; the latter under the
influence of Bucer, who had just arrived. Henceforward
Cranmer's writings exhibit a retreat from Zurich, rather
than an advance towards it: until at last, in the Oxford
Disputation, the mode of expression was so characteristically Suvermerian, that hardly a suspicion of Zwinglianism remained.

It would be tedious and unprofitable to multiply
quotations, but a few are essential: and the following may
be regarded as representative of the works from which
they are taken.

But there be all these things together in the holy communion:
Christ himself spiritually eaten and drunken, and nourishing
the right believers; the bread and wine as a sacrament declaring
the same; and the priest as a minister thereof. (*Defence*, II. xii.)

And where of this word 'there' you would conclude
repugnance of my doctrine, that where in other places I have
written that Christ is spiritually in them that receive the
sacrament, and not in the sacraments of bread and wine, and
now it should seem that I teach contrary, that Christ is

spiritually present in the very bread and wine; if you be pleased to understand my words rightly, there is no repugnance in my words at all. For by this word 'there' I mean not in the sacraments of bread and wine, but in the ministration of the sacrament, as the old authors for the most part, when they speak of the presence of Christ in the sacrament, they mean in the ministration of the sacrament.... I say that Christ is but spiritually in the ministration of the sacrament,... [not that he is] but after a spiritual manner in the sacrament. (*Answer*, I. *Cran.* 74, 91.)

(This marks his divergence from Bucer. The following extracts are a vigorous repudiation of Zwinglianism.)

And where you speak of the participation of Christ's flesh and blood, if you mean of the sacramental participation only that thereby we be ascertained of the regeneration of our bodies, that they shall live, and have the fruition of God with our souls for ever, you be in a most horrible error.... For Christ's flesh and blood be in the sacrament truly present, but spiritually and sacramentally, not carnally and corporally. And as he is truly present, so is he truly eaten and drunken, and assisteth us. (*Answer*, I. *Cran.* 89.)

The flesh liveth by the bread, but the soul is inwardly fed of Christ.... We ought not to consider the bare bread; but whosoever cometh to the sacrament, eateth the true body of Christ. (*Disputation*, April 1555, I. *Cran.* 408, 421. And cf. p. 66.)

It seemeth to me a... sound and comfortable doctrine, that Christ hath but one body, and that hath form and fashion of a man's true body; which body spiritually entereth into the whole man, body and soul: and though the sacrament be consumed, yet whole Christ remaineth, and feedeth the receiver unto eternal life (if he continue in godliness), and never departeth until the receiver forsake him. And as for the wicked, they have not Christ with them at all, who cannot be where Belial is. And this is my faith, and (as meseemeth) a sound doctrine, according to God's word, and sufficient for a Christian to believe in that matter. (*Letter to Queen Mary*, September 1555, II. *Cran.* 453–4.)

It is not easy to make a satisfactory collection of extracts to illustrate Cranmer's sacramental doctrine: but I have tried to make at least a fair and an honest one. The difficulty is that the manner of expression varies so very greatly. By judiciously selected passages, a partisan could make Cranmer appear inconsistent with himself, or a consistent Lutheran, Zwinglian, Suvermerian, or even (by suppressing a few contexts) an orthodox Roman Catholic. But there is no real inconsistency. Gardiner's *Explication* is full of contradictory statements, as Cranmer and Ridley showed. But in the *Defence*, the *Answer*, or the *Disputation*, though the mode of expression varies considerably, the doctrine expressed is invariably the same. It is impossible to judge any one of these fairly without reading the whole of it: but if that be done, the details, however superficially discordant, sink naturally into place in the pattern of the complete design. Cranmer himself always claimed to have been consistent. At his Examination before Brokes (Sept. 1555) it was to the *Defence* that he appealed for his vindication: 'My book was made seven years ago, and no man hath brought any authors against it. I believe, that whoso eateth and drinketh that sacrament, Christ is within them, whole Christ, his nativity, passion, resurrection and ascension, but not corporally that sitteth in heaven.' 'I taught but two contrary doctrines,' he declared, on the same occasion: the first was, of course, transubstantiation: the second, this Suvermerian doctrine of the spiritual eating, learned from Ratramnus through Ridley's agency, modified by à Lasco, fortified by Bucer. Nor was this claim to consistency unjustified. Except for that brief period of doubt and confusion in the winter of 1548–9, Cranmer's doctrine was always clear: and it was not Zwinglianism. The rest of this essay will be devoted to showing the strength of the Zwinglian influences that were brought to bear upon him: and there can be no more solid tribute to the strength of his character than his consistent, resolute, indomitable resistance. Nor is that the least of the debts of modern Anglicans to the first Protestant Archbishop of the English Church.

The charge of cowardice, so often levelled against Cranmer, still remains to be answered: but it is based principally upon the charge of inconsistency, and if that be demolished, it involves the other in its ruin. However, this admirable passage from Professor Pollard's biography[1] demands quotation:

He alone, so far as we know, tried to save the monks of Sion from the block; he alone interceded for Fisher and More, for Anne Boleyn and for the Princess Mary, for Thomas Cromwell and Bishop Tunstall. He told Henry VIII that he had offended God, and Cromwell that the Court was setting an evil example. He maintained almost unaided a stubborn fight against the Act of Six Articles, and resisted longer than anyone else the Duke of Northumberland's plot....

The last is perhaps the most splendid instance of his courage, if by Northumberland's plot be understood not merely the plot for the succession, but rather the plot for the spoliation of the English Church. For Cranmer in his old age was suddenly called upon to face the most determined and the most ruffianly antagonist that he had yet encountered. John Dudley, Duke of Northumberland, had successfully disposed of his rivals: he had disgraced the Catholic nobility, and imprisoned the Catholic bishops: and the young King, never an entirely negligible factor in the history of this reign, was confirmed in his own doctrinal opinions by finding them so firmly held by his minister. So, with the approval of the King already secured, and with the Papists silenced, Northumberland entered secretly into an unholy alliance with John Hooper:

[1] *Thomas Cranmer*, p. 328.

the terms of this alliance were, that the Puritans were to rule the Church, and the nobility were to despoil it. Hooper was perfectly sincere: he was determined that Zwinglianism should be forced upon the Church of England by any means and at any price. Northumberland was sincere in nothing but his insatiable ambition. And so, from very different motives, the Puritans and the New Nobility joined in this nefarious alliance, and the attack on the ecclesiastical revenues began. But one man stood between them and the realisation of their plans—Cranmer, who was determined that if it cost him his life he would never allow the Church which had been entrusted to his care to be delivered from the bondage of Rome only to be thrust into the more constricting bondage of Zurich, nor its revenues to be squandered by a pack of upstart peers. Cranmer was an erastian: he believed in the Divine Right of Kings: but he did not believe that it embraced their ministers. Had Edward VI lived a few years longer, Northumberland might have succeeded in getting rid of Cranmer and making Hooper Primate. But the time was short, and the resistance of Cranmer endured long enough to frustrate for ever the plans of that unholy combination. It is impossible to exaggerate the gravity of the issue. Had the plot succeeded, Northumberland would have reduced the Church to abject poverty and abject dependence on the State: Hooper would have reduced its doctrine to a slavish imitation of the theology of Zurich. The strength of the popular opposition that would have been provoked is quite incalculable: but it may be said with certainty that the reign of Queen Jane would have made it as impossible for England to remain Protestant as the reign of Queen Mary made it impossible for England to remain Papist. Had the Church of England ever come to be identified with the objects of Northumberland and Hooper, it would have lost all its hold upon the people.

It was the resistance of Cranmer that prevented this identification: and if by his death he saved the Church of England from the supremacy of Rome, so by his life he saved her from the supremacy of Zurich.

APPENDIX

THE DATE OF CRANMER'S LITURGICAL PROJECTS

The MS., published (with a facsimile) by the Henry Bradshaw Society under the title, *Cranmer's Liturgical Projects* (edited by Dr Wickham Legg), and previously printed by Gasquet and Bishop in *Edward VI and the Book of Common Prayer*, is in two parts. Part I, which resembles certain Lutheran *Kirchenordnungen*, supplied the groundwork of the offices of Matins and Evensong in the Prayer Book of 1549: Part II, which was composed under the influence of the Reformed Breviary of Cardinal Quignon, did not lead to any practical result that we know. Consequently it has generally been assumed that Part I is the later in date: Gasquet and Bishop assign it to 'an early period in the reign of Edward VI,' and Part II to 'some date between 1543 and Henry's death in 1547.' Certainly Part II was written during the Catholic Reaction (1539–47). 'It may be described as Sarum material worked up under Quignon influence.... The body of the book shows the ancient Sarum arrangement, whilst the table of lessons drawn up by his [Cranmer's] own hand adopts the changes initiated by cardinal Quignon.... In places he enriches the modern baldness of Quignon from the ancient Catholic storehouse of Sarum.' Now the Sarum Breviary (early thirteenth century) was the most important of the three great diocesan Uses (Sarum, York, and Hereford) that had evolved in Britain during the Middle Ages: though Lincoln, Bangor, Aberdeen, and various monastic orders and collegiate churches had their own Uses also. In 1542 the Convocation of Canterbury had passed an act prescribing, for the sake of uniformity, the Sarum Use for the entire Province. This suggests that Part II was at least subsequent to that date. Further, in 1543 Cranmer proposed to Convocation a new examination and reformation of the liturgy: a very material point. On the other hand, the office for the Feast of Corpus Christi expresses so unmistakeably if not transubstantiation at least the Roman doctrine of the real presence, that it was probably written before Cranmer's conversion in 1546. It is true that it was in 1546 that Cranmer tried to persuade Henry VIII by his royal authority to suppress all marks of veneration of the Cross in the service books—a request that Henry first granted, and then refused—and that the stanzas of veneration in the *Vexilla Regis* and the Invention of the Cross in the Calendar do not appear in this draft: but it is probable that Cranmer merely hoped to persuade the King to sanction, as if on his own initiative, a step that had already been taken. These considerations point to the conclusion that Part II was written between 1543 and 1546.

But there is no necessity to reject the natural supposition that Part I was written before Part II. There is no reason to assume that 1543 was the first year in which Cranmer contemplated a revision of the liturgy. There is on the other hand strong internal evidence for the assumption that Part I was written before, and not after, the Catholic Reaction. First, the stanzas of veneration in the *Vexilla Regis* are retained, and the Invention of the Cross (May 3) in the Calendar: which makes it almost certain that Part I was put together at least before 1546. Secondly, this Part contains two drafts for a Calendar, one of which is extremely empty, the other so full as to be entirely fantastic. 'It may be described in one sentence as scripturalism without discretion. It commemorates Abel, Noe, the good Thief, Benjamin, Lydia and Deborah, Gideon and Sampson, Booz and the Centurion, king David and Nathan, Judith and Esther with others.' It is incredible that this curious production should be an amplification of the reasonable Calendar of Part II, instead of that the latter should be a contraction of this. Thirdly, the Preface, which is an abridgment of the preface of Quignon's Second Recension, and which was retained in the Prayer Book of 1549, appears in Part I, but not in Part II: it may be inferred that it was understood to be carried over from Part I to Part II, to save the labour of copying: for how else should it be absent from Part II, which in all other respects follows Quignon closely?

Now for Part I, so clearly Lutheran in its ancestry, to have been composed during the Catholic Reaction would have been pointless: consequently it must have been written before 1539. The next question is, what is the earliest date at which it could have been written?

Its Preface is derived from Quignon's Second Recension. Now Cardinal Quignon's *Brevium nuper reformatum*, which had been commissioned by Pope Clement VII, and which represents that nascent Catholic demand for reform without Reformation which found effective voice at the Council of Trent, was first published in February 1535, and the Second Recension—a carefully revised edition—in 1536. This work was extremely popular, more than a hundred editions of the Second Recension being issued before it was finally superseded by the reform of Pius V in 1568.

Moreover the Lutheran *Kirchenordnung* with which, as Dr Wickham Legg has noted, this draft has the closest affinity, is Bugenhagen's *Pia et vere Catholica et consentiens veteri Ecclesiae ordinatio*, published in 1537. A copy was presented by Bugenhagen to Henry VIII, with an inscription on the fly-leaf, *Inclyto Regi Angliȩ* &c. *Henrico octavo; doctor pomeranus*: and it is not improbable that this was the copy that Cranmer used.

On this evidence, Part I may be said to have been composed between 1537 and 1539.

Happily it is possible to date it with even greater precision by means of a letter written by the Archbishop to Crumwell on April 11, 1538. Jenkyns, who did not know of Cranmer's *Liturgical Projects*, conjectured that the reference was to the revised Sarum Breviary published in 1541: but there is no indication that either Cranmer or Malet had any hand in that revision. On the other hand, everything seems to point to the conclusion that the reference is to Part I.

My very singular good lord; forasmuch as this bearer, your trusty chaplain, Mr Malet, at this his return towards London from Ford, where as I left him, according to your lordship's assignment, occupied in the affairs of our church service, and now at the writing up of so much as he had to do, came by me here at Croden [Croydon] to know my further pleasure and commandment in that behalf; I shall beseech you, my lord, that after his duty done in seeing your lordship, he may repair unto me again with speed, for further furtherance and final finishing of that we have begun. For I like his diligence and pains in this business, and his honest humanity declared in my house for this season of his being there so well, that I can be bold to so commend him to your lordship, that I shall with all my heart beseech the same to declare your goodness and favour to him by helping his poor and small living. I know he hath very little growing towards the supporting of his necessaries; which is much pity, his good qualities, right judgment in learning, and discreet wisdom considered. Thus fare your good lordship heartily well. From Croden, the 11th of April. [1538.]

Your own assured ever, T. CANTUARIEN.

Upon the hitherto neglected evidence of this letter it is possible, then, to assign Part I with confidence to the earlier months of 1538, for we know that Cranmer was at Ford from at least January 14 to March 14 of that year. On this hypothesis, the unknown Hand A (ff. 4–6 b) and probably Hand B also (ff. 7–47), which is very like it—the additions to both are in the handwriting of Cranmer himself—can be attributed to Malet. (A slight difficulty is created by the suggestion of Gasquet and Bishop that Hand D (ff. 157–195 b) can be identified with A: but Mr A. J. Herbert and the authors of the British Museum Catalogue of the Royal MSS. agree that this identification 'seems very doubtful.')

Our conclusion is, then, that Part I of Cranmer's *Liturgical Projects* was composed in the earlier months of 1538; Part II between 1543 and 1546.

CHAPTER THREE

ENGLISH REFUGEES
IN SWITZERLAND

Quanta haec tua sit humanitas, agnosci-
mus; nosque propterea tuos esse totos
fatemur, dum nostri esse poterimus.
Quod hic tuis pro meritis rependamus
nihil est: quae in Anglia habemus, omnia
tam tua esse puta quam quae sunt
maxime tua.

*John Butler, Nicholas Partridge, Nicholas
Eliot, and Bartholomew Traheron to
Bullinger.* [Bern, November 1537.]

Cupio enim tibi et Tigurinis omnibus
inservire; nam meipsum Tigurino-
Anglum duco.

John Burcher to Bullinger, Strassburg,
September 1, 1550.

If but a Zurich dog should come over to
me (though I am not acquainted with any
except Gualter's Wartley) I would make
the most of him, and not treat him after
dog-fashion.

Bishop Parkhurst to Bullinger, Ludham,
April 28, 1562.

CHAPTER THREE

ENGLISH REFUGEES IN SWITZERLAND

IT is one of the difficulties of historiography that the historian is constantly under the necessity of harking back. To maintain a consecutive narrative is seldom possible. The stage is continually being invaded by new and unfamiliar characters, whose presence requires some explanation: and in this period especially, where these entrances are so frequent, the desperate and never quite satisfactory expedient of footnotes, 'which' (as Mr Beresford has wittily said) 'one hates to read and fears to miss'[1], proves quite inadequate to cope with the situation.

It is therefore necessary now to return to the reign of Henry VIII, in order to discover the origins of the connection between the English Reformation and the Church of Zurich.

One of the first links may perhaps be discerned in the visit to England in 1531 of Simon Grynæus, Rector of Basel University, who was promptly entrusted by Henry with an important commission—to obtain for him the written judgments of the leading Continental Reformers, Melanchthon, Zwingli, Bucer, Œcolompadius, Phrygio, Capito, Hedio, and others, upon the proposed Divorce.

A less conspicuous but far more solid link was forged a few years later, when Reyner Wolf, a Swiss printer, came to England and set up his business at the sign of the Brazen Serpent in St Paul's Churchyard. 'The flower of London booksellers,' the author of the massive but unfinished *Universal Cosmography*, from which his employee, Raphael Holinshed, quarried the material for his *Chronicles* after Wolf's death in 1574, he was for many years the chief intermediary between London and Zurich: he used to attend the Frankfort Fair every year, there

---

[1] *The Diary of a Country Parson*, 1751–1781, ed. John Beresford, p. viii (1924).

handing over the letters entrusted to him to the Zurich printer Froschover or his representative, and receiving others in exchange: and he it was, in all probability, who first pointed the road to Zurich to English travellers.

The English came to Zurich in four main detachments. From 1536–9 they were for the most part travellers, and some of them even commercial travellers, in the general sense that they always had an eye to possible business openings in Switzerland. The second batch (1539–47) were refugees from the Catholic Reaction and the Act of Six Articles. During the reign of Edward VI most of them returned home, and (with one exception) the only Englishmen who came to Zurich were mere passing visitors. But the accession of Mary (1553) brought to Zurich a stream of refugees, more numerous, and more distinguished, than those who had fled under the Six Articles.

The first Englishmen to arrive in Zurich were John Butler and William Woodroffe. They arrived on August 18, 1536, and lodged with the learned Hebraist, Conrad Pellican: a few weeks later they were joined by a third boarder, William Peterson. Meanwhile, in August, Nicholas Partridge, while on his way to Italy, had fallen dangerously ill in Zurich, and Bullinger had taken him into his own house till he recovered. There he made great friends with Bullinger's foster-son and destined successor, Rodolph Gualter: and when he returned to England in January, he was allowed to take the boy with him, and also a letter for Cranmer. The visit was brief, for on June 8 they were back in Zurich, bringing three more Englishmen with them: Nicholas Eliot, John Finch, and a third—possibly 'Mr Maltravers' (*D. Mautrena*), who seems at any rate to have been in Zurich in August 1538, but of whom nothing further is known. Meanwhile Pellican's English lodgers had brought him only misfortune. His wife, who had been ill before their arrival,

had died at the end of October. Pellican was inconsolable.
He sent away all his boarders—it was now, I think, that
Butler moved to the house of Bibliander[1]—and on
December 2 he wrote to his old friend J. Fries declaring
mournfully that he would never marry again. His next
letter (Dec. 23) was, however, couched in a more cheerful
tone: his friends had persuaded him to change his mind:
further, 'Ultra xx. foeminae verbis et scriptis e proximo
et remotis uxores mihi offeruntur, juvenes et vetulae,
divites et egenae. Tam sum pulcher et felix!' He selected
one of these: as he wrote in his *Chronicon*, he had never
seen her before, but she had excellent references, and
nobody knew anything against her. The banns were read
on January 20, 1537, and he married her at the beginning
of February. Now 'the two Englishmen'—Woodroffe and
Peterson—'returned to my table': but again they brought
misfortune, for on July 7 his daughter died. They
remained with him, however, 'until the winter and so
[*sicque*] went away to Geneva.' But meanwhile, in September, Bârtholomew Traheron arrived, 'vir doctissimus,'
and commended himself to Bullinger by writing him some
adulatory Latin verses, beginning—

> *Bullingere tuae captus virtutis amore*
> *Huc veni patrios deseruique Lares,*

which pleased Bullinger so much that he copied them out
at length into his *Diarium*, and took Traheron into his
own house, where Partridge and Eliot were already
lodging.

Of two of these men something is known. Butler was
a gentleman of considerable private means, with a brother-
in-law at Court, who in the following reign became 'one
of the four stewards of the royal household,' and (according

---

[1] Cf. Egli, *Analecta Reformatoria* (1901), II. 96; *Das Chronicon des
Konrad Pellican*, ed. B. Riggenbach (1877).

to Hooper) 'most honourably defended the cause of
Christ in the palace.' Traheron had been adopted as an
orphan by Master Richard Tracy of Toddington (Glos.),
son of the famous Squire Tracy who had left a long
testament, full of texts and Lutheran opinions, for which
his body was exhumed and burnt two years later, and
which had consequently run to several editions. It is not
surprising that Traheron had been brought up 'to forsake
the puddels of sophisters, and to fetch water from the
pure fountains of the Scripture'[1]. It is surprising, however,
that he had become a Friar Minorite while still a boy. Sent
to Oxford, he had fallen under the inquisitorial eye of
Dr London, the infamous Warden of New College, and
had fled to Cambridge, where he had taken his degree in
1533. Soon after, relinquishing his friar's habit, he had
gone abroad, visiting the German and Italian universities,
and eventually coming to Zurich.

All the Englishmen, except Maltravers, left Zurich in
the winter. Traheron and Butler visited Geneva and won
the friendship of Calvin and Farel, whose banishment
(a few months later) they foresaw[2]. They then went on to

[1] Dedication to Richard Tracy of Traheron's translation of *The
moste Excellente Workes of Chirurgerye made and set forth by maister
John Vigon, heed chirurgien of our tyme in Italie* (1543).

[2] Prof. Pollard, in his article on Traheron in the *D.N.B.*, states
that towards the end of Henry's reign Traheron found it expedient
to go abroad again, and that in 1546 he was once more with Calvin
at Geneva. I suspect that he was misled by Traheron's letter to
Bullinger, which is number CXLIX in the Parker Society's edition,
where it is wrongly dated '[Before *Feb.* 18, 1546].' The correct date
is probably January 1538; this may be shown by comparing the sentence,
'Te filiolo auctum esse, et eo quidem primo etiam die Χριστοφόρῳ, ex
animo gratulor,' with the entry in Bullinger's *Diarium* (p. 26),
'Decembris 16. [1537], paulo ante 8. antemeridianam natus est mihi
Christophorus filius. Hunc levarunt e sacro fonte Christophorus
Froschover et Barbara Wyssin'; to which Dr Egli adds this note,
'Taufbuch 16. Dezember 1537: Stophel (!): Stoffel Froschauwer und
Barbara Wyssin.' This letter was therefore written during Traheron's
visit to Geneva in the winter of 1537–8.

Strassburg, where they lodged with Sapidus. Peterson went to Glarus to buy wood which a local carpenter called Schentz was to make into bow-staves for export to England: but he was a bad business man and made a bad bargain, for (as Butler told him) the wood was quite unsuitable. He and Finch spent a short time in Strassburg, lodging (apparently) with Conrad Hubert: they joined Partridge and Woodroffe at Frankfort, and, picking up Eliot on the way, returned to England, arriving probably in May. They brought with them 'a parcel of letters and books' from Bullinger 'to the leading men of our kingdom': the books were copies of Bullinger's *De Scripturae Sanctae authoritate, certitudine, firmitate, et absoluta perfectione; deque Episcoporum, qui verbi Dei ministri sunt, institutione et functione, contra superstitionis tyrannidisque Romanae antistites*, in two volumes, just published (March 1538), and dedicated to the King. There was a copy and a letter for Cranmer, who received it somewhat coldly, was reluctant to present Henry's copy to him, and deliberately omitted to reply to Bullinger's letter: another for Crumwell, who showed more pleasure: while the King, they heard, politely 'expressed a wish to those around him, that it might be translated into English.' There were also copies for Latimer, for Sir Edward Wotton, and probably for others.

Partridge was back at Frankfort in September for the Fair, possibly selling English cloth and Oxford gloves. Butler seems to have been back at Zurich then[1]: in February (1539) he returned again to England, where he found Traheron in Crumwell's service, in which he remained until his patron's fall; Eliot studying law with

---

[1] 'Ad autumnum venerunt Butlerus, Risenstein et Johannes Cellarius, quia iterum grassabatur pestis Basileae, Buthlerus infirmus, donec famulam quoque impraegnavit.' (Pellican's *Chronikon*, p. 149.) Evidently Butler had first settled down in Basel.

a pension from the King; and Partridge in the service of the Bishop of St David's as one of his readers in divinity, 'until better provision can be made for him.' Butler was offered a place at Court, but declined it: he was a rolling stone, and preferred to wander about Switzerland and southern Germany for the rest of his life. In the autumn of 1540 we find him at Strassburg courting a widow, and then falling dangerously ill of a quartan fever. In the spring of 1542 he returned to England for the last time, to sell out all his property. He met Eliot, now a successful barrister with an income of 200 florins. Eliot died not long after: Partridge, who had been employed as tutor to the Mayor of Dover's family, had died in the preceding winter. Peterson had conformed to the Six Articles: 'but I hope,' said one of the English refugees, 'that he still continues to savour of Christ in some measure': that is the last we hear of him. Woodroffe and Finch had vanished into obscurity, though Finch reappears in June 1550 as one of Bishop Ridley's ordinands. Traheron, deprived of his employment by Crumwell's fall, had fled from the Court, and was about to marry the daughter of 'a gentle-man who favours godly doctrine,' and who gave her an excellent dowry which Traheron intended to supplement by 'teaching grammar and keeping a school for little boys in some small town in that district.' But he was destined to more important public service. Six years later he was a Member of that Parliament which met for its second session in November 1548, when it debated chiefly the doctrine of the Eucharist to be adopted in the new Prayer Book. He spoke strongly against leaving any ambiguity in the form of celebration; 'but it was not in his power to bring over his old fellow-citizens to his view.' On December 14, 1549, on Cheke's recommendation, he was appointed Keeper of the King's Library at West-minster in place of Roger Ascham (who was extremely

angry[1]), with a salary of 20 marks; a post which he retained
until the accession of Mary. In February 1550, he was
nominated by the Council as tutor to the young Duke of
Suffolk and his brother: but his pupils were carried off
by the sweating-sickness on July 6, 1551, whereupon
he retired to the country. During these years, he was
gravitating towards Calvinism: in 1550 he had quarrelled
violently with Hooper over Predestination. He was
recalled from his retirement in September by the Council,
who gave him the Deanery of Chichester, and wrote to
the Chapter telling them to elect him to it. The Chapter
made some difficulty, on the very reasonable ground that
Traheron was not in orders, and it was not until January 8,
1552, that their objections were finally overruled. Even
then the new Dean was not popular in Chichester, and
in September he exchanged his deanery for a canonry
of Windsor. Meanwhile, on October 6, 1550, and again
on February 10, 1552, he had been nominated as one of
the civil lawyers on the Commission to reform the Canon
Laws. On Mary's accession he fled to Frankfort, where
he took part in the famous 'Troubles' of 1555: shortly
afterwards he removed to Wesel, where he lectured on the
New Testament, and where he died, probably in 1558.

But to return to Butler. Having sold all his property,
he came back to Switzerland and resumed his wanderings.
He was first at Basel (1542–3), because the damp climate
of Strassburg was bad for his health: he is next heard of
at Constance in October 1548; we then find him, in
March 1549, married and settled down in Zurich, with
Jan Utenhove, an old acquaintance, lodging with him in
the following month. But in February 1550 he was at
Winterthur, and anxious to buy a small estate there, which
would cost him 500 florins. By this time his circumstances

---

[1] *Ascham to Cheke*, Augsburg, January 14, 1551. (*Aschami Epp.*
II. ix.)

were much reduced. He had spent generously and lent generously: for example, he had lent money to Thomas Blaurer, son of the pastor of Constance, and a far larger sum to John Stumphius, pastor of Stammheim and dean of the chapter of Stein, a friend of Zwingli and a noted historian, to maintain his son, John Rodolph Stumphius, at Oxford. Stumphius ignored all requests for repayment, and at last (Feb. 2, 1551) Butler had to notify his agent in England to stop the allowance to John Rodolph (who was left in a far worse plight than Butler, for his father would send him no money to enable him either to leave Oxford or to stay there: in the end he borrowed some from Hooper and came home). By the refusal of Pastor Stumphius to repay this loan, Butler was reduced to considerable straits. The last reference to him occurs in a letter from young Stumphius to his father, dated July 7, 1553, and mentioning without comment that Butler had just died at Lindau.

Meanwhile the Catholic Reaction with which the Act of Six Articles (the 'Act abolishing Diversity of Opinions') of 1539 is primarily associated had driven many Protestant refugees to the Continent. Maitland, it is true, had little difficulty in showing that the 'Whip with Six Strings' did not draw much blood: but the real importance of the Act was that it gave a royal and a legal sanction to the individual efforts of persecuting bishops. These local persecutions brought Bullinger the two most assiduous of his English correspondents: John Burcher and Richard Hilles.

Hilles was a London cloth-merchant who had fled from England with his wife in 1540 because he thought Gardiner was after him for having refused to contribute to the placing of 'large wax candles' before the crucifix and the sepulchre in his parish church, though his contribution had been paid for him privately by his mother. But in his own eyes the adventure assumed heroic proportions:

...When I perceived that there was absolutely no place left

for us in England, unless, as Ustazades replied to the king of
Persia, we were willing to be traitors to God and men, we
departed thence, but for the pretended reason of carrying on
my trade here. Which pretext is known by all our godly
acquaintance to be false, and is also suspected by the impious
dogs. However because I had not been indicted for heresy,
nor summoned before the law-courts, all my property yonder
is up to the present safe enough....I mention this in order to
inform you of our condition, lest perchance any report among
you of our exile in these parts [as being] voluntary should be
the occasion of [your] overlooking our troubles in England.
Meanwhile I freely confess to you (although it would not be
safe to reveal myself to everybody like this), I have determined
not to return thither, unless God deigns first to effect such
a change, that we may be able to serve God there without
hindrance and [without] approbation for the evil face of evil.
My wife (thank God) looks after our condition here as well
as, or even better than myself. Although in God I do not
doubt of my perseverance even to the end, I beg you to pray
the Lord for us that the same good work which He hath begun
in us He may perfect until the day of Jesus Christ....

Hilles was a very timorous man, and wrote execrable
Latin (which he found 'a troublesome business'), but, as
Burcher observed later, 'he is not accustomed to be
[a retailer] of rumours and gossip, but a writer of truth;
and for that reason he somewhat rarely writes to me [any]
news: but what he does write is generally true.' He settled
down in Strassburg, and built up a business there.
Bullinger, to whose favour his friend Butler had commended him, had recommended him to deal with a Zurich
cloth-merchant, Henry Falckner, who unfortunately, like
most of the Swiss during this period, in their dealings
with the English, could not be induced to pay his business
debts, which led to a good deal of correspondence.
Actually, Hilles only visited Zurich once, in the summer of
1542: Butler went with him, and Myles Coverdale, who

was then in Strassburg, was to have done so, but did not, partly from illness, mainly from poverty. There were not many English refugees in Alsace: Coverdale had just arrived at Strassburg from Tübingen (1541), and in 1543 he was appointed schoolmaster of Bergzabern, where he earned barely enough to support himself and his wife until his recall to England in 1548: for a friend of his, a certain Edmund ——, he procured the post of assistant master at Landau, where there also seem to have been some English boys at school: one John Dodman was appointed pastor of Bissweiler in 1544: and John Abel was, like Hilles, a merchant at Strassburg; he was a generous friend to the exiles in Queen Mary's reign. Hilles was the only one to visit Zurich, and his visit was brief: but as one of the most faithful of Bullinger's correspondents he is entitled to our attention.

Not long before this date, a very different figure had arrived in Strassburg. John Burcher had left England, abandoning 'excellent prospects,' in 1538, shortly after Lambert's condemnation. After his flight he had sent Crumwell a somewhat defiant letter, demanding protection against the bishops; a letter that naturally went unanswered. He stayed for a time in Strassburg, and then, in the autumn of 1541, went to Basel, where he lodged with Myconius for six months: during that time he visited Zurich, and, undeterred by Peterson's failure, bought wood for bow-staves: the wood he required grew in a forest belonging to the municipality, and Bullinger, at the request of Butler and Hilles, used his influence with the magistrates on his behalf. Burcher returned to Strassburg, where he lodged first with the bookseller Oporinus, and afterwards with Michael Falcon, until 1543, when he seems to have settled down in Zurich, where he married a Swiss[1]: in 1545 he

---

[1] Mörikofer, *Geschichte der evangelischen Flüchtlinge in der Schweiz* (1876), p. 47.

obtained the privileges of citizenship, which he found useful for his business. In December 1546 he went back to England on business, to sell 'his wares'—presumably the bow-staves—returning to Zurich in the spring of 1548.

Meanwhile Hilles, infinitely relieved at the death of Henry VIII, had visited England to make certain that there was no longer any danger, and, having assured himself on that point, made bold to return by the next Frankfort Fair. For his business, he took Burcher into partnership 'for two or three years, or even longer.' Accordingly, Burcher bought a house in Strassburg and settled down there, and Hilles left the city for ever on August 22, 1548. Henceforward his letters to Zurich become rarer: he left it to his partner in Strassburg to translate and forward all his news, which Burcher did most industriously, writing to Bullinger almost every month. And it was through Burcher that Bullinger sent all his letters and books to England, though Burcher had more than once to remind him that postage cost something:

An ounce is conveyed for five kreutzer from Spires to Antwerp; not to mention the charge of the courier from here to Spires, which, if it be slightly over weight, is usually not less than a batz...sometimes they despise the just price, and will refuse the letter unless you pay what they choose to demand.... I know that you do not wish me to be at any loss....

Burcher visited England again in September 1550, after the Frankfort Fair, to see his friends, whom he had not seen for twelve years. He took with him young Christopher Froschover, who was going to Oxford. He arrived back in Strassburg on November 13. His letters for the next few years have been lost: we have none between August 10, 1551, and May 1, 1553. In the summer of 1553, Bullinger

was thinking of sending his son to Oxford, but Burcher
warned him of the King's illness, and then (Aug. 16) of
his death: he offered to receive the young man into his
own house instead, and the invitation was accepted.

Hilles also wrote (July 9) upon the death of Edward VI,
which he regarded as 'a punishment for our heinous sins,'
though he had great hopes of Queen Jane. But on Mary's
accession he recanted: he therefore did not write to
Bullinger again till February 28, 1559.

For...as long as our cruel and superstitious queen Mary
reigned in this country, I was so afraid for my property,
and of getting into danger, yea, even for my life itself, that
I scarcely dared to write to persons of your character, or to
receive letters from them. Man, you say, is prone to fall, and
we all of us offend in many things. It is not therefore to be
wondered at, if I also should have stumbled, and begun to
stand in awe and fear of men more than I ought to have done;
as well also as to entertain opinions which many years since
I held in the greatest abhorrence. To that I was drawn over
by reading the volumes of some of the holy fathers....I do
not choose however to write more upon this subject...: it is
so irksome to me to write Latin, and I am now almost entirely
out of practice.

But Bullinger was forgiving: it was he, indeed, who made
the first advances towards a reconciliation: and, during the
reign of Elizabeth, Hilles continued to correspond with
him without any further embarrassment, while his son,
Barnabas Hilles, took over his father's duty of acting as
intermediary between the divines of Zurich and those of
England. Hilles' last letter, addressed to Gualter, is dated
from London, January 10, 1579, four years after the death
of Bullinger.

Burcher was more adventurous. In 1557 he went to
Poland, accompanied by William Barlow, lately Bishop of

Bath; partly to assist à Lasco and Utenhove in the work of reformation (at their own invitation), but mainly to introduce the West European style of brewing. His enterprise was not very successful: he had to wait a year before he received the royal license, and then it was only valid for Lithuania, not for the whole of Poland. He returned home in 1560, only to find that his wife and her relations had been taking advantage of his absence: a young kinsman of hers, John Billinger, with whom Burcher had taken great trouble, and for whom he had found employment in Strassburg, had taken to drink and bad company, and was living extravagantly on Burcher's slender income: another of her relations, Christopher Rotaker, a minister at Zurich, was plotting with her to get hold of Burcher's capital: while she herself was living in adultery. In 1561 he divorced her, turned out her detestable relations, married again, and, in the summer of 1562 returned to England, 'very wretched and miserable,' according to Bishop Jewel, who promised to do what he could for him. The last mention of him is in a letter from John Abel to Bullinger, August 23, 1563:

John Burcher has become a clergyman in the country not far from London, where he preaches the word of God faithfully, and is much beloved, and does much good. His wife has been delivered of a little girl, and is also well and hearty.

John Burcher is a remarkable and a significant figure in the history of this period. He was a forerunner of the new spirit in English life. In spite of his more amiable qualities—his loyalty and his affection—he was a puritan and a bigot: he prevented Hales from having portraits painted of Gualter and the leading Swiss theologians, 'lest a door shall hereafter be opened to idolatry,' and he hated Bucer's doctrines with such uncompromising hatred that he prayed for and rejoiced at Bucer's death. In him

are exhibited the salient characteristics of puritanism
strongly developed: courage, intolerance, and business
ability: the foundations on which Britain's greatness is
undoubtedly, though perhaps somewhat regrettably, laid.
But Burcher and Hilles were not the only English
refugees at Zurich during the Catholic Reaction. Butler,
in his letter of February 24, 1540, commended to Bullinger
the bearer, 'an exiled and destitute Scotsman,' whom it
is difficult to identify: John Bale, afterwards Bishop of
Ossory, but chiefly famous for his obscene polemics
(against the Roman Catholics), a category of English
literature in which he has often been rivalled, but never
surpassed, was almost certainly there in 1543, when he
published, under the pseudonym of 'Johan Harryson,' his
'*Yet a course at the Romyshe foxe*[1]*: A dysclosynge or
openynge of the Manne of synne, cōtayned in the late
Declaratyon of the Popes olde faythe made by Edmonde
Boner, byshopp of London,*' 'imprented [at] Zurik by
Olyuer Jacobson'[2]: and, above all, John Hooper arrived
at Zurich on March 29, 1547, and stayed there until
March 24, 1549.

The accession of Edward VI, which took so many of the
English refugees back to their own country, also brought
to Zurich a number of casual or curious visitors. Among
these were Thomas Harding, Fellow of New College
and Professor of Hebrew at Oxford, who was entertained by Bullinger on his way to Italy in May of the
same year: Christopher Hales, who, after lodging with

---

[1] As a sequel to Dr William Turner's *The huntyng and fyndyng out
of the Romyshe foxe which more then seuen yeares hath bene hyd among
the bisshoppes of Englonde, after that the Kynges Hyghnes had commanded
hym to be dryuen out of hys Realme. Foxes haue holes* &c. Basel,
1543.

[2] *Englische Flüchtlinge in Zürich während der Ersten Hälfte des* 16.
Jahrhunderts: von Theodor Vetter. (Neujahrsblatt herausgegeben von
den Stadtbibliothek in Zurich auf das Jahr 1893.)

Burcher for some time, came to Zurich in September
1549, hoping to have Gesner for his host—although,
according to Mont, he lodged with Gualter—where he
was joined, in the summer of 1550, by his elder brother,
John Hales, later Clerk of the Hanaper and Commissioner
on Enclosures for the Midland Counties, who came over
from Augsburg: and Christopher Mont (or Mount), an
English merchant at Strassburg and diplomatic agent of
the Crown under Henry, Edward, and Elizabeth. Mont
first came to Zurich in December 1549—though he had
already corresponded with Bullinger—with letters of
greeting from Edward VI to the Senates of Zurich and
of Bern, to negotiate for a Protestant General Council.
Cranmer, we know, had already abandoned hope of such
a Council, but it would seem that the inquisitive and
imperious boy on the throne now took up the idea, and
tried what could be done with the Swiss. Providentially,
nothing came of it: but Mont had a great admiration for
Bullinger, and continued to correspond with him regularly
about Continental politics: he died in July 1572, and
Burghley appointed Johann Sturm, a Strassburger, to
succeed him.

The list of the Englishmen at Zurich may be a short one,
but it contains many distinguished names. The attitude
of the Swiss towards them is fairly evident. They were
generous with their hospitality, and anxious to convert
their guests to Zwinglianism, but in all their financial
relations they exploited them without shame. It is true
that the leading citizens and theologians of Zurich
welcomed the refugees as their guests: but only one of the
refugees (and he the only one of whom we hear nothing
further) could not afford to pay for his lodging. The
conduct of Schentz to Peterson, of Falckner to Hilles, of
Billinger to Burcher, and, worst of all, the conduct of
noted ministers of religion like Stumphius, Rotaker, even

of Bullinger himself, shows that the quality of their mercy was somewhat strained.

By far the most important of all the English visitors to Zurich was John Hooper. He was born in Somersetshire about 1495—being therefore about ten years older than Bullinger—though the exact date and place of his birth are unknown. He was the only son of well-to-do parents. He is known to have studied at Oxford, where he took his B.A. degree in 1519, but the tradition that he was at Merton College seems to be due to a confusion between him and a kinsman of the same name who was elected a Fellow of Merton in 1510. Beyond this point, the accounts of his life up to his arrival at Strassburg at the end of 1545 are confused and contradictory. I venture to suggest the following as approximately correct, without setting out all the evidence on which it is based. (It reconciles most of the other accounts: I only discard as improbable Strype's conjecture that he was in the Black Friars monastery at Gloucester and remained there until the Dissolution in 1538.)

On leaving Oxford after taking his degree in 1519, Hooper became a Cistercian monk and entered Cleeve Abbey, in Somerset[1]. Some time later—probably after the Dissolution—he returned to Oxford, and there 'through Gods secret vocation was styrred with feruēt desire to the loue & knowledge of the Scriptures': coming under the suspicion of the authorities, he was 'compelled to voyde the Uniuersity,' and entered the service of Sir Thomas Arundel as his steward. There, while in his own words 'a courtier, and living too much of a court life in the palace of our king,' there came into his hands 'certain

---

[1] 'John Hopper that some tyme was a whyth monnke.' (*Grey Friars Chronicle*, p. 63.) In the sentence pronounced on him by Gardiner (Jan. 29, 1554) he was described as 'presbyterum, olim monachum domus sive monasterii de Cliva, ordinis Cistercien.' (Strype, *Mem.* VI. 276.)

works of Master Huldrich Zwingli' and Bullinger's com-
mentaries on the Pauline epistles, which he studied 'with
all zeal.' Arundel was perturbed, and sent him to Bishop
Gardiner, whom he asked 'by conference of learning to
do some good upon him, but in any case requiring him to
send home his seruant to him agayne.' (This was probably in 1544 or 1545.)

Winchester after long conference with M. Hooper 4. or 5.
dayes together, when he at length perceiued that neither he
could do that good, which he thought, to him, nor that he
would take any good at his hand, according to M. Arundel's
request, he sent home his seruant agayne, right well commending
his learning and wit, but yet [says Fox, with a glorious confusion of metaphor] bearing in his brest a grudging stomacke
agaynst Mayster Hooper still.

Hooper had not been arrested, but it was obvious that
he soon would be, if he stayed: and so he fled to Paris,
and from there made his way to Strassburg. Certainly on
January 27, 1546, he was at Strassburg in the house of
Richard Hilles, where he had been nursed back to life
after a very serious illness. At that time there were two
other guests lodging in Hilles' house: two sisters of a noble
Flemish family (de Tserclas), refugees on account of their
sacramentarian opinions. Romance triumphed: Hooper
fell in love with Anna de Tserclas, and made plans to
return home to demand from his father (who was a
staunch Roman Catholic) some portion of his inheritance,
on which, if his father did not refuse it to him, he hoped
to marry and 'live economically among you in Zurich,'
'in sanctity and with a good conscience, far from the
impurity of Babylon.' This visit to England was a dangerous undertaking: Hooper wrote to Bullinger asking
whether it might be allowed him to attend Mass, citing
Elisha's words to Naaman, and the case of the seven

thousand who had not bowed the knee to Baal, and enclosing a long memorandum—*Quae Melanchthon, Œcolompadius, Bucerus, Martyr de hac quaestione senserint.* Bullinger's answer was uncompromising, and Hooper felt much fortified by it. He left Strassburg in March, and apparently did not return until nearly twelve months later: he was successful in the main object of his mission, but he had not exaggerated the risk. Fox (who antedates this episode) records that he was 'agayne molested and laid for: whereby he was cōpelled (under the pretence of being Captayne of a ship going to Ireland) to take the Seas, and so escaped he (although not without extreme peril of drowning) through Fraunce, to the higher partes of Germany.' This tallies with Hooper's own account (written on a somewhat obvious model) in his next letter to Bullinger, which Simler correctly dates 'about the middle of March, 1547':

I will tell your excellence in person about my long and very dangerous journey to England: I suffered many things on land, twice I endured bonds and imprisonment; having been marvellously delivered, by the mercy of God, but at a heavy loss to my fortune, for three months I was miserably harassed at sea by enemies and by storms; but the end is not yet: what remains of this calamitous life, I pray that it may be to the glory of God's name and to the edification of his church. Having been delivered from fire and water, I came upon War: I see nothing but the death of all godliness and religion....

Hooper married Anna de Tserclas immediately after his return, and on March 29 (1547), as Bullinger recorded in his *Diarium*, they arrived at Zurich[1]. They stayed with

---

[1] 'Venit ad me ex Anglia Ioannes Hopperus una cum uxore Anna von Tserclas 29. Martii, et egit in aedibus meis aliquot diebus.' (Bullinger's *Diarium*, p. 35.) See *Johannes Hooper, Bischof von Gloucester und Worcester, und seine Beziehungen zu Bullinger und Zürich*, by Theod. Vetter, published in *Turicensia: Beiträge zur zürcherischen Geschichte* (Zurich, 1918).

Bullinger until a suitable lodging could be found for them: then they probably lodged with Johann Jacklj, 'qui praetorem urbis egit, iam vero collegii nostri camerarius est,' though at the time of their departure they were lodging with one Huldrich Zingk, whose son Daniel acted as Hooper's secretary. Their residence in Zurich was uneventful. Hooper studied theology under Bullinger, and Hebrew and Old Testament interpretation under Pellican. During this period he wrote three books: *An Answer unto my lord of wynthesters booke intytlyd a detection of the deuyls Sophistrye* (published Sept. 1547): *A Declaration of Christe and of his offyce* (Dec. 1547), dedicated to the Lord Protector Somerset: and *A Declaration of the ten holy comaundements of allmygthye God*. The latter is dated '1548' on the title-page, but the Preface is dated November 5, 1549: presumably when Hooper left Zurich it was unfinished, but already in the press, and was not completed, nor the preface added, until after Hooper had returned to London: where, indeed, he was already revising it and making 'certayne new addicions' with a view to its immediate republication by a London printer, Richard Jugge (July, 1550). A year after his arrival a daughter was born to him: she was baptised by Bullinger, and he and Bibliander's wife were the god-parents[1]. In October 1548 he stayed for a short time with Butler at Constance, and was actually there when the city, which had resisted the Interim, was sacked by the Emperor's Spanish troops (Oct. 18): it was the one exciting incident in his exile. On March 24, 1549, he left Zurich for England[2], together with his wife and daughter Rachel, and John Rodolph

---

[1] The Taufbuch of the Grossmünster contains this entry, under March 29, 1548: 'Ioannes Hopperus ex Anglia: Rachael; M. Heinrich Bullinger und Rosilla Buchmann.'

[2] 'Martii 24. abit d. Ioannes Hopperus una cum uxore sua et filia Rahele, quam ei e sacro fonte levavi, in Angliam.' (Bullinger's *Diarium*, p. 37.)

Stumphius, who was going to Oxford to study. It was almost exactly two years since he had arrived in Zurich.

The account Fox gives in his *Actes and Monuments* of Hooper's farewell to Zurich has frequently been quoted. Bullinger had entreated him not to forget his old friends when he was back in England. Hooper assured him that he could never forget.

...As touching the forgetting of his olde frendes, although (sayd he) the remembraunce of a mans countrey naturally doth delight him, neither could he deny, but god had blessed his country of England with many great commodities: yet neither the nature of country nor pleasure of commodities, nor newnesse of frendes should ouer induce him to the obliuion of such frendes and benefactors, whō he was so intirely bound unto: therfore you shall be sure (sayd he) from time to time to heare from me, and I wyll write unto you as it goeth with me. But the last newes of al I shal not be able to write: for there (sayd he) taking M. Bullinger by the hand) where I shall take most paynes, there shall you heare of me to be burned to ashes: and that shalbe the last newes which I shal not be able to write unto you, but you shall heare it of me.

Wherever Fox had this story from—perhaps the substance of it from Bullinger himself—it certainly bears the stamp of truth. Over and over again there emerges from Hooper's letters the fact that he was a man who gloried in the prospect of martyrdom: though this does not in the least detract from the heroism with which he endured it. He lived in an atmosphere of fierce suspicion: his manner was severe, his sermons violent and provocative. He always imagined himself as the first victim of a papist *coup d'état*. The apparition of Gardiner and Bonner tormented him as the apparition of the Devil tormented Loyola and Luther. He invariably exaggerated the perils which he ran and the providence by which he escaped them. A thinker less than a man of action, he flung himself with

almost daemonic energy into the work of Reformation.
The letters from England to Zurich mention repeatedly
his untiring zeal: his wife became anxious for his health.
Not unnaturally, he was never popular, except in Gloucester, where curiously enough he was beloved: but he
became the natural leader of the extreme puritan party
in the Church, and the most formidable adherent of
Zwinglianism in England.

One thing made him particularly formidable. Unlike
most of the leaders of the English Church during the
reign of Edward VI, his creed was not in process of
formation or of modification: it was already formed, rigid,
hard-cast, susceptible of little alteration: the passage of
time, the occurrence of new situations and new problems,
made it not more flexible, but more rigid. During his
residence in Zurich his theological opinions, already
coloured with a Zwinglian complexion, had been cast in
the iron mould of Tigurine orthodoxy.

His creed was ruthless in its simplicity. One of his
letters to Bullinger contains a very characteristic reference
to 'the use of the holy supper, which as it is most simple
among you, so it is most pure'—*ut est simplicissimus, sic
est purissimus*. He condemned 'vestments, and such other
detestable pomps and Judaical apparels,' and called
aspersion 'a stinking ceremony.' This passion for simplicity is, of course, reflected in his eucharistic doctrine.
Of that doctrine, as it was when Hooper arrived in London
on May 16, 1549, we have ample evidence in the *Answer*
(1547) and in two of Hooper's letters—one to Bullinger
(Jan. 27, 1546) and one to Bucer (June 19, 1548).

His arguments against transubstantiation are the objections of uninspired common-sense, expressed with brutal
candour. Naturally, to him 'Lutheranism...is in that
particular [i.e. consubstantiation] more erroneous than all
the papists.' The Roman theory itself is 'idolatry':

The mother of this idolatry was Rome, and the father unknown. A bastard is this transubstantiation doubtless.

[Christ's body]...is taken out of the world, and shall not be in the world till the great day of judgment, Acts iii....If Christ's body be in heaven, wherefore is any man so hardy [as] to resort unto the place, where the priests of Baal make a piece of bread both God and man, and teach the people to honour it.

If it were the very body of Christ corporally present, Christ's words were not true; for he bid them do it in remembrance of him. Now the remembrance of a thing is not the selfsame thing that is remembered.

The words, *Hoc* EST *corpus meum*, proveth that the bread is already the body, before the words be spoken, or else they misname the thing, and call bread flesh.

If *Hoc est corpus meum* can alter the substance of the bread, then can *Hic calix est novum testamentum* alter the substance of the chalice; and thus, as they eat the bread, they should drink also the chalice.

Of a new singing loaf, that hath been consecrated with *Hoc est corpus meum*, sometime hath creeping worms been engendered, yea, and sometime cast into the fire and burned, as Benno Cardinalis writeth of Gregory VII, otherwise called Hil[de]brandus. Good proof hath been taken, that bread remaineth after the consecration; for by the sacrament poisoned there was an emperor [Henry VI] and a bishop of Rome [Victor III] poisoned. In what subject should this poison remain?...And when these men say, the mould and rot of the bread is nothing, every man that hath his senses knoweth it is a manifest lie: for so long it may be kept, that it will run round about the altar.

Until such time as they show me that glorious and perfect body of Christ, their saying, 'Believe, believe,' shall not come into my belief; for Christ saith, *Nolite credere*.

Now, mark, although man cannot comprehend which ways a miracle is done by reason, yet must the miracle be perceived and known by reason....All the world seeth the bread remain, and no body of Christ present; yet, say they, it is there. Is

God so much the enemy of man, to give him his senses to his destruction? No. He hath of his abundant mercy given them to discern white from black, sour from sweet, chalk from cheese, the glorious body of Christ from the sign of a sacrament, which is bread.

Believe Christ's body to be really and corporally in the sacrament, when thou seest him there with thine own eyes, and not before.

How, then, are the words, *Hoc est corpus meum*, to be understood? Metaphorically: like the words, 'I am the door,' 'I am the vine,' '*Ecce agnus Dei*,' '*Ecce mater tua*,' 'Elias is now come.' The phrase 'spiritual eating' cannot be avoided: but 'to eat the body of Christ is nothing else than to believe, as he himself teacheth in the sixth of John': to believe in him, to meditate upon, and so participate in, the merits of his death and passion. The important thing in the celebration of the communion is not the sacrament, but the receiver. 'Where faith is not, no sacrament availeth.' 'This sacrament and all other be but the confirmation of Christ's promises, which be in the person that receiveth the sacraments before, or else these external signs availeth nothing.' 'It is necessary therefore to bring Christ to the sacraments by faith, and not to look for him there.' It was on these grounds that Hooper desired that a sermon on Christ's death and the redemption of mankind should precede the administration, and that he attached such overwhelming importance to 'preparation unto the sacrament' by self-examination and penitence. It may even be said that he attached greater importance to preparation for the Communion than to the Communion itself.

To Hooper, the bread and wine are symbols, not so much of Christ's body and blood, as of the promise of grace, of remission of sins and everlasting life, secured for us by his death. Yet he insisted that the sacraments are not to be considered as bare signs: 'Far be such a belief from the most unlearned Christian!'

The holy supper is a testimony of grace and a mystery of our redemption, in which God bears witness to the benefits conferred on us by Christ....And as the promise of grace is received by faith, so also the sacraments, of which [promise] they are the testimonies and the seals. There are many other ends, but this is the chief. They who thus use the sacraments do not make them bare signs.

It is upon this conception of the sacraments as 'testimonies and seals annexed unto the promise of grace' that Hooper's contention is based.

I put as much difference between the sacraments of Christ, and all other signs and tokens not appointed for sacraments, as I do between the seal of a prince that is annexed unto the writing or charter that containeth all the prince's right and title that he hath unto his realm, and the king's arms painted in a glass window. Such seals, annexed unto so weighty writings, be no less esteemed than the whole right, title or claim that is confirmed by the seal, though the matter of the seal be nothing but wax, not for the value of the matter (for twopence will buy ten times as much wax), but for the use that the matter is appointed unto. And he that would take upon him to deny the king's seal in such a purpose, and say, it is but a piece of wax, it were no less than treason, and a very contempt of the king himself; because the king hath appointed that seal to be honourably received and reverently used of all men. And as the writings sealed doth confirm and declare the right of the owner unto all the world; so doth the sacraments confirm the assurance of everlasting life unto the faithful, and declareth the same to all the world. And as the matter, substance, and land itself is not corporally nor really contained in the writing, nor annexed to the writing, neither brought (when any matter of controversy is for the land) before the judge with the writing; no more is the corporal body of Christ brought before the church, *neque cum pane, neque in pane, neque sub pane, neque per panem, neque ante panem, neque post panem.*

The analogy is very ingenious. But what Hooper failed to perceive was that a wax seal visibly stamped with the royal arms (which is not the same thing as 'a piece of wax' not so stamped—the comparison is unfair) is, after all, a mere symbol, a 'bare sign' of the king's authority: he failed to appreciate that a symbol is merely a symbol, whatever its sanction and whatever its significance: it does not cease to be a 'bare sign' because the thing that it signifies is of transcendent importance.

'They [i.e. the sacraments] be not the thing that they represent [i.e. God's promise of grace], but signs and remembrances thereof. Weigh the scripture diligently, Christian reader, and search for the truth there.' That was the sum of Hooper's sacramental doctrine: and for its support he appealed from human tradition and from the authority of bishops and priests to the word of God upon the one hand, and on the other—which was more useful— to the authority of the King and Council.

So I doubt not but our most virtuous and noble king will deliver unto his subjects the only bible, to be preached in the congregation, and suffer none other man's writings to be preached there, to seduce his faithful subjects, and say with this noble king Josijahu [i.e. Josiah] unto all the bishops and priests of his most noble realm, *Auferte de templo Domini cuncta vasa quae facta fuerant pro Baal, pro lucis, et pro universa militia coeli.* Cast out all vessels, vestments, holy-water bucket, with *placebo* and *dilexi* for the dead, with praying to dead saints, all other such trinkets as hath blasphemed the name of thy God; and use the testament and such sacraments there prescribed, and as they be prescribed by the word. O how great shall the king's majesty and the council's reward be for their thus doing! They shall triumph for ever with God in such joys as never can be expressed with tongue or pen, without end in heaven, with David, Ezechias and Josijahu.

The answer to this appeal is the history of the Reformation under Edward VI.

A final word is necessary upon the English refugees in Zurich during the Marian Persecutions. 'Here,' says Strype, 'were Jewel, Horne, Lever, Parkhurst, Humphrey, Beaumont, Mullings, and others, men of great note and eminency afterwards in the Church of England.' The Zurich Letters are full of their expressions of gratitude: while Zurich possesses a more solid memorial of their residence in the so-called Bullingerbecher presented by Queen Elizabeth in 1560, and in the three silver cups presented by Bishops Jewel, Horne, and Parkhurst in gratitude for their admission as honorary members into a select ecclesiastical drinking-club[1].

---

[1] *Notice of three Silver Cups, preserved in the Public Library at Zurich*: communicated by Ferdinand Keller (*Journal of Archaeology*, vol. XVI.)

CHAPTER FOUR

OXFORD AND
PETER MARTYR

'There is yet among us two great learned men, Petrus Martyr and Barnard Ochin, which have a hundred marks apiece: I would the king would bestow a thousand pound on that sort.'

LATIMER'S *Third Sermon preached before King Edward the Sixth*. (March 22, 1549.)

Quod optaram proximis literis, Bullingere amicissime, en mitto ad te, D. P. Martyris disputationes et libellum de Eucharistia.... Acriter dimicatum est cum hominibus acutis nimium et perversis. Palmam tamen tulit, quod certe omnibus bonis gaudio maximo est. Simili si posset Cantabrigia ornari viro, quam felicissima foret Anglia nostra!

John Burcher to Bullinger, Strassburg, August 10, 1551.

CHAPTER FOUR

OXFORD AND PETER MARTYR

THE strategic importance of the Universities was perceived clearly enough both by the advocates and by the opponents of the Reformation. The Universities were the principal theological seminaries of the day ('for all masters of arts are supposed to learn theology, except four only in each college, of whom two have to study medicine, two law'[1]): and not only did they provide priests for livings, but also, to a very considerable extent, livings for priests. Therefore in no other town, not even in London, was every inch of the ground so stubbornly contested as in Oxford and Cambridge. Bale, in Act IV of his *Comedye concerynge thre lawes*, puts the following speech into the mouth of *Hypocrisis*[2]:

And I wyll rayse up, in the uniuersytees,
The seuen slepers there, to aduaūce the popes decrees
As Dorbel & Duns, Durande & Thomas of Aquyne
The mastre of sentens, with Bachon the great deuyne
Hēricus de Gādauo. And these shall read ad clerñ [= clerum],
Aristotle and Albert, de secretis mulierum,
    With the com̃entaryes, of Auicen and Aueroyes,
And a Phebo Phebe, whych is very good for boyes.

The Catholics could count on Oxford with more confidence than on the sister university, where their position was already very largely undermined. Oxford, which had not taken kindly to the Renaissance, was violently hostile to the Reformation. 'The Oxonians,' wrote John Rodolph Stumphius to Bullinger (Nov. 12, 1550), 'are still up to the present pertinaciously sticking in the mud of popery, as they have been used to do; and in opposing them Doctor Cox [the Vice-Chancellor] seems to favour too

---

[1] *Bucer to Calvin*, Whitsunday 1550.

[2] This, however, is probably a slip on the part of either the author or the printer. The speech clearly belongs not to *Hypocrisis* (the Grey Friar) but to *Pseudodoctrina* (the Popish Doctor).

much the Fabian tactics.' Stumphius was impatient that 'such putrid limbs of antichrist may be altogether cut off and expelled from the entire university,' but his wish was as impracticable as Caligula's. The University was Catholic almost to a man: the few 'gospellers' that had arisen there in the time of Henry VIII[1] had been hunted out by the authorities: the whole of Peter Martyr's work was an almost single-handed struggle against overwhelming odds. Occasionally Oxford declared itself openly. On the fall of Protector Somerset, when every one believed that the Mass was about to be restored, Town and Gown broke prematurely into wild rejoicings: in 1553 they committed themselves with enthusiasm, while the issue was still doubtful, to the cause of Queen Mary against Queen Jane, 'and threatened burning, hanging, crucifixion and drowning to all the godly.' It cannot however be pretended that the Protestants had given no provocation. In the summer vacation of 1550 they had caught a mass-priest, 'the Alpha of all the papists,' and had thrown him into prison and fined all his congregation £10 a head: but, far worse, the looting of the Oxford libraries by Warwick's agents, under the specious name of reformation, created considerable ill-feeling, not only among Catholics; even Bale and Fuller were disgusted. Gregory Martin, in his *Discoverie of the manifold corruptions of the holy scriptures by the Heretikes of our daies, specially the English Sectaries* (Rheims, 1582), relates an anecdote of 'those good searchers in Oxford (as it is said, masters of arts) who, having to seek for papistical books in a lawyer's study, and seeing there books with red letters, cried out, Mass books, Mass books: whereas it was the code or some other book of the civil or canon law': an anecdote which suggests the extent of the destruction.

Consequently, on Mary's accession it did not take long

[1] For a list of their names, see Strype, *Mem.* I. 569.

to undo the laborious work of Peter Martyr. His own friends, like Sidall and Curtop, canons of Christ Church, and Harding, Professor of Hebrew, recanted promptly. Little mercy was shown to the imprisoned Reformers: 'It is reported to us of our keepers,' wrote Ridley to Bradford, from Bocardo, 'that the University beareth us heavily [i.e. hath ill will to us, *margin*].' The seed of Protestantism had indeed fallen upon stony ground. 'At Oxford since your departure,' wrote Jewel to Peter Martyr (March 20, 1559), 'two famous virtues, ignorance and obstinacy, have unbelievably increased: religion and all hope of learning and ability has utterly perished.' Writing to Bullinger two months later, he added:

Our universities are so afflicted and ruined, that at Oxford there are scarcely two [individuals] who think as we do, and they are so abject and broken that they can [do] nothing. That friar Soto and another Spanish monk[1], I know not who, have so torn up by the roots all that Peter Martyr had very beautifully planted, and reduced the Lord's vineyard to a wilderness. You would scarcely believe that so great a devastation could have been effected in so short a time.

But though the achievement of Peter Martyr in the University of Oxford was so superficial that it did not survive the withdrawal of the protection of the State, yet he left an abiding mark upon the theology of the Church of England.

At the beginning of 1542 the Curia had become alarmed at the spread of heresy in Italy, which had been brought to their notice by the prosecution of Aonio Paleario. The Inquisition was given more drastic powers, and spurred on to greater activity. As a result, many eminent priests and scholars, who had long been suspect, found proceedings instituted against them. A disciple of Juan

[1] Juan de Villa Garcia.

Valdez, Giulio Terenziano, was arrested at Venice and imprisoned by order of the Papal Nuncio. Now it so happened that a friend of Terenziano, the Vicar-General of the Capuchin Order, Bernardino Ochino (1487-1564), was at that time delivering a course of Lenten sermons in Venice. Ochino, the son of a barber of Siena, had the reputation of being the greatest Italian preacher since Savonarola—his sermons had moved the Emperor to admiration, and Aretine to repentance: and he was, moreover, hardly more famous for his eloquence than for his austerities. But his scholarship was far inferior to both. His theology was unsound: twice at Naples he had been accused of heresy, and the publication of his *Sette Dialogi* in 1539 had encouraged the suspicion that he leaned dangerously towards Lutheranism. Now, in a sermon preached before the Senate and the chief magistrates of Venice, he denounced the arrest of Terenziano. The Nuncio promptly inhibited him from preaching, but was forced by the popular clamour to withdraw his inhibition, and, apparently, to release Terenziano. But the harm was done. The Nuncio had examined Ochino and sent a report to Rome, in consequence of which Ochino, who had retired to Verona, where he was lecturing on the Pauline Epistles to the preaching friars of his Order, was cited to Rome to give an account of his doctrine. With some hesitation, he journeyed south, halting at Bologna to consult Cardinal Contarini, who was too ill to advise him, and thence proceeding dubiously to Florence.

Meanwhile the spread of heresy in Lucca had been engaging the attention of the Holy Office and of Guidiccioni, the Cardinal-Bishop of the diocese. Here the head of the offending[1] was a man very different from

---

[1] 'Reports had already been spread at Rome, amongst those who are conversant in these matters, that it was chiefly owing to me that

Ochino, but hardly less distinguished: Peter Martyr
Vermigli (1500–63), the Prior of the great monastery of
San Frediano. Peter Martyr was a younger man than
Ochino, and came of an ancient family: we may recall
Strype's comment (*Mem.* III. 55) on 'how insufferably he
was affronted, undermined, and belied by the popish
party at Oxford, who, one would think, might have better
entreated a man of quality by birth.' He had entered the
Augustinian Order at sixteen, to the annoyance of his
parents, and his promotion had been rapid: selected for
a preacher in 1527, Abbot of Spoleto in 1530, Prior of
S. Pietro ad Ara at Naples (1533), Visitor-General of the
Order (1540), Prior of S. Frediano at Lucca (1541), he
also enjoyed the friendship of many members of the
Curia, including Contarini and Reginald Pole. As a
preacher he was eloquent, though without Ochino's genius:
but he had what Ochino lacked—scholarship. He was a
D.D. of Padua, a good classical scholar—he had once
lectured on Homer—and skilled in Hebrew: moreover his
study of Aristotle at Padua had given him a genius for
clear reasoning and lucid exposition rare among contemporary Reformers. It was at Naples that he began 'to
see the verity of the Gospel,' from reading Bucer's Com-
mentaries on the Gospels (1527) and on the Psalms (1529),
and Zwingli's *De Vera et Falsa Religione* (1525). In 1541
the Theatines accused him of preaching heresy—mainly,
of denying purgatory—and Toledo, the viceroy at Naples,
inhibited him from preaching: but Martyr's powerful
friends at Rome quashed the inhibition, and the charge
was dropped. At S. Frediano he took great pains for the
education of the monks: he lectured himself, in Italian,
on the Pauline Epistles, and engaged three other lecturers
for them: Paolo Lacisio, of Verona, who taught Latin;

your city continued in error.' (*Peter Martyr to the faithful of the
Church of Lucca*, Strassburg, January 6, 1543.)

Count Celso Martinengo, Greek; and Emanuelo Tremellio, Hebrew. Tremellio (1510–80), the son of a Jew of Ferrara, had been converted to Christianity by Cardinal Pole (c. 1540): he was now converted to Protestantism by Martyr. All these three afterwards held honourable posts abroad: Lacisio became Professor of Greek at Strassburg, Celso became pastor of the Italian Church at Geneva, and Tremellio succeeded Fagius as King's Reader in Hebrew to the University of Cambridge.

But in 1541 the Pope had visited Lucca, and his attendant clergy carried back a bad report to Rome: the Cardinal-Bishop Guidiccioni complained to the magistrates of the spread of heresy there: and on July 21, 1542, a papal bull was published, introducing the Inquisition into Lucca. Martyr promptly withdrew, 'doubting not that this persuasion was inspired by God,' and Lacisio, Tremellio, and Giulio Terenziano fled with him. He lay hid for a while at Pisa, and then went on to Florence, where he met Ochino, who was on his way to Rome. Quoting Matt. x. 23 he persuaded Ochino to flee also but by a different route. Ochino went first: he visited Siena, to take leave of his brethren, where he very narrowly escaped arrest, and was pursued by his enemies to Florence; there he lay hid for a while; then at the end of August he left Florence, disguised as a layman, and, accompanied by three monks, made his way across the Alps to Zurich, and thence to Geneva. It is a tribute to his importance that the Pope was so enraged at his flight that he thought of suppressing the whole Capuchin Order.

A day after Ochino had left Zurich, Martyr and his companions, who had come by Bologna, Ferrara, and Verona, arrived there: they stayed for two days, enjoying 'godly, learned, and sweet communication' with Bullinger, Bibliander, Gualter, and Pellican: then they went on to Basel, and stayed there till November 16 (1542). At this time

Martyr's theological opinions, though better grounded than Ochino's, were in the melting-pot: if anything, his natural bent was towards Sacramentarianism. But it so happened that Zurich and Basel had no post to offer him: while at Strassburg the death of Capito, the Professor of Theology, created a vacancy which Bucer invited him to fill. He accepted the invitation, and lived there on terms of closest intimacy with Bucer, who characteristically begged him to be a little more ambiguous in his lectures, for the sake of union. At Strassburg he inevitably absorbed the Suvermerian point of view: it delayed his natural acceptance of Zwinglianism by some years. There also he married, as all quondam monks and priests were now expected to do: his wife was a lady of Metz, Catherine Dammartin, a quondam nun. Lacisio and Tremellio were also given posts at Strassburg: Lacisio was made Professor of Greek: Tremellio taught Hebrew in the famous School, and received a prebend of the Cathedral.

Then, in the winter of 1547, Martyr received an invitation from Cranmer to come to England. It was six months after Mühlberg, and the shadows of persecution were already lengthening across the territories of the Empire. Ochino, who had married in Geneva, and had accepted in 1545 the pastorate of the Italian Church at Augsburg, had fled to Basel, where he received a similar invitation. He was then in some poverty. He came to Strassburg with his wife, about whom we know nothing except from one of those spiteful observations so frequent in Hooper's letters—'I hear that Bernardino's wife now exhibits herself in England in dress and behaviour as a French noble-woman. But I shall soon know more about her, and so shall you': he left her in Strassburg with Martyr's wife, and himself, with Martyr and Giulio Terenziano, now Martyr's servant, departed under the escort of John Abel, an English merchant in Strassburg, arriving in

London on December 20[1]. (Their wives were brought over by Terenziano in the following spring: Tremellio, after vainly trying to obtain a post in Switzerland, probably accompanied them, and having for some time 'solicited at Court' with Cecil's aid, was appointed to Cambridge in November 1549.)

Ochino, as I conjecture, stayed with Cranmer for four months, until his wife's arrival, and then took a house in London. On May 9, 1548, he was given a prebend at Canterbury, apparently without any obligation of residence. He also received a pension of 40 marks a year from the Crown. He devoted himself to literary activity: 'Bernardino employs his whole time in writing, and that too with such vigour and speed as never before, as he told me; and he has lately had a son born to him, in whom he takes great delight.' Many of his sermons were translated and published: but more notable was the publication, in 1549, of *A tragoedie or Dialoge of the uniuste usurped primacie of the Bishop of Rome, and of all the iust abolishyng of the same.* The *Tragedy* is a very dull piece of work, which consists of nine interminable dialogues between characters ranging from 'Lucifer and Beelzebub' to 'King Henry the Eighth and Papista, and Thomas, Archbishop of Canterbury,' or from 'The People of Rome and the Church of Rome' to 'Thomas Massuccius, the Master of the Horse, and Lepidus, the Pope's Chamberlain.' Its main interest derives from the fact that two editions appeared in 1549, one before, the other after the fall of Somerset: in the first, the Ninth Dialogue is between 'King Edward the Sixth and the Lord Protector'; in the

---

[1] Abel's bill of the expenses of their journey is in the Bodleian Library. It has often been reprinted, e.g. in Young's *Aonio Paleario*, I. 576–7, and in Gorham's *Reformation Gleanings*, pp. 38–40: but both these are reprints from *Archaeologia*, XXI. (1827), No. XXVIII., 469–73, where it is published with interesting notes by N. H. Nicholas, Esq.

second, it is between 'King Edward the Sixth and the Councillors,' and from the three leaves on which Somerset's name had appeared in the first edition it was now omitted. But the man responsible for this change is generally held to have been the translator, '*Master John Ponet Doctor of Diuinitee*': who certainly had a bishopric not long after.

Ochino is often said to have been pastor of the Italian Church in London, from a conjecture of Gerdes (followed by Simler) that he is referred to in à Lasco's letter to Bullinger of January 7, 1551:

Iam vero et Itali suam habebunt Ecclesiam, quibus et templum iam et Minister peculiaris ordinatus est, vir et pius et doctus, et singulari dicendi gratia praeditus, proque Christi gloria plurima passus.

But the reference (as Kuyper noted) is to Michael Angelo Florio[1]: Ochino was too much of a Lutheran for à Lasco to have allowed him such an office.

On the accession of Mary he was deprived of his prebend, and fled to Zurich, where he was made pastor of an Italian congregation of refugees from Locarno. Unfortunately in 1563 he published at Basel his notorious *Thirty Dialogues* (translated into Latin by Castalio), one of which seemed to deny the doctrine of the Trinity, while another treated very regrettably of Polygamy, in the form of an argument between *Telipolygamus* and *Ochinus*, in which *Ochinus* had very much the worst of it. Zurich was shocked: the ministers complained to the Senate, who

---

[1] If Ochino had been a pastor in this Church, à Lasco, Micronius, or Utenhove would certainly have mentioned the fact to Bullinger in their letters. Moreover, Florio in a letter (undated) to Cecil, printed by Strype (*Cran.* II. 881), wrote, 'All these [Italians] promised his grace of Canterbury to provide me with all things needful, and *since the month of January* I have received from them so much, five pounds.' It is, of course, possible that the reference is to January 1552, not 1551: but the coincidence of the date of à Lasco's letter (Jan. 7, 1551) makes this improbable.

directed the dialogue on polygamy to be translated into German, that they might judge it for themselves: while Ochino, reckless with desperation, made his case worse by publishing an apology which contained slashing attacks on Bullinger; in it he alleged, for example, that he was being persecuted because he would not bow down before Bullinger as before a Pope or a God. After this, no mercy could be expected. His petition to be allowed to stay the winter was disregarded, and Bullinger wrote triumphantly in his *Diarium*, 'Sub finem mensis Novemb.' —the exact date was November 22—'eiicitur urbe Bernhardinus Ochinus propter prava dogmata in dialogis eius sparsa. 30. dissipata est Italica ecclesia.' Basel, Mulhausen, Nuremberg refused to receive him: he turned to a Polish Lutheran, Nicholas Radziwil, Count Palatine of Vilna and Duke of Lithuania, to whom the obnoxious volume had been dedicated, and for a short time was allowed to minister to the Italian residents in Cracow: but, in deference to the wishes of the Roman Curia, he was banished from Poland by royal edict on August 6, 1564. He died at Slakow in Moravia towards the end of the same year, at the age of seventy-seven.

It was a melancholy end to a long and futile career. He had influenced no one, and created nothing: his reputation as a preacher was purely ephemeral: he left nothing by which to be remembered except a sordid and unpleasant scandal. Members of all Churches combined to blacken his memory, for his mental instability had rendered him odious to them all. His career offers the rare example of a Reformer who was not a theologian: a limitation, in a popular preacher, of which his age was more impatient than our own. The years he spent in England, his intimacy with Cranmer, produced nothing of any value: of all the foreigners, Ochino had probably the least influence: and Peter Martyr probably the most.

Martyr it was who first made public the dispute on the nature of the Presence in the sacrament, and carried the controversy into the market-place by way of the lecture-room[1]. After spending some weeks at Lambeth, at the end of March 1548 he was appointed Regius Professor of Divinity at Oxford, in place of Dr Richard Smyth, deprived: on May 9 he was assigned (like Ochino) a royal pension of 40 marks a year for life. He began to lecture on the Epistles to the Corinthians, and then, in the spring of 1549, upon the Eucharist. These lectures on the Eucharist created a great stir: in April there was something of a riot at one of them, Smyth, the Papist's champion, who had packed the hall with his supporters, challenging Martyr to an immediate disputation. Martyr said that he was unprepared, not having been furnished with the propositions beforehand: but he offered to dispute against Smyth later, under the regular conditions, with judges and moderators presiding, and public notaries present to record the arguments. The audience becoming rowdy, the Vice-Chancellor intervened, and took the protagonists to his own house, where the propositions were agreed on, both sides undertaking (at Martyr's instance) to use only the words *carnaliter* and *corporaliter*, *realiter* and *substantialiter*, instead of the complete Scholastic terminology: further it was agreed that the disputation should be held on May 4, and that the Council should be notified[2].

The situation was critical. This was recognised by the Council, who decided themselves to appoint the moderators —who were, in fact, the royal Visitors of the University, who arrived at the beginning of May. At that, Smyth lost his nerve, and fled to Scotland: whereupon Martyr, fortified by the presence of the Visitors, published an open challenge, which was accepted by Dr Tresham and Dr Chedsey. The disputation was held on May 28–

[1] Dixon, III. 110 *n*.　　　　[2] Strype, *Cran.* I. 284 ff.

June 1. At the conclusion, the president, Dr Cox, declined to give a decision, and so both sides claimed the victory: a circumstance which spread the fame of the disputation even farther. The Catholics, being in a vast majority, were certainly unlikely to admit defeat. Martyr published a report of the disputation, though with a few alterations which Bucer recommended: it was translated by Udall. Tresham complained to the Council that Martyr's account was unfair: he had tampered with the order of the arguments, omitted some and added others, and inserted 'calumnious annotations' in the margin. However the Council allowed neither him nor Chedsey to publish their versions of the debate. Only Smyth, from the security of Louvain, published two tracts attacking Martyr, entitled *De Coelibatu Sacerdotum* and *De Votis Monasticis*: but their effect was rather impaired by the common knowledge that Smyth was an evil liver[1], and by the fact that no sooner were they in the press than he offered to write *De Sacerdotum Connubiis*, 'as a just satisfaction for anything he had written against the same,' if Cranmer would obtain for him the King's pardon.

On January 20, 1551, Martyr was appointed to a vacant canonry at Christ Church. He took his wife into college with him, and Dr Cox did the same: 'the first women, as 'twas observ'd, that resided in any coll. or hall in Oxon.'[2] This gave rise to some scandal, and parties of undergraduates and townsmen used at night to stand outside his rooms (which were on the north side of Christ Church great gate leading into Fish Street) and shout out insults about 'stews' and 'concubines' and 'coney-burrows,' and often broke his windows, till he was forced to change his

---

[1] 'He had a man-servant who took to himself a wife: he lodged with them; and, as is generally reported, they had all things in common. Such are the advocates of "*The Celibacy of Clerks and Monks*."' (*Martyr to Bucer*, June 10, 1550.)

[2] Wood, *Athenae Oxonienses*.

lodgings with the Canon of the second Stall, who lived in the Priory House. Meanwhile on March 15 his opponent, Dr Chedsey, was 'called before the Council touching such seditious preaching as he had preached in Oxford at the beginning of this Lent,' and committed to the Marshalsea; and ten days later White, the Warden of Winchester, was committed for writing a verse-lampoon entitled *Diacosio-Martyrion*, which he had sent to Louvain to be printed: but his imprisonment delayed its publication until 1553. After that, Martyr seems to have been left in peace.

But his most important activity was not in Oxford. He was consulted by Hooper upon the Vestiarian Controversy, and probably by Cranmer too: he was invited to submit his recommendations for the revision of the Prayer Book, and certainly had a hand in that revision: after the death of Bucer, Cranmer seems to have relied increasingly upon his judgment. On October 6, 1551, he was appointed a member of the Commission of 32 for the Reformation of Ecclesiastical Laws, and on November 11 he was appointed on the select committee of eight who prepared the materials for revision: and thus during those critical months, November 1551 to April 1552, he stayed with Cranmer at Lambeth, returning to Oxford upon the dissolution of Parliament (April 15). He was at Lambeth once more at the beginning of October 1552, to complete his work on the Ecclesiastical Laws, and probably supported Cranmer in the controversy upon kneeling at communion. But at that time he and his wife were both suffering from the effects of a quartan fever, from which she never recovered. She died at Oxford on February 16, 1553. She was a fat, homely woman[1], involved in her husband's unpopularity,

---

[1] The Papists nicknamed her 'Flaps' and 'Fusteluggs' (meaning, 'a gross, fat, unwieldy person'—Boag's *Dictionary*, 1848). George Abbot, her vindicator, admitted that she was 'reasonably corpulent,' 'but of most matron-like modesty.' Her hobby was carving 'plumb-

and it was certainly regrettable that she should have been buried so near the shrine of St Frideswide in the Cathedral. Four years later her body was dug up by the Papists, and flung onto the dunghill in the Dean of Christ Church's stable: but on January 11, 1561, it was solemnly re-interred, being mingled, at Calfhill's suggestion, with the bones of St Frideswide, so that the desecration should not be repeated.

At the time of her death, Martyr himself was suffering a relapse, and he had hardly recovered before the Edwardine Reformation had run its course. On Mary's accession he was confined to his house under the custody of his old friend, Sidall. Giulio Terenziano went to London to present a petition to the Council: he was told to wait, but nothing was done. He and Whittingham then appealed to Sir John Mason, by whose influence Martyr received permission to come up to London and plead his cause before the Council: he was also allowed to remove all his property from Oxford.

Then followed an incident which reflects the very highest credit upon both Martyr and Cranmer.

Dr Peter comes to London. He goes to [the Archbishop of] Canterbury, his ancient and most saintly host. Who can express, how welcome he was? He had so much hoped for his coming, that he often importuned the councillors [to allow] it, and was willing to give all his property as a security, if they had any fear of Dr Peter's running away. When Dr Peter comes to him, Canterbury tells him, how he has caused bills to be posted all over London, in which he offers to prove that the doctrine which was received under Edward VI is sound, agreeable to the scriptures, also to the primitive church, and approved by the authority of the old Fathers, if they will admit Peter Martyr, and one or two others, to be his colleagues. Dr Peter praises the deed, [and] further says that had it not

stones' into 'curious faces.' These, and other entertaining details, are to be found in Strype's *Parker*, I. 199–201.

been done, he would have wished to persuade it. They prepare themselves for the disputations. You should know, moreover, that the popish preachers, when they saw many of ours already thrust into prison, and that others saved themselves by flight, bragged a great deal about disputing with us. However, when Canterbury's placards were posted up, they began to sing on another note, to the effect that no disputation ought to be held, that they ought to abide by the received [doctrine], that this was a matter of faith not of reason. But those placards of Canterbury so far strengthen the minds of the godly, that they no longer hesitate to die for the truth; but they so far exasperate [our] adversaries, that they instantly bring forward a new charge of treason against Canterbury, and summon him to trial, on what day of September I do not recollect, but I am sure it happened on a Thursday [Sept. 13]. Dr Peter then dined with Canterbury, [and] after dinner Canterbury came into Dr Peter's bedroom; he tells him that he himself must abide his trial, and that it is certain that he will never see him again; that he warns him to apply for a passport: if he obtains it, he should depart; if not, let him save himself by flight: no justice was to be expected from his adversaries[1].

Cranmer's challenge was magnificent. It rallied the scattered forces of the Reformation in the darkest hour of their despair, and infused them with new courage and a determination to resist. But Cranmer was thrown into the Tower: and at this point Martyr's adventures cease to be heroic. For four days later he received a safe conduct, and it is even said that Gardiner 'gave him wherewith to beare his charges': accordingly, after taking absurdly elaborate precautions, he departed, and reached Strassburg with Terenziano at the end of October, without much risk: although, in writing to Calvin, he compared his escape ('de ore leonis') with that of his namesake, the Apostle Peter, from prison.

[1] *Giulio Terenziano to John ab Ulmis*, Strassburg, November 20, 1553.

But the situation in Strassburg had changed greatly since 1547. Bucerianism was almost extinct in what had been its stronghold. Since 1548, when the city had been compelled to receive the Interim, Lutheranism had been gaining ground: the Consistory of the clergy (with whom Martyr had never been on the best of terms[1]) was now dominated by Jean Marbach, who demanded Martyr's subscription to the Wittenberg Concordat of 1536. Martyr, who by now had practically become a Zwinglian, refused. But, after two months of this deadlock, the Senate (which was still dominated by Johann Sturm) defied the Consistory, and appointed Martyr to his old post of Professor of Theology on January 1, 1554. The opposition of the Lutheran clergy, however, placed him in a difficult position: 'they will not teach and dispute of this matter [i.e. 'our doctrine of the Eucharist'] openlie in the schoole,' he wrote to Bullinger (May 7, 1556), 'whereas neuerthelesse in the Churches they utter speeches verie outragious and bitter.'

Martyr professed at this time a great admiration for Calvin, and seems to have embraced his doctrine of predestination. Early in 1555, therefore, Calvin invited him to accept the pastorate of the Italian Church at Geneva. But Martyr, though he warmly approved the burning of Servetus[2], preferred to approve it from a

---

[1] 'I never found any one in that College, yourself alone excepted, who cared much about me and mine.' (*Martyr to Bucer*, Sept. 6, 1550.) Apparently during Martyr's residence in England, his colleagues in the Strassburg School had put up new buildings and, since Martyr had not actually resigned but was in England only on leave of absence (like Bucer himself), had sent the bill to him.

[2] 'And as to the Spaniard Servetus, I have nothing else to say, except that he was a genuine son of the Devil, whose pestiferous and detestable doctrine ought everywhere to be overthrown, nor are the authorities who put him to death blameworthy, since no signs of amendment could be found in him, and his blasphemies were altogether intolerable.' (*Martyr to the Polish nobles who profess the*

distance: a naturally cautious man, he replied (March 8, 1555) that there was nothing he could desire more than a pastorate at Geneva, but that unfortunately it would be impossible for him to obtain permission from the Senate to leave Strassburg. When, however, in May 1556 he received an invitation from Bullinger to come to Zurich as Professor of Hebrew—the vacancy had been created by the death of Pellican on April 6—he quickly made it impossible for the Senate to permit him to remain. He complained against the other clergy, and, at the Senate's request, drew up a statement of his sacramental doctrine—in a form which he knew would not be acceptable: and by the end of the month Sturm had, reluctantly, to let him go.

He arrived in Zurich in July, bringing with him John Jewel (afterwards Bishop of Salisbury), who had been lodging with him in Strassburg. He also married again: his second wife was a member of the Italian Church at Geneva, Caterina Merenda, of Brescia, by whom he had three children. His old friend Ochino was also in Zurich, as will be remembered, pastor to the Italian Church there.

On the accession of Elizabeth, he was repeatedly invited to return to England: his Professorship at Oxford seems to have been kept open for him, and his friends in England, the puritan clergy (Sampson, Sandys, Jewel, Cox, and others) wrote to him frequently, asking his advice on the controversies on the use of vestments and of the crucifix, and urging him to come back. But, as he replied to the Earl of Bedford, whose invitations were pressing, 'Truelie if I might haue mine owne will I would no lesse serue the church of *Englande* than before time I haue doone: howbeit neither mine age nor the strength of my body wil any longer indure the same, being not able to

Gospel and to the ministers of the Churches, February 14, 1556. Cf. his letter to Calvin of May 9, 1554.)

indure a viage so long, so diuers and not altogether easie.'
Nevertheless he accepted, as Cecil and Grindal had hoped
he would, the King of Navarre's invitation to attend the
Colloquy of Poissy (Sept. 9–Oct. 19, 1561) under a safe
conduct: and he was certainly very useful there to the
Huguenots, speaking, as he did, in Italian, to gain the ear
of the Queen Mother, Catharine de Medici. But the
exertion proved too much for him at his time of life: he
returned to Zurich broken in health. On November 4,
1562, he fell ill of a fever, and died a few days later. He
was buried in great honour: and it is from Simler's great
funeral oration over him that most of the facts of his
biography are drawn.

In view of Martyr's influence on the Prayer Book of
1552, it is essential to discover, as accurately as possible,
what was his sacramental doctrine.

In the first place, it must be remembered that the
doctrine which he held when he arrived in England in
1547 was very different from that which he held when he
left it in 1553. In 1547 he was a Bucerian, albeit rather
by force of circumstances than by natural inclination; five
years with Bullinger at Zurich, instead of with Bucer at
Strassburg, would have brought him far sooner to that
solution of the sacramental problem at which he finally
arrived. But he had embraced the Suvermerian doctrine:
that is evident from the fact that both Hooper and Smyth
(as, later, the author of the *Chorus alternatim canentium*)
mistook him for a Lutheran.

'Peter Martyr,' saith he [Smyth, in the Preface to his
Confutation of 'The True and Catholic Doctrine'], 'at his first
coming to Oxford, when he was but a Lutheran [*sic*] in this
matter, taught as D. Smyth now doth [i.e. 'that our Saviour
Christ's body and blood is really and corporally in the sacrament']. But when he came once to the court, and saw that

doctrine misliked them that might do him hurt in his living, he anon turned his tippet, and sang another song'[1].

But a Swiss student at Oxford, John ab Ulmis, writing to Bullinger on Ascension Day, 1548, showed a more accurate appreciation of Martyr's teaching at this period:

He has maintained...that the eucharist and holy supper of the Lord is truly a commemoration of Christ, and a solemn proclamation [*praedicatio*] of his death, [and] not a sacrifice; meanwhile, however, speaking cautiously and with prudence (if indeed it is prudence) about the corporal presence, so that he has seemed to follow neither your opinion, nor that of Luther.

Then, however, there followed a misunderstanding between Martyr and ab Ulmis about the sacramental doctrine of Zwinglianism, which has led to much subsequent confusion. As early as June 21, 1548[2], ab Ulmis wrote to Bullinger, 'You may know that Peter Martyr... has lately declared his mind more openly concerning the eucharist'—the occasion must have· been his lectures on Corinthians—'nor, if I understand his words, does he differ at all, or [only] very little, from you.' On March 2, 1549, he was still more confident:

Peter Martyr this very day on which I write this letter has propounded publicly to us all what is his opinion on this, and he seemed to us all to differ not at all, or only a nail's breadth, from your opinion; further, he defended that most valiant man, Zwingli, by the testimony of your words, and guarded him against [his] opponents who object falsely [that he makes the sacraments] bare signs: besides he says that they are all mad who make the body of Christ ἄτοπον, ἀπερίγραπτον, πολύτοπον, ἀσχημάτιστον, [without place, uncircumscribed, in many places at once, shapeless,] and other things of that kind.

[1] I. *Cran.* [P.S.] p. 373.
[2] Letter CXCVI in the Parker Soc. edition, where it is misdated '[1550].'

In fact, ab Ulmis (who was not expert in theology) believed, and persuaded Martyr to believe, that the doctrine he taught was almost identical with that which was taught at Zurich. Thus we find Martyr writing, in his first letter to Bullinger (Jan. 27, 1550), 'You congratulate me upon the happy issue of the disputations, which however is rather to be attributed to you than to me, since you have for so many years taught and defended that doctrine which I there undertook to defend.'

But to what did ab Ulmis' letter of March 2, 1549, refer? Clearly, to Martyr's lecture on *Lutheranism*: which began with a caveat, 'I haue heard of persones right credible, that neither Luther was in veray dede of so grosse an opinion in thys matier, nor zwynglius of so slendre and light a belief concernyng the sacramentes.... We dooe not affirme that either zwynglius or els Luther wer of suche opinions as aboue saied, but we shall onely examin the said sentences and opinions suche as they are carryed about and supposed to bee': and proceeded, after citing the usual Lutheran arguments, to raise the following objections:

This reall and corporall presence bringeth no maner of utilytye or benefite unto us, whiche we haue not by that other spiritual presence. For in the sixt Chapter of John, the lorde hath promised euerlastyng life unto them that eate hym, and he hathe promised moreouer that he wyll abyde in them, and they shall abyde in hym. And what can we require more then thys?

It could not otherwise be graunted that we and the fathers of the olde lawe had one maner of sacramētes....

Moreouer it should folowe that both the godly and the ungodly do eate the body of Christ.

Also ouer and aboue that spyrytuall eatyng whych wee haue in the Syxte Chapiter of John, they brynge in an other fleshely and bodelye eatynge of Christe, which can not bee proued: whereas thys and yᵗ other are all but one, sauynge that in the latter there bee added outward material signes to confyrme the thyng so much the better [...*nisi quod in posteriore adduntur symbola, ad rem magis confirmandam*].

Also it shoulde folowe that whyle thei yeld so muche unto the woordes and yᵉ letter, they wade in yᵉ same difficultee and hardenesse, that yᵉ transubstancyatours are entangled wyth all, whan they saye: THYS IS MY BODYE....

It is perfectly true that these were characteristically Zwinglian arguments. But if ab Ulmis attended Martyr's next lecture, on *Zwinglianism*, it should have damped his enthusiasm. For here Martyr's Suvermerianism was manifest:

Thre [= They, i.e. the Zwinglians] dooe...lene and staygh altogether upon the speakynges of Paule, whan the lorde biddeth this to bee dooen in remembraunce in [*sic*] hym, and his death to bee shewed til he come, whych wordes seme unto them to declare the absence of Christes bodye, and not hys presence.

But, Martyr explains, Christ's body is only 'really, corporally, and naturally' absent:

forasmuche as it is receiued by feith, it is not understanded to bee utterly absent, though hys abydynge bee in heauen as touchyng his nature and his substaūce. For he is eaten spiritually, & is thereby in veray true dede ioygned and knitte unto us.

Moreover the favourite Zwinglian similitudes of an absent friend present in one's thoughts, of 'lookyng glasses' arranged in a circle round a single individual, of the sun shining everywhere at the same time, he rejected as 'some what to cold to agree well wyth thys misterie.'

This I lyke not, that they dooe seldome make mencion of the sacramental mutation of the breade & the wyne, whiche yet is no small matier. And the fathers whāsoeuer they seme to [dis]fauour the trāsubstanciatiō. Yet haue a respecte unto yᵉ said sacramētal mutation....

Neyther is it necessarye that for these thynges Chryste

shoulde bee dyspersed and scattered aboute throughoute infinyte places. For all that euer we dooe here teache is spirituall. And yet it is not a feygned thynge nor phantasticall. For phantasies, idolles, or thynges imagined and feigned, dooe not fede the solle as it is certayn that it is dooen here in this sacramente. For we haue saied, and dooe confyrme, that these materiall sygnes dooe moste truley sygnyfye, represente, and exhibite unto us the body of Chryste, to bee eaten, and not of the bodye....

But the most lucid statement of Martyr's doctrine— Suvermerian doctrine—is to be found in a speech of his at the Disputation of May 1549:

D. Martyr. I answer: when we receiue the sacrament faithfullie, two kinds of eatings are there, and also two sorts of bread. For the receiuing of the bodie of Christ, which we haue by faith, is called a metaphoricall eating: euen as the bodie of Christ, which we receiue, is a metaphoricall bread. There also haue we an eating of the sacramentall signes; the which is a proper eating, euen as bread is both true and naturall. In the sixt of *Iohn*, there is mention onlie of metaphoricall eating, and of metaphoricall bread: but in the supper of the Lord, wherein he communicated with his apostles, there was had a proper eating; and true bread was giuen for a signe: and so in the supper was giuen both sorts of bread, euen naturall and metaphoricall: and both sorts of eating is performed; to wit, both a naturall eating in signes, and also a metaphorical, as touching the bodie of Christ, which we receiue by faith.... But as for the words; *Take ye, and eate ye,* I saie, that they must thus be understood: As ye receiue this bread, and eate it with your bodie; so receiue ye my bodie by faith, and with the mind, that ye may be strengthened thereby in stead of meate.

This was Suvermerian doctrine: yet with a difference, for the shadow of Zwinglianism lay already across it. The use of the adjective 'metaphoricall,' the persistent reference to John vi, could but be disquieting to a strict adherent

of the Strassburg school. Moreover there were passages
in Martyr's lectures, beside the attack on Lutheranism,
which might have been written by Hooper. Bucer was, indeed, extremely disquieted: the master of Suvermerian
theology trembled at the defection of his pupil. He had
arrived at Lambeth on April 25, and had been delighted
to find Martyr there, with his wife and Giulio. Martyr
was probably there to inform the Council of Smyth's
challenge and to seek Cranmer's advice upon the forthcoming Disputation. Bucer was keenly interested: and
so, on June 15, Martyr sent Giulio to him with his account
of the debate in manuscript and a private letter, in which
he wrote that he expected Bucer would, in the main,
approve his arguments, though he admitted that in the
method of treatment he had erred, if anything, in the
direction of sacramentarianism, because he was confronted
by superstition: and he feared that Bucer would not like
his declaration that 'it is impossible for the body of Christ,
even glorified, to be in many places.' The last point
puzzled Bucer, who had never taught otherwise—'I, who
in these mysteries exclude all idea of place': later he
discovered that Hooper, on his return to England, had
been spreading everywhere the scandalous report that he
was an Ubiquitarian, like Brentius. But with the rest of
the Disputation he was not entirely satisfied. He was
more frightened of those who denied Christ's presence in
the sacrament than of those who maintained transubstantiation: the latter did at least honour the sacrament,
whereas the former brought it into contempt. He feared
that too many of those who might read the acts of this
Disputation would conclude wrongly that Martyr maintained the presence, not of Christ, but only of his Spirit
and of his influence: he disliked the form of the three
propositions in dispute, because, as they stood, they did
not repudiate Zwinglianism sufficiently clearly: above all,

he regretted that Martyr had persistently used the word *Significatio* instead of *Exhibitio*, and urged him to add a preface plainly declaring Christ's presence in the sacrament, to exclude the possibility of misconstruction. Martyr obeyed: he altered his account of the debate materially, and added a preface: but the three original propositions had to stand, unless (as is possible) Martyr omitted the word *realiter* from the second one.

To call Martyr a Zwinglian in the summer of 1549 is therefore premature: but he had already entered upon that transition stage whose climax is marked, though somewhat tardily, by his removal from Strassburg to Zurich in 1556. He had, indeed, been converted long before that date, although his doctrine bore traces of Bucer's influence to the end. It was also distinguished by one peculiarity; his theory that the *body* of the devout receiver of the sacrament is thereby, 'vi quadam sanctificationis,' made 'capax beatae resurrectionis & aeternae vitae'; a theory based, apparently, on Ephes. v. 30 and Gal. ii. 20. But his doctrine was preponderantly and essentially Zwinglian: and he had reached that position before he left England. Writing to Bullinger on March 8, 1552, for instance, he spoke of himself in the same breath as of Hooper and à Lasco, the puritan leaders: the phrase occurs in his description of the Commission of 32 for the Reformation of Ecclesiastical Laws—

of whom the majority are distinguished by profound erudition and singular piety, and among them we also are admitted; I mean Hooper, à Lasco, and myself.

More definite, however, was his letter to Bullinger of April 25, 1551, in which he declared his assent to the *Consensus Tigurinus*, the agreement between Bullinger and Calvin upon the sacramental controversy:

With what you have solemnly agreed between you concerning the sacrament of the eucharist I am delighted; and I desire

9–2

nothing more than that that doctrine concerning the matter may be set forth plainly and perspicuously in the churches of Christ; as to myself, I go along with you *manibus et pedibus* in that same opinion, and I teach practically nothing else here, when the Lord's supper is treated of or debated....I shrink from no dangers, from no labours, that I may fight for this sound doctrine: and unless God himself had been with me to strengthen me, sometimes I do not know how I could have survived; but as I have great confidence in your prayers, so also I do not doubt that I am very much aided by them.

Martyr's conversion to Zwinglianism may be dated, then, between June 1, 1549 and April 25, 1551. By what influences was it effected?

One of the most important was undoubtedly the malevolence of his opponents, and the deliberate misconstructions put upon the somewhat vague metaphysics of the Strassburg Compromise. For the sake of clarity, and for the avoidance of superstition, Martyr (like Cranmer himself) was driven to dangerous simplification. In this he was, moreover, encouraged by his friends. At Oxford he had very few friends among the Fellows, and no intimate friends: but he was surrounded by an admiring band of Swiss students, John ab Ulmis, John Rodolph Stumphius, Christopher Froschover, and others, Zwinglians to a man. Ab Ulmis, that importunate youth, constituted himself Martyr's private secretary, and introduced the penurious Stumphius as his assistant: both, it may be noted, entered the Zwinglian ministry on their return. It was ab Ulmis, too, who persuaded Bullinger to write to Martyr, and nursed that new-formed intimacy. Moreover Martyr was acquainted with Hooper, who, with Coverdale, visited Oxford 'three days before Easter,' 1551: 'We exhorted each other lovingly in the Lord,' wrote Martyr to Bullinger, 'and regard each other with the greatest affection and agreement.' But far more important,

probably, was à Lasco's visit in May 1550. What happened
on that occasion is uncertain: but we have a letter from
Martyr to Bucer, dated November 11, 1550, in which he
commended (as a thing he had approved of long before)
à Lasco's proposal that a Consensus of sacramental
doctrine should be drawn up and subscribed by the four
leading foreign theologians in England: à Lasco, Bucer,
Martyr, and Ochino.

Another circumstance of very considerable importance
was that the one man who might have held Martyr back
was himself progressing even more rapidly along the same
path. Bucer, his old master and colleague, spent a few
days of the Long Vacation of 1550 with Martyr at Oxford:
but on this occasion it was not Bucer who influenced
Martyr's theology, but Martyr who influenced Bucer.
The influence of Martyr was fortified by à Lasco, whose
visit to Bucer at Cambridge in September seems to have
completed his conversion. Stumphius, who was sent to him
not long after as the bearer of a letter from Martyr, wrote
to his father (Nov. 12, 1550) with perfect truth: *De
Sacramento Coenae Dominicae plane obmutuit.*

APPENDIX

SWISS STUDENTS AT OXFORD

The little colony of Swiss students at Oxford has been
strangely neglected by historians: even Strype merely remarks
(not very accurately), 'Bullinger in these days sent over divers
young men to Oxon, to study there': yet one at least of their
number exercised a very important influence upon the course
of the Edwardine Reformation.

The first to visit Oxford was Rodolph Gualter, Bullinger's
adopted son and destined successor, who, when he was
eighteen, paid a brief visit to England (Jan.–June 1537) under
the charge of Nicholas Partridge.

Apart from this flying visit, the first Swiss student to come to Oxford (and the last but one to leave it) was John ab Ulmis, the son of a gentleman of Thurgau. He came to England in the spring of 1548, against his parents' wishes, provided with very little money and two letters of commendation from Bullinger, one to Eliot (who was dead) and one to Traheron (who was away in the country). For some months his resources were therefore somewhat strained. He had, however, a genius for acquiring patrons. His system was simple: if he was introduced to any person of consequence, whom he thought likely to be useful or generous to him, he would pester Bullinger to write to him, and urge him to write to Bullinger: or, if the person was of very great consequence indeed (such as the Marquis of Dorset or the Earl of Warwick), he would importune Bullinger to dedicate to him his next book. Not being over scrupulous, he frequently represented his new acquaintances to Bullinger as being far more influential than they actually were: for instance, he called Barnaby Fitzpatrick, the King's whipping-boy, 'an Irish earl' (*comes Hyberniae*), and attributed an astonishing authority to Ralph Skinner, an obscure lawyer in Dorset's service. He was fortunate in having a friend at Court in the person of Traheron, who secured him his introductions to men like Dorset, Northampton, Warwick, Cheke, and others: while his patrons at Oxford—Cox, the Vice-Chancellor, Sidall of Christ Church, Peter Martyr, Caius of All Souls, Harding of New College, Oglethorpe of Magdalen—he managed to secure for himself. The system worked admirably. Bullinger had the gratification of knowing that the most distinguished and influential men in England had embraced his doctrine: various more or less important people at Court or at the University had the gratification of receiving a letter from the famous Reformer: and ab Ulmis had the gratification of receiving a lump sum in cash or a small annual pension. Hooper thought he was wasting his time and money by so·constantly running up to London from Oxford, and told Bullinger so: but, as ab Ulmis naïvely replied,

To sum up all in one word, if one's object be to procure the patronage of men of rank, I think that I must not be content with walking, but must hurry on horseback.

How else, indeed, could Bullinger have enjoyed what ab Ulmis called 'the greatest possible pleasure, that is, [receiving] the letters of distinguished men and princes'? Ab Ulmis was an invaluable publicity agent for Zwinglianism, for his audacity, his energy, and his enterprise were unlimited: no man did more than he to advertise and to advance the puritan cause at Court. His visit to London on October 20, 1549, to present a copy of Martyr's lectures on Divorce to the Earl of Warwick ('from which also I derived some emolument') may well be reckoned as a turning-point in the history of the Edwardine Reformation.

Curiously, however, ab Ulmis could never persuade Bullinger to dedicate 'any of his lucubrations' to Warwick. Bullinger, very properly, was jealous of his dedications, and it was only after a long delay that he was induced to bestow on Dorset the dedication of his Fifth Decade (published on March 1, 1551). Now, it seems that he had originally intended, on ab Ulmis' recommendation, to dedicate it to Dorset and Warwick jointly, but changed his mind, and thereafter, in spite of all Northumberland's (Warwick's) advances (as reported by ab Ulmis), and in spite of all ab Ulmis' frantic solicitations, could not be brought to dedicate anything to the all-powerful Duke. Yet between March 1551 and July 1553 he published nine books, and had another lying by him in manuscript. The only possible explanation is this, and it is significant: Bullinger distrusted Northumberland, and never forgave him for betraying Hooper to his enemies in the Vestiarian Controversy.

Meanwhile, by sheer importunity, ab Ulmis provided very well for himself. At the end of November 1548, his position had been desperate. He had spent one term at Oxford as a non-collegiate student, and feared that he could barely afford another. Traheron had offered him a post at Court, with 'a large and ample salary,' but, to his credit, he was genuinely unwilling to leave his studies. Then Cox, the Vice-Chancellor, and Dean of King's College [i.e. Christ Church], procured him a King's scholarship at that college. A little later, Dorset gave him a pension of 20 crowns a year: and he received (as has been noted) occasional presents of money from his other patrons. Emboldened by his success, he sent for a poor widow's son, Alexander Schmutz, in whom he was sufficiently interested to wish to save him from 'sordid and illiberal employment' 'in the workshop of some artificer.' Schmutz (whose uncle, Augustine Bernher, was already in England) arrived at Oxford in the late autumn of 1549, and ab Ulmis actually collected enough subscriptions from his numerous patrons to maintain him there.

Ab Ulmis took his B.A. degree in the summer of 1549, and his M.A. three years later: at the same time (1552) he accepted a fellowship at St John's College, and 'laid aside his longing for home.' But this did not please his family, who promptly recalled him. He obeyed, reluctantly: and after carefully providing for Schmutz, left England in October. He became an obscure pastor at Zurich, and died in 1580.

His correspondence is extensive—38 letters, mostly to Bullinger, of which 34 have been published by the Parker Society—but, for the reasons suggested, it is not very candid. It is too full of fawning adulation and insincere enthusiasm. Ab Ulmis was in an excellent position to acquire information, but he did not hesitate to distort it for his own ends: it is therefore unfortunate that most historians of this period have received his testimony with unquestioning faith.

The other Swiss students were of less consequence: as one of the Oxford dons observed, ab Ulmis was 'as it were their standard-bearer' (*eorum veluti antesignanus*). The next to arrive, in chronological order, were Andrew Croariensis, of Constance, a medical student, and Augustine Bernher, who shortly became Latimer's servant, and ministered to the martyrs in prison with singular devotion: these followed ab Ulmis to Oxford in the autumn of 1548. Then came John Rodolph Stumphius, who accompanied Hooper to England in the spring of 1549. Cox procured him a King's scholarship at Christ Church. His numerous letters home (for the most part unpublished) are mainly occupied with his financial difficulties and his father's obstinate neglect to send him any money, which was certainly disgraceful: but they contain scraps

of valuable information on events in Oxford after the fall of
Somerset, on Hooper's consecration, Bucer's conversion, the
depreciation of the currency, the Enclosures (which he alone,
of all the foreigners in England, remarked), and so forth. He
returned to Switzerland with Croariensis in November 1551,
with letters of commendation from Harding and Martyr.
After waiting querulously in Zurich for a benefice for eighteen
months (during which time he married), he at last (July 1553)
was elected pastor of Kilchberg. He subsequently became
Antistes, or chief pastor, of Zurich, in succession to Gualter.

In the autumn of 1549 came ab Ulmis' *protégé*, Alexander
Schmutz. On ab Ulmis' departure, Suffolk (Dorset) allowed
him the same pension that he had been giving to ab Ulmis,
increased by now from 20 to 30 crowns a year: he also,
apparently, received the fellowship that ab Ulmis vacated,
through the kindly offices of Cecil and the Council. He left
England—the last of all the Swiss—in December 1553. What
became of him is unknown.

The seventh arrival was Christopher Froschover, the great
printer's nephew, who, after six months at Marburg, came to
England in Burcher's company in September 1550. Like all
the foreigners, he suffered intensely from the cold, and missed
the gigantic stoves of his own country: he also resented having
to fast in Lent. He returned home in March 1552, and was
married a few months later. He probably entered his uncle's
business.

To these must be added Henry and Conrad ab Ulmis, the
sons of John ab Ulmis' uncle Gregory, who came over in the
spring of 1551, were twice courteously entertained by Cheke
in the King's palace, and presumably returned home with
their cousin in October 1552: and—though this is not absolutely certain—Albert and Walter Blaurer, the nephews of
Ambrose Blaurer, the pastor of Constance, who seem to have
spent three months of the summer of 1551 at Oxford 'at no
small expense,' and to have then returned home.

This brings the total to eleven, and, so far as we know,
completes it. There were others who had intended coming,
such as Georgius Cellarius, a relative of Gualter, and son of

a senator of Zurich, who changed his mind and went to Padua instead, and Bullinger's own son, Henry, who was only prevented from coming by the accession of Mary: but we hear of no others who actually came, and so may reasonably conclude that there were none. The presence of these students at Oxford was not unimportant. They bore an unflinching testimony to Zwinglianism in the heart of a Catholic University: they strengthened the resolution, and accelerated the conversion, of Peter Martyr: while the personal achievements of John ab Ulmis form a memorable chapter in the history of this reign. The letters of ab Ulmis and Stumphius contain valuable information on the state of the country, while the letters of nearly all the students (and the letters of their friends about them) afford extremely interesting descriptions of the University curriculum and of the expenses of the Oxford undergraduate in the reign of Edward VI.

It is noteworthy that upon the accession of Elizabeth the stream flowed once more in the old channel, and among the Swiss who were sent to English Universities to study are to be found the names of Rodolph Gualter, Rodolph Zwingli, Henry Butler, and John Rodolph Ulmer (ab Ulmis).

CHAPTER FIVE

CAMBRIDGE
AND BUCER

Neque tam perverse doctos Cantabrigiae, atque Oxoniis D. Petrus, inveniat. Suspecti enim semper erant hujus academiae alumni haereseos, ut vocant, apud veteres doctos et indoctos; quo facile judicare posses, horum studia sinceriora Oxoniensibus semper fuisse.

Burcher to Bullinger, Strassburg, August 10, 1551.

Tibi in mentem non venit, quantus vir Bucerus theologus extitit.

JOHANNES STURM, *Antipappus quartus* (1581).

Ibi facile, inter tot rerum discrimina, est ut pereas, quod avertat Deus; quae vero hic apud nos conderes, difficillime perirent. Vivent, mihi crede, in multa secula.

Martyr to Bucer, Oxford, December 26, 1548.

CHAPTER FIVE

CAMBRIDGE AND BUCER

CAMBRIDGE was more favourably disposed than Oxford towards the Reformation, and mainly for that reason Protestantism there assumed a milder and less radical form. Oxford was the battle-ground of the extremists of both parties: Papists and Puritans attacked each other with real malice: while, in the summer of 1549, in the villages of the surrounding county, two hundred priests swung from their own steeples. In Cambridge the opposing forces, being more equally matched, preserved the amenities of theological controversy, and, indeed, avoided it as far as possible. For Cambridge had but little experience of the ferocious puritanism that for a few unhappy years dominated and embittered the sullen Catholic majority in the sister University: and it was fortunate for the final establishment of the English Reformation under Elizabeth that Cambridge was called upon to make the larger contribution to the creeds and ceremonies of the English Church.

When, in the summer of 1551, Wolfgang Musculus was approached as a possible successor to Bucer, Burcher, who was anxious that he should accept the Professorship, wrote to Bullinger as follows:

He will not find them so perversely learned at Cambridge, as Dr Peter [Martyr did] at Oxford. For the students of this university were always suspected of heresy, as they call it, by the ancient members, learned and unlearned: from which you can easily judge that their studies have always been purer than the Oxonians'.

Indeed, quite early in the reign of Henry VIII, Reformation doctrine had begun to make headway in the University: under the leadership of Barnes, the prior of St Augustine's, who was afterwards burnt at Smithfield in 1540, a little group used to meet privately for discussion at the White Horse, which was therefore nicknamed 'Little Germany' by their enemies: and it was rumoured that the Master of Peterhouse 'kept a wife privately.' (Cranmer, then a Fellow of Jesus College, was not, however, of their number.) In 1525 Sir Thomas More, the High Steward, and in 1528 Cardinal Wolsey had tried to stamp out heresy in the University: but their persecutions were only partially effective. The ascendancy of Crumwell gave the movement wider freedom, and when, on Crumwell's fall, Gardiner, Bishop of Winchester, became Chancellor of the University, there was continual friction between him and the Vice-Chancellor, Dr Matthew Parker, the Master of Bene't (Corpus Christi) College. For during his term of office Gardiner discovered many 'matiers of innovation and disordre' in the University: and he had a long and heated correspondence with Parker in the summer of 1545 about 'a tragedie called Pammachius'[1] which had been played by 'the yought of Christes College,' with the approval of the Master and President and all the Fellows except two, in contempt of 'Lent fastinges, [and] al ceremonies, and albeit the words of sacrament and masse wer not named yet the rest of the matier wryten in that tragedie in the reproffe of them was expressed.' Parker, supported by 'the masters and presidentes of the Colleges with the Doctors of the university,' replied that all 'slanderous cavillations and suspitious sentences' had been sufficiently expurgated: Gardiner, after examining the version acted, indignantly

---

[1] With regard to this celebrated performance, see C. H. Herford's *Literary Relations of England and Germany in the Sixteenth Century* (1886), E. K. Chambers' *The Mediaeval Stage*, II. 217, 220 (1903), F. S. Boas' *University Drama in the Tudor Age*, pp. 22–3 (1914), G. C. Moore Smith's *College Plays* (1923), and Mullinger, II. 74. The text of *Pammachius*, which was written by the Lutheran pastor Thomas Kirchmayer (Naogeorgus) in 1538 and published with a dedication to Cranmer, has been printed by J. Bolte and Erich Schmidt (1891).

answered that they had not: but, seeing that it was useless
to pursue the argument further, closed the correspondence
with these ominous words:

I here many thinges to be very far out of order both openly
in the university and severally in the Colleges Whereof I am
sory...I was chosen chauncelor to be soo honoured (although
above my desertes) of them and I have geven noo cause to be
despised I wil do that I canne for the mayntenaunce of vertue
and good ordre there and chalenge again of dutie to be regarded
after the proportion not of my qualities but myn office Requiring
youe Master Vicechancellor to communicate these my letters
with the Masters Presidentes and Doctours and on my behalf
to desire them gravely to consider of what moment the good
ordre of yough is and to withstand the lewde conduct of such
as have neyther shame ne feare of punyshment and correction
The lesson of obedience wold be wel taught and practised and
I wylbe more diligent to knowe howe men proufite in it thenne
I have been....

This correspondence illustrates very clearly the temper of
the University at this time: and in face of it Gardiner
was impotent to do more than threaten darkly.

But, although favourably disposed to Reformation
doctrine, Cambridge, like other great mediæval cor-
porations, had suffered greatly from Reformation politics.
It had been visited in 1535, by Legh, and again in 1549,
by a Royal Commission, when the colleges of Clare and
Trinity Hall came dangerously near to being dissolved:
and having been continually pillaged it was now 'but in
a sorry declining condition'[1]. The type of student had
changed. Hitherto, the sons of the gentry had rarely gone
to an University: but the colleges were full of poor scholars,
maintained there by scholarships from the monastic

---

[1] On December 14, 1550, Thomas Lever, himself a puritan and a
Fellow of St John's College, the puritan stronghold, preached at
St Paul's Cross a very bitter and outspoken sermon on 1 Cor. iv. 1
('Let a man so account of us, as of the ministers of Christ').

schools (the Free Schools), and being trained for the priesthood. The dissolution of the Free Schools, involved in the general fate of the monasteries to which they were attached, struck a heavy blow at the Universities: and the subsequent rapid rise in the cost of living completed the disaster. The shortage of clergy was an inevitable consequence. 'It would pity a man's heart,' Latimer declared, in his Fifth Sermon preached before King Edward VI (April 5, 1549),

to hear that that I hear of the state of Cambridge; what it is in Oxford, I cannot tell. There be few do study divinity, but so many as of necessity must furnish the colleges; for their livings [i.e. means of livelihood] be so small, and victuals so dear, that they tarry not there, but go other where to seek livings; and so they go about. Now there be a few gentlemen, and they study a little divinity. Alas, what is that?...It is not that, I wis, that will keep out the supremacy of the bishop of Rome.

Here I will make a supplication, that ye would bestow so much to the finding of scholars of good wits, of poor men's sons, to exercise the office of salvation, in relieving of scholars, as ye were wont to bestow in pilgrimage-matters, in trentals, in masses, in pardons, in purgatory-matters....I require no more but that ye bestow so much godly as ye were wont to bestow ungodly. It is a reasonable petition; for God's sake look upon it. I say no more. There be none now but great men's sons in colleges[1], and their fathers look not to have them preachers; so every way this office of preaching is pinched at....

It was to Cranmer that the University turned in its destitution: and he, to strengthen the faculty of theology, and to attract more students to it, wisely sent a number of distinguished foreign theologians and Hebraists to teach there.

---

[1] Cf. Cheke's letter to Cranmer, quoted by Strype, *Cran.* I. 242.

In 1548 Francisco Dryander, who had come to England at the beginning of the year with letters of commendation from Melanchthon to Cranmer and to the King, was appointed Greek Reader to the University. Dryander—whose real name was Encinas—was a Spaniard of noble family, born at Burgos about 1515. His brothers James and John were both theologians distinguished in their profession, the latter by being burnt at Rome in 1545: two years earlier he himself had been arrested by the Emperor's orders. He had sat at the feet of Melanchthon when he was little more than a boy: since then, after a short residence in Paris in 1541, he had quartered himself on some rich relatives in Flanders, embraced Lutheranism, and, in 1543, published at Antwerp a translation of the New Testament into Spanish, which he boldly dedicated to Charles V. For this he was arrested (Dec. 13, 1543): but on February 1, 1545, he escaped from prison. The next few years he spent in wandering about Germany, never out of danger: he made or renewed the acquaintance of Bullinger at Zurich, of Vadian at St Gall, of Calvin at Geneva, of Bucer at Strassburg, of à Lasco at Emden. He seems to have been invited to England in the winter of 1547: there, after staying with Cranmer for a while, he was placed at Cambridge, thanking God for the breathing-space (*aliquam respirationem*). His residence there, but for an illness in March 1549, was uneventful. He rejoiced at the safe arrival of Bucer and Fagius in England, and at the delightful news that they were to come to Cambridge: but their coming was delayed by illness, and Dryander actually left Cambridge a day or two before Bucer's arrival. He went straight to Basel, in order to publish there what he had written in England, fully intending to return in the following spring. But he changed his mind, and settled at Strassburg instead, sending for his wife and family (whom he had left at Cambridge) to come out and join him: he died there on December 21, 1552.

Dryander must have had an extraordinarily attractive personality, for all the leading Reformers, whatever their theological opinions, were deeply attached to him (except perhaps Bullinger and Calvin, who were somewhat in-human in their friendships): à Lasco addressed him as 'Francisce mi dilectissime frater,' and Bucer began a letter to him with the words 'Ah mi Cor,' and after his death Melanchthon offered to adopt his orphan children. The only person who disliked him was Hooper, who made a characteristically acid comment on his departure: 'Do not be alarmed at Dryander's returning to you: he consults his own interests, and cares but little for ours, when there is no money in it': a criticism that was quite unfounded. Although a Lutheran, he had friends in every Protestant camp, even at Zurich; a remarkable achievement in one of the most remarkable periods of the history of Protestantism.

Dryander's residence at Cambridge is important not so much for what he did as for what he did not do. He did not antagonise the champions of the Old Learning: himself a Lutheran with somewhat radical leanings (he disliked the ambiguity of the Prayer Book of 1549), he yet did not attempt to thrust his opinions down Catholic or conservative throats. He seems to have made no enemies: and thereby he left the University prejudiced in favour of the next foreign theologian to come there— Martin Bucer.

Martin Bucer (Butzer) was born at Schlettstadt in Alsace on November 11, 1491. His father and grandfather were cobblers: but the existence in Schlettstadt of a famous Latin school, then at its prime under the head-mastership of Jerome Gebweiler, enabled them to provide him with an excellent education. But when he was fifteen, they could afford to keep him at school no longer: if he wished to continue his studies, he must take the cowl. He therefore entered the 'reformed' Dominican monastery in Schlettstadt. In the first year of his novitiate, they told him that by the grace of Our Lady no 'prediger münch' could be damned, though he must spend some time in Purgatory: but any Dominican who forsook the Order would come to a bad end and be doomed to everlasting perdition. Terrified, the boy took his vows. As he wrote in his *Verantwortung* (or *Apologia pro vita sua*), published in 1523: 'Uñ ist also gewiszlich an mir wor wurdē dz gemeyn sprichwort. Die verzweiflung macht ein münch. Uñ dz ist meiner müncherey anfang.'

'*And thus in my case the proverb certainly came true: Despair makes a monk.*' But it did not take him long to discover that he had been enticed into the cloister with false promises. The Classics were taken from him: the only works that he was allowed to study were the writings of the Schoolmen. He was bitterly disappointed: but even these he studied to such advantage that few contemporary Reformers could claim a knowledge of scholastic theology equal to his. He was rewarded by being sent to the universities to complete his education: first to Heidelberg, then for a short time to Maintz, and then back to Heidelberg again, where he took the degree of Bachelor of Theology, and was appointed Master of the Students. Heidelberg was then a centre of Humanism, and there Bucer fell under the spell of Erasmus' writings: the Prior of his monastery, a Humanist and a Basler himself, allowed him to lecture to the students on the *Encomium Moriae*, and Brentius, his Greek tutor, on Plato's *Symposium*.

Then followed an event which changed the whole course of Bucer's life. In April 1518 a chapter of the Augustinian Order was held at Heidelberg, which was attended by

Martin Luther, as District-Vicar of the Order: it concluded on April 26 with a public disputation between Luther and his opponents, which Bucer and Brentius attended. Both were completely won by the daring and novelty of Luther's doctrine; and from that moment Bucer became an enthusiastic 'Martinianer.'

This was a serious matter. The fact that Luther was three parts a heretic was not half so damnable, from the Dominican point of view, as the fact that he was an Augustinian. The Order of which Tetzel, Prierias and Cajetan were all members, was unlikely to tolerate any defection to the enemy's camp. Bucer's life was made a burden to him: in the summer of 1519 he was nearly stoned for a speech he had made in a disputation: his correspondence was continually opened. In 1520 Jacob Hoogstraten, the Inquisitor at Cologne and persecutor of Reuchlin, summoned Bucer before him, on a charge of teaching Latin and Greek to some of the younger brethren. The position had become intolerable, and in September 1520—'*aleae jactae*,' as he wrote to Spalatin—Bucer retired to Strassburg, where fortune drove him into the arms of Ulrich von Hutten. To the part author of the *Epistolae Obscurorum Virorum* any victim of Hoogstraten was *persona grata*: and while the influence of another friend at Rome procured him his release from his monastic vows (though he remained in priest's orders), Hutten's friend, Franz Sickingen, gave him the living of Landstuhl. While there, he married a quondam nun, Elizabeth Silbereisen. But the catastrophe of Sickingen's fortunes deprived him of his refuge: and he decided, in September 1552, to go to Wittenberg to study under Luther and Melanchthon.

His way led him through Weissenburg: and there the pastor, Heinrich Motherer, a devout Lutheran but unused to preaching, implored him to stay and help to proclaim the gospel. Bucer agreed, and laboured there as a preacher for six months: but the episcopal vicar of Speyer called on the magistrates to expel him, and the imprisonment of Sickingen gave him power to enforce his demand. The magistrates privately requested Bucer and Motherer 'to withdraw for a while,' and so (May 1523) they left the city and retired to Strassburg.

When Bucer entered Strassburg, he seemed to have reached the very nadir of his fortunes. He was an ex-communicate, married priest, almost penniless, devoid of the gifts of a popular preacher (for, as Luther told him, his sermons were too scholarly and involved), and lately deprived of his chief patron. He came to Strassburg an ecclesiastical outlaw. Within six years he threw out the Mass and drove the Bishop of Strassburg out of his own cathedral city. It is, however, unnecessary to enter into the details of his work in Strassburg, of his struggles against the Mass, against the Anabaptists, against Schwenckfeld and his followers, or of his establishment of the famous Strassburg School. But it is essential, for a true appreciation of his doctrine and of his work in England, to study the wider aspect of his policy: his work for Protestant Reunion.

In September 1524 Carlstadt, by denouncing Con-substantiation as a 'Romish' doctrine, flung the torch of dissension into the Reformation camp. The relations between Luther and Zwingli, which had long been strained, blazed up into open hostility. The cleavage was, indeed, inevitable: the only wonder was that it had come so soon. War was declared between the two irreconcileable forces of Protestantism, conservatism and radicalism, reform and reformation: between the last heretic of the Middle Ages and the first Protestant of modern times. In the acrimonious literary controversy that followed, the sympathies of Bucer lay with the Sacramentarians. He had lost none of his admiration for his old master: but he was then, like Zwingli, strongly under the influence of two Netherland Protestants, Hinne Rode and Honius, who were staying with him in November 1524, and who held the purely symbolic and commemorative view of the Sacraments, as taught by the Dutch pre-Reformer Wessel[1]: and his relations with Wittenberg happened to be somewhat strained because in his Latin translation of Luther's *Church Postil* and of Bugenhagen's *Commentary on the Psalms* he had interpolated some observations of his own which were quite alien from Lutheran doctrine. It is therefore not surprising that when in October 1525 an envoy was sent from Strassburg with the proposal that every man should be permitted to believe after the measure of the gift bestowed upon him, Luther declared that whosoever denies the real presence is of Satan, and stands outside the faith: and dismissed him curtly with the words, 'We are certain of our faith.' Meanwhile the struggle against the Anabaptists brought Bucer and Zwingli into a closer alliance: and at the Disputation at Bern in January 1528 Bucer distinctly declared in favour of Zwingli's sacramental doctrine.

But with the meeting of the Diet of Speyer in 1529, at which the Lutheran Estates submitted the historic Protest from which Protestantism takes its name, the need for unity became more urgent: and from this year Bucer devoted himself to the splendid but fatal project of finding a formula of sacramental doctrine to which both Luther and Zwingli could assent. After incredible labours, he and the Landgrave of Hesse induced the two leaders to meet at Marburg in October 1529. But this Conference did far more to accentuate the quarrel than to mitigate it:

---

[1] On Wessel's sacramental doctrine and its influence on Zwingli, see Ullmann's *Reformers before the Reformation* (tr. R. Menzies, 1855), II. 505–37.

and at its conclusion Luther refused to recognise even the Strassburgers as brothers: 'er schlug es rund ab und befahl uns dem Gerichte Gottes.' Moreover the Emperor seized the opportunity of this religious deadlock to detach Saxony from the Protestant League.

The Diet of Augsburg (1530) presented an opportunity to win back the Saxon alliance. Luther and Melanchthon had drawn up a Confession of their doctrine (the Augustana), which was presented to the Emperor on June 25. Bucer first proposed a general acceptance of the Augustana, with certain reservations as to the article on the Sacrament: but with this policy the Swiss would have nothing to do. Then, as a compromise, Bucer and Sturm drew up a separate Confession, conciliatory in tone and vague in its phraseology: the important article on the Eucharist (Art. XVIII) asserted that Christ 'through the Sacraments gives his very body and his very blood truly to be eaten and drunk, for the food and drink of souls, whereby they are raised up into eternal life.' But the Zwinglians thought that this conceded too much, the Lutherans that it conceded too little, and in the end only four of the South German cities—Strassburg, Constance, Memmingen, and Lindau—were willing to assent to this Confession, which was therefore called the Tetrapolitana.

The presentation of the Tetrapolitana to the Imperial Chancellor on July 9, 1530, marks the emergence of Suvermerianism as an independent doctrine, and of Strassburg as the focus of a Centre Party of Protestantism, the party of compromise. But the danger of a coalition between Lutheran Saxony and the Catholic Emperor against the Sacramentarians was not yet averted: Melanchthon was somewhat unscrupulously engaged in adding fuel to the fires of Luther's resentment. As a last resort, Bucer, finding his letters unanswered, dashed to Coburg and, much to Melanchthon's annoyance, demanded a personal interview with Luther. This was extremely successful: Luther declared himself willing for compromise with the Strassburgers, if not with the Swiss. At the beginning of October, Bucer set out on a tour of the Oberland, as the evangelist of Protestant Reunion. He visited Ulm, Memmingen, Isny, Lindau, Constance, Zurich, and Basel. Everywhere he was received with open arms. Blaurer, at Constance, and Œcolompadius at Basel, assured him of their support: Zwingli himself now appeared eager for a formula of union. Meanwhile Bucer's labours bore political fruit in the formation, at the New Year, of the Protestant League of Schmalkalde.

The next step was to persuade the Swiss to join the League and to accept the Tetrapolitana as the basis of negotiation. In February 1531 Bucer went to Basel to receive their consent. But in the meanwhile Zwingli had repented his concessions: it was generally suspected, not without foundation, that the Lutherans were treacherously using Bucer to detach the Oberland cities from the Swiss. Thus, when 'Luther's Cardinal *a latere*' arrived in Basel, he received from Zwingli a curt note, declining to accept any ambiguous formula which veils the truth and admits all the old errors of sacramental doctrine. With the words, '*Perstamus perpetuo; parce in hac re labori et chartae*,' Zwingli closed the door for ever to the Reunion of the Protestant Churches.

But Bucer did not abandon hope. He had at least persuaded the Oberland cities to join the League: and the rest of this year he spent in strengthening his position in Ulm, Memmingen, Biberach, and, above all, in Augsburg, which his missionaries Wolfhard and Musculus had turned from a stronghold of Lutheranism into an outpost of the Strassburg group. But the prospect of a Concordat seemed more than ever remote: he lamented that the Lutherans were more stubborn and intractable than before:

the Elector of Saxony was again becoming entangled in the web of Imperial diplomacy, and the League of Schmalkalde seemed on the point of collapse. To avert this disaster, a meeting of the Protestant Estates was held at Schweinfurt in April 1552, at which Bucer, speaking for Strassburg, proposed that all the Estates should subscribe to the Augustana without abandoning the Tetrapolitana: a curious plan which was regarded with distrust by all parties: even Constance began to waver in its loyalty.

But the crisis in Wurtemburg in 1534 accentuated the need for a settlement. Wurtemburg was the Fashoda of the Reformation. On the restoration of the deposed Duke Ulrich, the Lutherans regarded the duchy as their province: but Ulrich called in not only the Lutheran preacher Schnepf, but also the Suvermerian, Blaurer. Their inevitable rivalry carried the controversy into the heart of Germany. Bucer and Sturm stood firm in support of Blaurer, and succeeded in extorting from the Lutherans the Stuttgart Concordat of August 1534. This raised the hope of a general settlement. Bucer returned to Augsburg and to Constance, where he held a secret conference with his supporters (Dec. 14–17), and then rode through the snow to Cassel, where Melanchthon awaited him. The interview, which took place on December 27, was on the whole satisfactory: Melanchthon declared himself ready for compromise, though he could not speak for Luther. Hardly had this point been reached, when Bucer received the news that Constance, afraid of these ambiguous formulae, had deserted to the Swiss. The following year was therefore spent by Bucer in strengthening his position in the Oberland: meanwhile he sent his friend Gereon Sailer, an Augsburg doctor, as an envoy to Luther, who allowed himself to be persuaded and himself proposed a conference to be held in the following year.

This conference met at Wittenberg on May 22, 1536. It was the crown of Bucer's labours: but the issue was still doubtful. 'Sextum iam annum saxum volvo,' he wrote: and would this rock roll back once more upon the Sisyphus of Protestantism, and crush him? The object of his diplomacy was to secure a formula sufficiently ambiguous to cover both the Lutheran doctrine of consubstantiation and his own doctrine of the sacramental eating, and even, perhaps, to be accepted later by the Swiss. He proposed, therefore, to substitute for the words 'corporally,' 'substantially' and 'carnally' in the description of Christ's presence in the sacrament, the words 'truly' and 'really,' which admitted of a far wider interpretation. It was a dangerous policy. Bucer may be called the Trimmer of Protestantism: and the position of a Trimmer, while it is sometimes commanding, is always insecure: moreover at Wittenberg he laboured under an additional disadvantage, for the influence of a Centre Party is naturally precarious where the Party of the Left refuses to attend. The outward expressions of goodwill were something, but the path of compromise was still beset with difficulties. Luther, sick in body and mind, was as stubborn as ever in his demand for a clear statement of the doctrine of consubstantiation, and only Bucer's tact and Melanchthon's generosity secured even the use of the word 'vere': while the Articles finally agreed on were so patently Lutheran that Bucer was only able to explain them in any other sense by a gloss three times as long as the original. Blaurer, representing Constance, refused to sign, and it was only by consummate tact that Bucer and Capito persuaded the other Oberland cities not to stand out also. The compromise had at last been achieved, but the victory lay with Luther.

At Basel in September and, twelve months later, at Bern, Bucer made a last attempt to win the Swiss for this

Concordat. But the task was hopeless. Zwingli was dead, it is true, but Bullinger was as implacable: while, since the death of Œcolompadius, Bucer's friend, the Church of Basel had been absorbed by Zurich. Nevertheless, in spite of the resentful attitude of Constance and the incredible malevolence of Zurich, he certainly effected a *rapprochement* between Luther and the Swiss greater than any accomplished either before or after.

Meanwhile it soon became evident that the Concordat was built on a foundation of sand. Within a few years it became impossible to restrain Luther. The Articles of Schmalkalde almost undid the work of Wittenberg, while Luther's heated denunciations of the Swiss were being replied to with less heat but more malice. On the other hand, Bucer had not entirely failed. He had secured a Concordat at a time when that was a vital necessity, although at a higher price than he should have allowed himself to pay: he had saved the League of Schmalkalde: he had succeeded in modifying Melanchthon's opinions, and was able to co-operate with him in the work of reformation in Cologne (1541-3), though Luther denounced the alliance, implacable to the last.

Yet from the moment of Strassburg's submission to the Wittenberg Concordat, the Central Party was doomed. It is the tragedy of the Reformation that the one man who had vision to see how vital was the need for unity should have been made a mere cat's-paw of the Lutherans. Bucer's chief limitation was that he attached too much importance to external uniformity, and assumed too readily that internal unity would follow: if he could find a formula of sacramental doctrine to which all Protestant Churches could subscribe, he would be willing to allow to each the fullest liberty of interpretation, for, to his mind, the difference was not so vital as the agreement. Perhaps, in that age of confusion between religious controversy and political intrigue, he was right. His own sacramental doctrine had originated as an ingenious attempt to make Zwinglianism acceptable to Luther: although, certainly, he came to hold it for its own sake, convinced that in his pursuit of a somewhat more worldly object he had, as it were, stumbled upon the truth. He failed to realise that any such compromise, even had it been accepted, could only have been a temporary expedient. But neither Luther nor Zwingli had any use for formulae of compromise that made men uncertain of their faith, or, worse, embraced each other's doctrines. Inevitably, after Bucer's exile, Suvermerianism on the Continent was squeezed out of existence between the two parties that it had been designed to reconcile. After the publication of the Interim, Lutheranism, by sheer weight, crushed all elements of doctrinal independence in the South German cities, and captured Strassburg itself: while those who would not submit to Lutheranism could find no other refuge than the Zwinglian camp.

But there was one country to which the Strassburg Compromise was more congenial, and whose climate (if Halifax is to be trusted) prejudices its citizens in favour of Trimmers. The echo of the six long years in which Bucer had laboured for Protestant Reunion was heard at Lambeth in 1549 and at Cambridge in 1550 before the author of this doctrine relapsed from it himself: and in the theology of Archbishop Cranmer and in the Elizabethan Settlement the Strassburg Compromise at last bore fruit.

It was natural that the third Protestant theologian of the age had some connection with England before his coming there. In 1531 he had been one of the foreign theologians whom Henry VIII had consulted, through the agency of Grynæus, upon the validity of his marriage with Catharine of Aragon. Bucer gave his opinion that marriage with a deceased brother's widow was not contrary to natural law, but suggested that, if absolutely necessary, Henry might commit bigamy, which he thought permissible because it had been permitted to David[1]. (Henry, who was genuinely scrupulous in this matter, was not at all pleased with his suggestion, as Bucer learned from the Bishop of Hereford four years later.) In 1535, when Henry was in negotiation with the Schmalkaldic League, the Germans agreed to send an embassy to England, to consist of Sturm and three theologians—Melanchthon, Bucer, and George Draco: but the disgrace and execution of Anne Boleyn destroyed the opportunity. Yet, though Bucer never visited England till 1549, his writings had a wide circulation there: he was denounced as a heretic by the Northern rebels in the Pilgrimage of Grace, and he enjoyed a controversy with Gardiner on the question of sacerdotal celibacy: above all, *The Consultation of Archbishop Hermann of Cologne*, the product of his collaboration with Melanchthon, which had been translated into English in 1547, exerted, as has already been explained, a profound influence on the liturgy of 1549.

It is, therefore, not surprising that, upon the publication of the Interim, Cranmer (to whom Bucer had dedicated his Commentary on Romans) should have offered him a

---

[1] Œcolompadius indignantly declared that such an opinion savoured more of Mohammed than of Christ. He, with Zwingli and Grynæus, held that the law of Leviticus xviii. was still binding, and that Henry was therefore morally obliged to put Catharine away. But Luther wrote, 'It might be permitted that the king should take another wife according to the example of the patriarchs, who had many wives even before the Law, but it is not right that he should exclude her [Catharine] from the royal family and from the title of Queen of England': while Melanchthon declared, 'It is most certain that polygamy is not prohibited by divine law,' and hinted, correctly enough, that the Pope would make no difficulties about granting a dispensation for bigamy. There was thus a curiously sharp demarcation of opinion between those theologians who were within the Empire of Catharine's nephew, and those who were not. (See Hastings Eells, pp. 30–43.)

refuge in England, though the Archbishop's real object was, of course, the convocation of that 'godly synod,' that Protestant General Council, to which his hopes were now directed. His invitation is dated October 2, 1548.

The grace and peace of God in Christ. I have read your letter to John Hales, in which you recall to mind the most miserable condition of Germany, and write that you can scarcely preside any longer in the ministry of the word in your city. With groanings therefore have I exclaimed with the prophet, 'Shew forth thy marvellous loving-kindness, O thou that savest them that trust in thee from those that rise up against thy right hand.' Nor do I doubt but that God will hear this and the similar groanings of the godly: and will both preserve and defend the true doctrine, which has hitherto been sincerely propagated in your churches, against all the rages of the devil and the world. Meanwhile those who by the tempestuous fury of the waves are unable to sail out into the deep must flee to the harbour. For you, therefore, my Bucer, by far the safest harbour will be our kingdom, in which. by the blessing of God, the seeds of true doctrine have already happily begun to be sown. Come therefore to us; and become a labourer with us in the Lord's harvest. *You will be of not less benefit to the universal Church of God when you are with us, than if you retained your former post. In addition, you will be better able to heal the wounds of your afflicted country in your absence, than you are now able to do while present.* Laying aside therefore all delay, come to us as soon as possible....

The sentences I have placed in italics seem to hint at Cranmer's project. Further, the Archbishop implored him to take all precautions ('You are aware of those that pursue your life: do not deliver yourself into their hands'), and to confer with 'a certain English merchant, Richard Hils' about the arrangements for the journey.

Bucer was, indeed, running a serious risk by staying on in Strassburg. Early in the year he had been summoned to Augsburg by the Elector of Brandenburg, whose courage had been broken by the disaster at Mühlberg, and who kept him virtually a prisoner for three weeks in order to make him accept the Interim, which was shortly to be laid before the Council. Bucer was indomitable: but this enforced detention was an ominous sign of what might follow. The days of his supremacy in Strassburg were evidently numbered. But still he remained there. Martyr, now at Oxford, was tormented with anxiety on his behalf. 'I cannot be easy in my mind about you,' he wrote (Dec. 26), 'for I am always afraid lest you should rashly expose yourself too long to danger, until there remains no longer any way of escape....There, amid so many dangers, you may easily lose your life, which God forbid; but what you might found among us could hardly perish. It will live, believe me, for many centuries....' This letter crossed one to him from Bucer, dated December 24, assuring him that all was not yet lost, though the situation was indeed hopeless, and, characteristically, enquiring whether three of his colleagues—probably Sleidan was one of them, but the other two are unknown—might also be invited. Martyr's reply is dated January 22, 1549:

I would advise you, since you now see the case to be hopeless, not to delay too long, nor wait till the last moment. If you do, I fear that the means to escape will slip away from you. You know what I mean. The antichrists are thirsting, I tell you, thirsting for your blood and for the blood of all men like you: and so take care, if you love Christ's church, to withdraw yourself before that time....You and Paul Fagius[1], who have been invited, ought to come hither; how welcome and accept-

---

[1] Paul Fagius (Buchlein), the son of the schoolmaster of Rheinzabern, born in 1504, had been a minister in the Church of Constance (1542–4), and had laboured to promote the Reformation in the Palatinate at the request of the Elector (1546): he was now Professor of Hebrew at Strassburg. He was not only a great Hebraist, but also a great preacher, 'more eloquent,' according to John Burcher, than Bucer himself.

able you will be, there is no need for me to write to you: for besides that he [Cranmer] is ardently longing for you both, you are greatly needed in the universities; and when you are here, I do not doubt that it will be very easy to provide for the three others whom you mention, and they will soon be invited, I am confident.... Only look to it that you escape thence in safety. Greater perils await you than you are aware of....

Cranmer also was becoming anxious; and on March 24 Peter Alexander of Arles (late chaplain to Mary of Burgundy, Regent of the Netherlands) wrote to both Bucer and Fagius from Lambeth on his behalf, urging them to delay no longer, for it was known that the authorities had already bade them leave the city.

'As I and my very dear friend Fagius could not give up the liberty of preaching the whole of Christ's kingdom, our [Senate] dismissed us on March 1, as being [considered] in the emperor's court (as it was said) moιe criminal than the rest.' So Bucer wrote to his friend Hardenberg. Burcher notified Bullinger of their dismissal, and added piously, 'The Lord preserve our England from both of them!' They had indeed been invited elsewhere, by Melanchthon, Calvin, and Myconius, and they had hardly left Strassburg before they were offered professorships at Copenhagen: but the presence in England of Martyr and of Fagius' son, Paul, who was at school at Canterbury at Cranmer's personal expense, doubtless determined their choice. They left Strassburg secretly on April 6, and arrived safely at Calais, 'the first English city,' on the 18th: there they found Peter Alexander, whom Cranmer had sent to meet them. Their crossing was delayed by unfavourable winds, but they eventually reached London on the 25th, picking up young Paul Fagius at Canterbury on their way, and thence 'proceeded by water to Lambeth, the palace of the archbishop of

Canterbury, who received us with the greatest kindness.' They were also delighted to find there 'our very dear [friend] Dr Peter [Martyr] with his wife and his [servant] Giulio, Dr Immanuel [Tremellio] with his [wife], Dryander also and other certain godly Frenchmen[1] [whom] we sent before us thence [i.e. from Strassburg].' Cranmer, who had temporarily abandoned hope of his 'godly synod,' proposed to place Bucer at Cambridge and Fagius at Oxford. 'But we are urging his Grace not to separate us, but to allow us to remain together for a time, which would be a comfort to us both.' It was then decided to place them both at Cambridge: not, however, immediately (as they hoped), but at the beginning of the academic year: in the meantime they were set 'to translate the Bible into Latin from the originals, with some explanations of the difficult passages in each chapter, and with the addition of summaries and parallel passages. All of which they wish to be translated afterwards into the English tongue, for the use of the preachers and the people. It is certainly a laborious task. God give [us] strength!'

It is evident that they were regarded with great respect. On May 5 'we were taken to the king's palace, where immediately after dinner we were granted an audience with his majesty. I cannot express how kindly he and the Lord Protector and other nobles received us, and how delighted he was at our arrival: at which indeed we were overjoyed beyond measure.' Moreover, while at Lambeth, Bucer had a curious visit from Roger Ascham, who said he was being badly treated by the other members of the Princess Elizabeth's household, and asked Bucer to write to her on his behalf, 'ut tuis literis me reponeres in gratiam Dominae meae, quae nulla mea culpa, teste deo

---

[1] Valérand Poullain, who was on the point of returning to Strassburg on a visit, and 'Antoine the Frenchman,' whoever this may be. Cf. *Fagius to Marbach*, April 26, 1549 (Gorham, p. 80).

loquar, sed iniqua aliorum opera, nonnihil a me abalienata fuit.' They stayed with Cranmer during the summer, on terms of the closest intimacy: there is, for example, an unpublished letter (dated June 15) from Fagius to his son-in-law, John Ulstetter, who was expected to follow them to England, in which he wrote: 'When you come, bring the songs with you, and do not forget *He, he, nur*...[two words illegible]..., which we used often to sing at Strassburg. We often sing here at the Archbishop's, who is extremely fond of music.' The Zwinglians were disgusted: 'I pray they may not pervert him or make him worse,' wrote Burcher to Bullinger, while on June 25 Hooper gloomily observed, 'Bucerus est cum Cantuariensi tanquam alter Scipio et individuus comes.' His influence on Cranmer's *Defence* is certainly evident.

They were at Croydon, the Archbishop's summer residence, from May 1 till the beginning of August, though Bucer went to visit Bishop Goodrich at Ely in July, passing through Cambridge on his way. At Croydon they worked at their translation of the Bible, and Fagius began to prepare a course of lectures on Isaiah. But the move to Lambeth, at the beginning of August, did not agree with them: on August 28 Fagius fell ill of a quartan fever, to which Bucer also succumbed a few days later. On September 26 a grant of £100 was made to each of them by the Crown. But for Fagius it was too late. He was so seriously ill, that it was thought that a change might do him good, and he was taken to Cambridge on November 5: but there he rapidly became worse, and on November 13 he died in the arms of Bucer, who, seriously ill himself, had hurried to his side. 'Vix...ingenij & eruditionis prima indicia dederat, cum ad superos emigraret.' He was buried in St Michael's, Cambridge, on November 24. His place, as King's Reader in Hebrew to the University, was given to Tremellio, whose son-in-law, Antoine-Raoul

le Chevalier of Montchamps, a French exile, was afterwards (in 1552) sent there to assist him.

The death of Fagius was a heavy blow to Bucer. The
University received him with great honour: he had been
appointed Regius Professor of Divinity, Madew retiring in
his favour: he was elected Doctor of Divinity by acclama-
tion, but the speech of thanks which he made to the Senate
on that occasion expressed the inward misery and loneli-
ness of his heart.

...For what else could have moved them to such great
benevolence and beneficence toward me, to me, I say, an old
man, sick, useless, foreign, and so scantily furnished in every
way, but that they esteem me, far above what I have ever
deserved, because for some years the Lord has deigned to use
me, although unworthy, in the ministry of his Gospel?...
...For my years forbid me, especially with my body now
so broken by ill health, to hope that I may anywhere discharge
my ministry in the Church of Christ more commendably or
more fruitfully by the evidence of this rank and dignity....

It was for Bucer a miserable winter. He was extremely
ill, for from the illness that had attacked him in August
he never fully recovered: he was uncomfortable in his
lodgings: he complained bitterly of the cold, to which he
was very sensitive, and he missed the enormous stoves of
his own country: his means were slender, his pension was
paid very irregularly: he was worried because the patent
of his Professorship was not signed till December 4, he
was worried about the change in Martyr's opinions, about
the safety of his friends in Strassburg, about the condition of the University which he was helpless to amend.
However, after Christmas he was a little better, and very
soon after the New Year he was well enough to begin his
public lectures (on Ephesians), to preside at disputations
in the Schools, and to preach in Latin on Sundays a series
of sermons on John vi. This last alarmed the Zwinglians,

and Valérand Poullain officiously wrote admonishing him 'not to raise any controversy upon the matter of the Eucharist.' But the warning was unnecessary, for Bucer had no such intention: he was far too deeply engaged in denouncing the laxity of University life and discipline, for he saw clearly that the failure of Oxford and Cambridge as theological seminaries lay at the root of the shortage of Reforming clergy. As he wrote to Calvin (Whitsunday, 1550),

Both universities have very many distinguished colleges, furnished with large endowments and many excellent statutes, such as no [other] university in the world possesses. For not only are a very large number of students magnificently educated in these colleges, in most of them more than a hundred, but they also have honourable money pensions for clothes and books. From these colleges swarms of faithful ministers ought to be sent forth continually to the churches....But that old connivance formerly obtained, and is at this time especially so strengthened, that by far the greater part of the Fellows are either most bitter papists or dissolute epicureans, who, so far as they can, draw over the young men to their ways, and imbue them with hatred of sound Christian doctrine and discipline.

Again, to Brentius (May 15, 1550) he wrote: 'In the universities the Balthazars [i.e. Belshazzars: men given over to feasting] are almost supreme; though there are not lacking several even of the heads [of colleges] of solid piety and well instructed to [the kingdom?] of God.'

He was unsparing in his attack. A contemporary, Thomas Horton, of Pembroke, recorded in a letter (unpublished) to Dryander his impression of Bucer's campaign:

...Dr Bucer cries incessantly, now in [his] daily lectures, now in frequent sermons, that we should practice penitence, discard the depraved customs of hypocritical religion, correct the abuses of feasts, be more frequent in hearing and having sermons, [and] constrain ourselves by some sort of discipline. Many things of this kind he impresses on us even *ad nauseam*, for we are so insensitive that, notwithstanding, we sleep with both ears, 'we eat, we drink, we take wives, and expose them as it were to be gazed at, &c.' but suddenly he concerning whom we are all heedless hammers on our inner doors[1].

But this strenuous activity overtasked his strength. In the middle of March he had so dangerous a relapse into his old malady that ab Ulmis feared, and Burcher hoped, that he would die: but fortunately his wife and two daughters had now come over to him, in the care of his son-in-law, Christopher Söll, to his great comfort, and he was carefully nursed back to health. Early in May he was convalescent, and, since his enforced idleness oppressed his mind with 'an incredible melancholy and dejection,' he promptly resumed his work with unabated vigour. His wife was sufficiently assured of his recovery to return to Germany at the beginning of June, though intending to come back in the winter: and from July 16–27 he took a holiday, and, with his son-in-law and John Bradford (a Fellow of Pembroke, whom Bucer had persuaded to be ordained: he was one of the first martyrs under Mary), visited Martyr at Oxford, and preached twice in the Cathedral, returning 'much refreshed in body and mind.'

Meanwhile, however, in his absence, and in the absence of the Vice-Chancellor, Walter Haddon, the Papists had opened their offensive. Towards the end of the previous month Bucer had, rather as a matter of form, engaged in a Disputation with three Catholic theologians, Sedgwick, Perne, and Young, principally on the question of Justification by Faith. The opposition to Bucer was, in general, friendly—*sine stomacho et aculeis*, as Ascham said: but unfortunately John Young (whom Bucer's friend, Conrad Hubert, persisted in calling *fungus*, instead of *Iungus*) flattered himself that he had done brilliantly in this

---

[1] '...at repentinus pro foribus instat interioribus, de quo omnes securi sumus.'

Disputation, and was ambitious to add to his laurels; whereupon, in Bucer's absence, he began a course of lectures on 1 Timothy, in which he impugned and ridiculed Bucer's teaching on Justification, and accused him before the Senate, 'with great excitement,' of being in serious error. Bucer and his friends were present at Young's lecture on July 30, and subsequently tried to pacify him: but Young continued his attack, though somewhat more calmly, and Bucer was driven to retort in his public lectures and from the University pulpit. Affairs having reached this stage, on August 23 the Vice-Chancellor and the Heads of houses intervened, and required from each of the disputants a written statement of the case. Both complied: and Bucer further requested the authorities to end the dispute by appointing a public Disputation on September 9, and as many following days as objectors could be found, from 7–10 a.m., and from 2–4 p.m. Young agreed to this, though he asked for a postponement, on the score of ill-health. Martyr indeed, whom Bucer had consulted on various points of this doctrine of Justification, was alarmed at the possible consequences of such a general challenge: he pointed out that the Papists had everything to gain and nothing to lose from such a contest, and that since neither Visitors nor Official judges were to preside, they would undoubtedly claim the victory and, probably, publish a garbled report of the debate. But in this he drew too much from his own experience. The Disputation seems to have taken place on the date Bucer suggested, September 9: it was only semi-official, since no judges presided, and no official report was taken of it: from the fact that it was concluded so soon it may be inferred that Young was the sole disputant on the Catholic side, for early next morning Bucer was able to send a messenger post-haste to Martyr at Oxford with the news of his triumph. This was the only serious challenge to Bucer's authority during his residence at Cambridge: the important point is that the challenge was directed against his views on Justification, and not against his sacramental doctrine.

The challenge to Bucer's sacramental doctrine came not from his enemies, but from his allies. In September he received a visit from John à Lasco. À Lasco had stayed with Martyr at Oxford in May, as has been noted, and it appears that he had intended with Martyr to visit Bucer at the end of June: but he was detained at Lambeth, trying to raise a loan in London for the Fürstenbund, which two of their mercenary captains, Hans von Heideck and Count Mansfeld, had come over to negotiate, and was further delayed by the cause of the Strangers' Church in London. Meanwhile Bucer visited Martyr, who had come strongly under à Lasco's influence, and who in turn shook Bucer's adhesion to Suvermerianism: thus à Lasco's visit, in September, supplied the decisive influence in Bucer's conversion to Sacramentarianism, which Martyr had initiated in July.

At this point, some examination of Bucer's sacramental doctrine is essential.

The essentials of that Suvermerian doctrine of the sacrament, which Bucer held when he arrived in England, have already been described. A *résumé* of it (though not entirely adequate) may be taken from Article XIX of the *Epitome, that is, a brief summary of christian doctrine and religion, which has been openly proclaimed at Strassburg for the past 28 years*, which Bucer compiled before his expulsion, and bequeathed as a testament and charter to the church he had served so long.

Concerning the very substance of the Sacrament of the body and blood of the Lord, we believe and teach..., That undoubtedly this bread, which we break (i.e. we consecrate, distribute, and partake, as the Lord commanded us) is a

communication of the body of Christ, which was given for us: 1 *Cor.* 10
and that this cup is a communication of his blood, which was
shed for us: and that that communication is such, that ever *Ephes.* 5
the more we are made flesh of his flesh, and blood of his blood, *John* 6
and bones of his bones: by which also we remain and live in
him, and he in us, and we are in him one body and one bread.
Thus, together with St Irenæus, bishop and martyr, and all
the ancient Apostolic churches and the fathers, we confess two
things [to be] in the Sacrament: an earthly [thing], viz., bread
and wine, which in their nature and substance, as the godly
Pope Gelasius I rightly confesses, remain unchanged: and a
heavenly [thing], i.e. Christ our Lord himself, the whole true
God and man: who does not on that account leave heaven,
nor is he mingled naturally with the bread and wine: but gives
himself in a heavenly manner for the food and sustenance of
eternal life, and for a testimony of the blessed resurrection....

This summary, which does not guard sufficiently clearly
against the Zwinglians the Suvermerian concept of a
double eating—the natural eating, with the mouth, of the
symbols of bread and wine, and the spiritual eating, with
the soul, of Christ's true body and blood—should be read
in connection with two other documents: Bucer's letter
to Martyr, of June 20, 1549, criticising the Oxford
Disputation, and his letter to Calvin, written towards the
end of August 1549, criticising the Consensus Tigurinus
(between Zurich and Geneva), of which Calvin had sent
him a copy.

In his letter to Martyr, among the schools of thought
that he condemned were those who held 'that undoubtedly
nothing more is here exhibited than bread and wine, the
symbols of Christ who is utterly absent, by which we
ought to make only a remembrance of him, and to advance
in the faith of him,' with whom he included those who,
by a refinement of that doctrine, held that 'by this remembrance, however, [their] minds are lifted up into
heaven, that they may enjoy Christ there.' Christ, he

insisted, is really—that is, genuinely, undoubtedly—present in his sacraments, though not locally, nor after any fashion of this world. Christ is not merely signified, but actually exhibited in the sacrament and spiritually eaten by faith and by the power of his Spirit, for our salvation, of those who receive him worthily and by faith.

In his letter to Calvin, he expressed his general approval of the Consensus Tigurinus, but propounded three searching criticisms: (1) he regretted (as Calvin himself did) that they 'so carefully avoided using the words of Christ and of Scripture'—'This is my body'—because these make for a real presence in the Sacrament: (2) he wished that they had not so strictly localised Christ in one place in heaven, and made that an article of faith, although, as he declared, he did not himself believe in a local presence in the sacrament, nor was he an Ubiquitarian: (3) he was sorry that in their somewhat unfounded vehemence against Lutheranism they had gone too far in the opposite direction. Further, he was extremely distressed that Musculus had gone over to the Zwinglians.

These letters make Bucer's position perfectly clear. The first hint of change occurs at the beginning of Bucer's second year in Cambridge—that is, after his visit to Oxford and à Lasco's visit to him. À Lasco was anxious at this time to draw up a Confession on the sacramental question to be signed by the four leading foreign theologians in England, Bucer, Martyr, Ochino, and himself, presumably as a standard for the English Reformers—Martyr alludes to it in his letter to Bucer of November 11—and this was probably the object of his visit. Certainly on October 13, Micronius, a pastor of à Lasco's church, wrote to Bullinger:

Dr à Lasco...paid a visit to Dr Bucer last month. They came to an agreement on every point except that of the corporal presence in the supper. Bucer wrote out the heads of his

opinion respecting the Lord's Supper. He left them for Dr
à Lasco to examine, and this good and learned man is writing
annotations on them, and most strongly confutes Bucer's
opinion. When he has finished, he will send back to Bucer
his heads with the annotations. I pray that God may see fit
to open his mind.

À Lasco's visit had indeed plunged Bucer into a period
of doubt. Stumphius, who visited him soon after, wrote
to his father (Nov. 12), 'Concerning the Sacrament of the
Lord's Supper he has plainly become silent.' He began
carefully to avoid the question, as a matter *sub judice* in
his mind, while privately he continued to correspond with
à Lasco on it: externally, therefore, the change was not
apparent.

Meanwhile, considerable anxiety was felt by his friends
as to whether he would survive another English winter.
The King sent him £20 to build a stove with, and begged
him not to hold himself bound to lecture: a liberty of
which he availed himself to some extent. His most loving
patron, the widowed Duchess of Suffolk, gave him a cow
and a calf (which the Papists believed to be two devils
who taught him what he should lecture in the schools):
her two sons came up to the University this term, and, in
order to be near them, she took a house in Cambridge,
at which Bucer was a welcome and a frequent guest.
His wife also returned to him from Strassburg. He
resumed his lectures on November 9, lecturing now *On
the power and practice of the sacred ministry*, but not so
frequently as before: he devoted most of his time to
literary activity. Bishop Goodrich, of Ely, had asked him
to write out his judgment (*Censura*) on the Prayer Book
of 1549, in view of the need for its revision: about the
same time he was engaged in writing his *De Regno Christi*
as a New Year's gift for the King.

The *De Regno Christi* delicately avoids all sacramental

theory, though one of its chapters concerns the practical administration of the Communion. Out of 76 chapters, no less than 33 are devoted to marriage and divorce, which was then a matter of controversy. The rest are a mine of curious suggestions, such as the chapters *De honestis ludis*, *De coercendo luxu et noxijs sumptibus*, and *De Ciuilium legum repurgatione & explicatione* (which suggests that the reformed code of Civil Law might be put 'after the manner of the ancients, into certain brief epitomes and songs, which may be quickly learnt by the young, and may be chanted by the whole people'). Most characteristic in this book is its extreme candour and outspokenness. Bucer never attempted to curry favour with those in power. Here he told the King that by taking tenths and first-fruits he incurred the guilt of sacrilege, that the nobles ought to be taxed for the upkeep of the Church, and that the Universities stood in need of immediate and drastic reform: he commented sharply on the negligence of the bishops, denounced the New Nobility who had defrauded and despoiled the Church of its possessions, and told the King pointedly, in several places, that a reformation could not be carried out by royal edicts without 'godly suasions' also.

The *Censura* is said to have been delivered to Goodrich on January 5, 1551. Though it, also, deals more with the use than with the theory of the Eucharist, yet in it Bucer's approval of the sacramental doctrine of the Prayer Book of 1549 is at least implicit. À Lasco had not won him over yet: but he was coming slowly into line. He was lecturing, as has been said, *On the power and practice of the sacred ministry*: and a comparison of the seventh section of this series ('*On the power and efficacy of the Lord's Supper*') with the *Epitome* previously quoted marks the process of his conversion.

And so when we are asked, what is the power and efficacy

of the holy Eucharist, or Supper of the Lord, that is, what the Lord offers and bestows on us through this sacrament, when it is both administered and received as he himself commanded, and what he effects in us thereby: so far as the Lord has given me to understand his own words, I reply before him, that he gives three things to us: One, true bread and wine, almost unaltered in their nature....

Another, the very body and blood of the Lord, and thereby the Lord himself, God and man, as he sits and reigns on the right hand of the Father: but he must be received and enjoyed as our eternal saviour, the giver and supporter of the blessed life: and thus must be received not by the senses, nor by any natural understanding, nor in any way and understanding of this generation, but by faith, and by the inward working of the holy Spirit: and must be enjoyed, not for the food of the belly, but to the increasing of that communion of him in us, and of the life of God, which he gave to us in baptism, in which we remain and live, not unto ourselves, but in the Lord himself, and he in us.

The third thing, which is here given and received, is the confirmation of the new Testament, that is, of faith concerning the grace of God and the remission of sins....

Here we may see what indeed he bade them [the disciples] receive, eat and drink. It is more certain than certainty, that the Lord gave bread and wine. But because he added, This is my body, this is my blood, and especially since a reasonable particle [*particula rationalis*] has been added, which undoubtedly pertains not less to the bread offered, than to the cup offered, it is a synecdoche: from one thing two are understood: as also the phrase must be understood, when the Lord breathed on the disciples, and said to them: Receive the holy Ghost....

Further, since it is agreed that those words, λάβετε, φάγετε [Take, eat], are synecdochic, and refer to two things, and those very different indeed: it must also here be observed, that when they refer to the symbols, they are taken literally [*simpliciter*], so that the symbols, to wit, are taken into the hands and eaten and drunk with the mouth: but that when they refer to the identical body and blood of the Lord, [they are taken] meta-phorically [μεταφορικῶς]. For to eat, if taken literally, signifies the action of the body, by which food is taken with the mouth, chewed by the teeth or swallowed, and so passes into the belly: and thus also, to drink signifies the action of the body, by which drink is swallowed with the mouth and passes down into the belly. Now it has always been acknowledged in the Church, and the Scripture also manifestly teaches, that Christ's body and blood are not the food and drink of the body, nor are they bestowed literally by these [words], to be eaten and drunk, but by a similitude, and therefore metaphorically. For as the bread eaten, and the wine drunk, nourish the body, and support strength and life; so the body and blood of the Lord, received by faith and by the inward working of the Holy Spirit, nourish a man unto new life, support the strength for this life and the life itself, the life in which the just live by their faith....

But this course of lectures was never finished, and the lecture on the sacrament was the last to be delivered, if, indeed, it were delivered at all. On February 13 Bucer was taken ill: on the 28th he died. 'Dr Bucer,' wrote à Lasco to Bullinger (April 10), 'began a treatise on the sacraments [probably these lectures] shortly before he died, but did not finish it. He had also begun, as I hear, to reply to me'—that is, to à Lasco's 'annotations' on his sacramental doctrine, previously mentioned—'but I have seen nothing of that, though I should like to have seen it. But as far as I understand, he persisted in his opinion of the presence of Christ and of the real exhibition of the body and blood of Christ with the signs or in the signs or through the signs. I will send to you shortly what he had sent to me, and what I had answered to him in return.' But à Lasco's arguments had been far more effective than their author had dared to hope. Bucer's reply was forwarded to him, and on May 31 he wrote triumphantly to Hardenberg, 'He entered into a correspondence with me, which will perhaps be published, and at length he wrote to me, that *he assented to my doctrine, which I left in Friesland*,' and on June 7, to Bullinger, 'The correspondence I had with Bucer before his death concerning the sacramental question, I have not [with me] now: for it is in the hands of my Lord of Canterbury'—presumably à Lasco had sent it to Cranmer with a view to publication—'who is now away from here. When I have it again, I will send you a copy. *You will marvel, I know well, when you have read it through.*'

But since this correspondence was never published, and that course of lectures never completed, the change in Bucer's opinions was not generally known and exercised no material influence. His contribution to Anglican theology and practice had been made before his conversion: he had strengthened Cranmer in Suvermerian doctrine, had supplied the groundwork of the English Ordinal, and had composed a document—the *Censura*—by which he was yet to exert a strong though posthumous influence upon the Revision of the Prayer Book of 1549. Nor did the change disturb the impress of his Suvermerian theology upon the University of Cambridge. It was from among those Cambridge theologians who had enjoyed his friendship and attended his lectures—men like Parker, the Master of Bene't College, Sandys, Master of Catharine Hall, Grindal, Vice-Master of Pembroke—that the great statesmanlike prelates of the Elizabethan Reformation were drawn. The influence of Bucer upon that Reformation was paramount: but it was the influence of his first year at Cambridge, not of his second. It was perhaps providential for the English Church that the process of his conversion was interrupted by the return of his old malady.

This time his illness was of short duration. Nicholas Carr wrote a long intimate account of his last days.

...It was a grievous spectacle for us, and indeed miserable also for his own household, when from the extreme debility of his whole body, the enervation of his limbs, the difficulty of digestion, and a perpetual choking for breath, he was in such great pain, that he could hardly bear to see or talk with anyone. Not that either his kindness towards us or his piety towards all was in any degree diminished: but he felt...that his hour was at hand....When Bradford...was going [out] to preach, and said that he wished to be remembered in his prayers, [Bucer] said, weeping, Cast me not away, O Lord, in the time of my old age, when my strength has failed: then he added, Let him stoutly chastise me, yet he will never cast me away, he will never cast me away....Now I ought to mention that the physicians and his other friends were afraid lest when the moon waned [in eclipse], his strength too might wane, and he might be overcome by the strength of his disorder: when on the following day he seemed a little better, Bradford came to him as usual and explained to him the fear of the physicians and the anxiety of his friends on account of that eclipse of the moon and perturbation of the heavenly ‘bodies, and he is said to have held up three fingers and, raising his eyes to that eternal heaven, cried, It is he, it is he who ruleth and ordaineth all things....No tearful words escaped him, no complaint of his illness, no sorrowful cry. Thus constantly and patiently he bore the cruelty of his continuous pain. His death was like his life: if you know how he lived, you cannot be ignorant how he died....Even as he lived, as no man better; so he died, as no man more blessedly: even as he bore his illness, that no man might see him lament it; so he passed away, that no man could perceive him dying....

Martyr was heart-broken: the death of Bucer brought home to him for the first time the bitterness of exile. ‘I haue often in my time beene holpen and refreshed of him...I can neuer forget how ready his sound and faithfull counsels haue alwayes beene unto me....Nowe I feele my selfe to liue a banished man. Now I perceiue my selfe to be out of my countrie, & those things which

I counted no discommoditie before while he liued, nowe
when I am left alone, I finde a griefe and disquietnesse
of them. ....He died most constant, and in the faith of our
Lorde Jesus Christe: he sawe not a multitude of euils
which hang ouer our heads and ouer the Church because
of our sinnes. I would to God that wee also might be
loosed from hence before the floud of calamities ouer-
flowe.' Calvin, who, already anxious to set his mark upon
the Church of England, had corresponded frequently with
Bucer, with the most satisfactory results, was also acutely
disappointed: the death of Bucer presented an unexpected
check to his plans. As Farel wrote to him, 'We lament
our lot and that of the Church in being deprived of a man
not only very useful but inexpressibly necessary for the
Lord's work': to which Calvin mournfully replied, 'I feel
my heart almost like to break when I think of the great
loss the church of God has sustained in the death of
Bucer....He would have been very useful to England.
I was hoping still more from his writings than all he had
accomplished up till now.'

'The great architect of subtleties,' as Bossuet called
him, was buried with great honour and ceremony on
March 2 in the choir of Great St Mary's, 'all the whole
university, with the whole town,' as the King noted in his
Journal, 'bringing him to his grave, to the number
3000 persons.' Haddon, Parker, and Redman delivered
funeral orations; 'which three sermons made the people
wonderfully to lament his death. Last of all, all the learned
men of the university made their epitaphs in his praise,
laying them on his grave.'

The death of Bucer raised an important question: who
was to succeed him? On March 9, Cheke wrote to Parker,
'Although J dout not but the K.M. wil p̊vide sūme grave
lerned man, to maintein goddes true learning in his
uniuersítee, yet J think not of al lerned men in al poíntes

ye schal receiue M. Bucers like, whither ye consider his deapnes of knowlege, his earnestnes in religion, his fatherlines in life, his authorítee in knowlege.' This was quite possibly true: but the immediate question was this, was the Regius Professorship to be given to a Zwinglian, a Suvermerian, or a Lutheran? Many names were canvassed, and à Lasco hastened to Lambeth to give Cranmer the benefit of his advice, but met with an unexpected rebuff. 'I proposed Musculus, Bibliander, and Castalio. But he added also Brentius. But when I said that he does not agree with us on the sacramental question'—Brentius was a Lutheran, and chaplain to the Duke of Wurtemburg —'he answered, that he had already been warned of that. I could indeed ardently wish, most holy man! that we had here some of your [ministers]. I already number Musculus among yours.' So he wrote to Bullinger (April 10). Apparently, however, Cranmer instructed John Hales to approach both Musculus and Bibliander, and the English Zwinglians were most anxious for Musculus to accept the post: but it seems that the Council of Bern, who had lately given him the Professorship of Divinity there, held him inexorably to his contract, while Zurich could certainly not spare Bibliander. The post therefore seems to have been left vacant, until, in May 1553, the King wrote offering it to Melanchthon[1].

The death of Bucer had been mourned by friends and opponents alike: but the leaders of the Catholic Reaction could not suffer his bones to rest in peace. At the beginning of 1556 a Royal Visitation of the University of Cambridge was held, at the direction of Cardinal Pole: and, after the elaborate and lengthy mockery of a formal trial for heresy,

[1] 'Regiis litteris vocor in Angliam, quae scriptae sunt mense Maio. Postea secuta est mors nobilissimi adolescentis, qui etiam est exemplum humanae imbecillitatis.' (*Melanchthon to Camerarius*, Aug. 10, 1553.)

on Saturday, February 6—the day was specially chosen because it was market day—the bodies of Bucer and Fagius 'were taken up owt of their graves and about ix of the clock brent in the market place and a cart lode of Bookes with them, for betwyxt 8 and 9 my L. of Lynkolne preched in St Mary's and stood tyll almost xi setting furthe BUCER'S wyckedness and heretycall doctryn'[1]. This ghastly ceremony concluded with a shower of comminatory verses and epitaphs, and a very eloquent sermon by the Vice-Chancellor on Psalm cxxxiii.—'Behold, how good and joyful a thing it is, brethren, to dwell together in unity!'

Therefore whereas in euerye singular place, was executed a singuler kind of crueltie: insomuche that there was no kinde of cruelnesse that could be deuysed, but it was put in ure in one place or other) This was proper & peculiar to Cambridge, to exercise the crueltye uppon the dead, whiche in other places was extended but to the quicke....[2]

But in July 1560, upon the receipt of letters from Archbishop Parker, the Senate restored Bucer and Fagius to their former honours, and on July 30 a great Memorial Service was held in Great St Mary's, at which Acworth, the Public Orator, made a Latin oration, and Pilkington preached. There followed a third shower of verses and epitaphs, this time eulogistic once more. It is gratifying to human frailty to recall that the same Vice-Chancellor, Perne of Peterhouse (in memory of whose prompt re-cantations the word *pernere* was coined), presided at both ceremonies—both at the burning and at the restitution.

---

[1] *Quene Mary's Visitation. By J. Mere present* (Lamb's *Documents*, p. 216). The journal of John Mere, Esquire Bedell, covers the period from November 26, 1556, to May 31, 1557. References to the trial of Bucer and Fagius may be found under January 12, 13, 15, 18, 20, 22, 25, 26, 27, 31, February 1, 2, 4, 6, 7.

[2] 'The oration of Acworth oratour of thuniversitye,' from *A briefe Treatise concernynge the burnynge of Bucer and Phagius, at Cambrydge ...with theyr restitution* (tr. A. Goldyng, 1562).

CHAPTER SIX

THE STRANGERS'
CHURCHES
JOHN À LASCO

Je voy les feux brûlants en lieux divers
. . . . .
Je voy passer de la mer au travers
Une grand' troupe, et un Roy sur le port
Qui tend la main pour les tirer à bord.
Que Dieu te doint, ô Roi, qui en enfance
As surmonté des plus grands l'espérance,
Croissans tes ans, si bien croistre en ses
　grâces
Qu' après tous Rois toy mesme tu sur-
　passes.

*Théodore de Bèze à l'Église de Nostre
　Seigneur.*

Hic exilii locus est....Magnum est,
posse habere receptaculum hoc tempore,
ubi nobis ipsi et nostris, quos eiusdem
spiritus vinculum in Domino nobis
coniunxit, in fidei nostri Confessione
vivere possimus.

À Lasco to Dryander [Lambeth?],
　September 21, 1548.

CHAPTER SIX

THE STRANGERS' CHURCHES. JOHN À LASCO

THIS brief notice of the change in the opinions of Martyr and Bucer points the way to some account of the chief agent of their conversion—John à Lasco. John à Lasco was born in 1499, the second son of a Polish junker, Jaroslav Laski [à Lasco], lord of the manors of Lask and Krowicz, Palatine of Leczyc and Sieradz. The family had an invaluable patron in Jaroslav Laski's brother, the Archbishop of Gnesen, Primate of Poland, and subsequently Papal Legate and Chancellor of the kingdom. The Archbishop designated his other two nephews for a diplomatic, but John for an ecclesiastical career: he educated them in his own palace at Cracow, the capital of Humanism in Poland, and sent John to the University of Bologna (1513–17), and, five years later, to travel in Europe. From 1524–5, à Lasco studied in Basel, learning Hebrew from Conrad Pellican (then still a Minorite friar), and lodging with Erasmus, who was engaged in supplementing an already comfortable income by taking aristocratic boarders on exorbitant terms: among these was Karel Utenhove, a nobleman of Ghent. Erasmus at this time was standing on the threshold of the Reformation, though hesitating to advance: but he influenced à Lasco, who afterwards wrote of him, 'It was he who first brought me to apply my mind to sacred things, or rather he truly was the first who began to instruct me in true religion.' But disquieting rumours of à Lasco's heretical tendencies began to reach Poland, where the Archbishop's enemies seized the opportunity to strike at him through his favourite nephew, on whom, in his absence, ecclesiastical preferments had been lavishly showered: the canonries of Plock and Cracow, the Coadjutorship to the dean of Gnesen, and then the deanery itself. It was known that à Lasco had visited

Zwingli: it was rumoured that he had broken his vows and taken a wife. In September 1525 he received an urgent message from his uncle to return home, avoiding heretical Germany. On his return, he was made to clear himself of the charge of heresy by a solemn oath of purgation: after which he retired to his deanery of Gnesen, and watched with cynical indifference the efforts made to check the advance of Reformation doctrine into Poland.

In 1531 he was appointed Provost of Gnesen and Leczyc, and then Bishop of Vesprin. But in that year his uncle and protector died: and although King Sigismund still favoured him, and in 1538 gave him the archdeaconry of Warsaw and offered him the bishopric of Cujavia (which he declined), yet he was generally suspected of being a secret Lutheran. His position had, indeed, become intolerable: and at the end of the summer of that same year the noble pluralist dramatically crossed the German frontier, leaving his enemies to divide the spoils.

For the next few years à Lasco wandered about Germany and the Netherlands. At Frankfort he became acquainted with a Bernardine monk, Albert Hardenberg, whom he ultimately (in the spring of 1543) persuaded to leave the Roman Church: at Louvain, where he studied for a year, though under grave suspicion, he won the admiring friendship of a young Spaniard, Francisco Encinas (Dryander), who was translating the Bible into Spanish: there also he became a member of a secret pietistic brotherhood, heretical rather than Protestant, and married a burgher's daughter. But the spread of Protestantism in the Netherlands, accompanied by anti-Catholic riots, brought the Emperor to Ghent and initiated a period of persecution. Hardenberg was denounced and banished: Encinas was arrested: à Lasco himself fled with his wife to Emden, in the hospitable duchy of East Friesland, where, three years later (1543), he was prevailed on to accept the Superintendency of the Church—'ἐφορείαν ecclesiarum omnium totius regionis.'

In Emden his environment was sacramentarian and radical: for though the original impetus to the Reformation there had come from Luther, that influence had been quickly superseded. Aportanus, the Reformer of Emden, had taught that Baptism and the Supper are, like circumcision and the passover, 'only certain and infallible signs and seals on the part of God regarding the things mentioned.... To know Christ and to receive him with the whole heart through faith, that is truly to drink his blood and truly to eat his flesh.' In this sacramentarian mould à Lasco's sacramental doctrine, as yet unformed, was now hard cast. The influence of his environment was paramount: moreover, at the time of his arrival, the churches of East Friesland were fighting for life against three enemies—the Lutherans (who were strong in Bremen and Norden), the Franciscan monks (to whom the Countess herself was somewhat favourably inclined), and the Anabaptists (whom the persecution in the Netherlands had driven in great numbers into the duchy, under the leadership of Carlstadt, Menno, and David Joris). It was à Lasco's task, as Superintendent, to restore order out of anarchy, to expel his adversaries, to erect a system of church government (of which the centre was the famous *Coetus*, a peculiar ecclesiastical court for the maintenance of order and uniformity), and to organise religious education.

But his sacramental doctrine did not immediately crystallise out into a rigid sacramentarian pattern. He was anxious to consult with the leading non-Lutheran Reformers—with Bucer, as well as with Bullinger—before making any final decision. In March 1544 he had taken steps to get into touch with Bullinger, and had written him a letter introducing himself to his care, 'because I ardently love

you and therefore am anxious also for all my [works] to
be approved by you, although I do not know you. Now
if you wish to know who I am.....You know my motives,
now it will be your [part] to receive me into your friendship
and have me henceforward as a brother': whereupon
Bullinger, having carefully checked à Lasco's account of
himself (for this letter is endorsed in Bullinger's writing,
'*Ioannes à Lasco nobilissimus Poloniae Baro, quondam
Gnesenis praepositus, singularis D. Erasmi Rot. amicus,
Regis Poloniae legatus. Cuius patruus, et ipse Ioannes à Lasco
dictus, fuit Archiepiscopus Gnesenis in Sarmatia...*), sent
him an unpleasantly fawning reply, enclosing a copy of his
*De Auctoritate Verbi Dei, & De Officio et Functione
Praelatorum Ecclesiae*. Pellican, who had been at Zurich
for the past nineteen years, and who was now delighted
to hear news of his old pupil whom he had believed to be
dead, also wrote to him, and renewed their friendship.

À Lasco's motive in writing to Bullinger was that he
had just prepared an *Epitome of the doctrine of the churches
of East Friesland* for his clergy, and was waiting to publish
it until he had 'heard the judgment of learned men' upon
it: he therefore sent a copy to Hardenberg, who was then
at Strassburg, bidding him show it to Bucer, and then
send it on to Bullinger. (Another copy was sent to Duke
Albert of Prussia, who forwarded it to Melanchthon, and
a third to Entfelder, the pastor of Konigsberg.) The
manuscript met with a not very favourable reception, and
so à Lasco decided not to publish[1]. On the other hand,

[1] It is briefly summarised by Dalton. 'Faith is an affection of the
spirit, wrought in us by the Holy Ghost through the instrumentality
of the preaching of God's Word, in virtue of which we believe in
God, love Him, steadfastly purpose henceforth continually to cleave to
Him, although, by reason of our weakness, we sin ever afresh. In
order to afford provision against this our weakness, God gives us
means by which we strengthen and renew our faith. As such means
are to be regarded the preaching of the Word and the visible tokens
of His grace, whereby He seals in our hearts that which He has

a little later in the year he published a less official, and more detailed statement of his sacramental doctrine in the form of an open letter—*Epistola ad amicum quendam*—of which he sent Pellican a copy (Aug. 31). This pamphlet, which had a wide circulation, belongs to the experimental stage of à Lasco's theology, and was probably issued in order to see what criticisms would be passed upon it.

It may be briefly summarised. À Lasco declared his independence of both Carlstadt and Zwingli: for although he agreed with them in denying the real (or corporal) presence in the sacrament, yet he differed from them in the interpretation of the words of administration, '*This is my body*,' and proposed a more literal interpretation than theirs. The word 'THIS,' he claimed, refers not to the substance of the bread, but to the whole action or ceremony of the Lord's Supper—the breaking of bread, the partaking, the drinking of the cup, the giving of thanks. In support of this he cited St Paul, who wrote, 'The bread which we break, is it not the communion of the body of Christ?' (1 Cor. x. 16). It is not 'the bread,' but 'the bread *which we break*'—that is, therefore, the breaking of the bread, or the entire rite of the Lord's Supper—which is 'the communion of the body of Christ.' This is confirmed by the fact that in verse 21 he uses the phrase 'the Lord's table' as synonymous with 'the bread which we break.' (The same interpretation follows, of course, from the words, 'The cup of blessing *which we bless*, is it not the communion of the blood of Christ?') Secondly—

Since he expressly says that we *are*, not that we *become*, one body, to wit, of Christ, and that on account of the partaking of the one bread, not on account of the distribution of the body, it is evident that in this place he was not thinking at all

promised us by the testimony of His Word: two sacraments under the new covenant—Baptism and the Supper, corresponding to circumcision and the paschal meal under the old covenant ' about the distribution or extension of the body, but wished rather to teach that we who feed on the bread of the Lord in his Supper have also the communion of the bread of the mysteries, that is, of the body of Christ: although the bread be one thing, but the bread of the mysteries another, to wit, the body of Christ; even as in Israel they who ate the sacrifices had also the communion of the mystery of the sacrifices, although the sacrifices were one thing, but the mysteries of the sacrifices another, nor were the mysteries in the sacrifices themselves, far less were they offered to the hands....

...And we call the symbols of the Supper σφραγῖδας with Paul, i.e. seals of that very communion, which [symbols], while we receive them according to the Lord's institution, bring before our eyes in a mystery that same communion and renew it in our minds, and seal us wholly in certain and undoubted faith in it, by the operation of the holy Spirit, although we place in them no physical or real inclusion of the body or blood of Christ....

In this pamphlet, a few points are to be noted. First, à Lasco's claim to independence, which was characteristic: for later, in his pamphlet against Westphal, while admitting the influence of Zwingli upon him, he yet denied that he was a Zwinglian, since he was baptised in the name of no man, and neither Zwingli nor Luther was crucified for him. Secondly, his affinity with the Zwinglians, which Luther noted with abhorrence, and his fondness for the essentially sacramentarian concept of the sacraments as *seals*, which was as strongly emphasised in the unpublished *Epitome*. Thirdly, a slight tendency to Suvermerianism, in his conception of a double eating.

For some time, indeed, à Lasco failed to see how wide a gulf separated his doctrine from that of Bucer. On June 23, 1545, having lately received from Hardenberg Bucer's criticisms of the *Epitome*, he wrote back that there seemed to him to be little difference between Bucer's theory that in the Supper the communion of the body and blood of Christ is '*given and received*' (dari ac percipi), and his own, 'following that similitude which Paul proposes in [his] explanation of circumcision,' that it is '*sealed*' (obsignari).

For when I say that faith in [God's] promises is sealed in our minds by the use of the Supper, I include also under the name of the promises the communion of the body and blood of Christ, seeing that we have it delivered and laid open to us by the promise. And thus also your *dari ac percipi* does not seem to be very far from my *obsignari*. For if the communion of the body and blood of Christ is so given to us in the Supper, that of course it does not then first begin, but also was ours before, before taking the Supper; if, again, it is there [as] food, though only of the soul—how much difference will there be now, I beg, between your *dare* and my *obsignare*?

They continued to correspond upon this question, though it seems that they never met: and as late as March 1546 à Lasco still imagined that there was but little difference between them, as he told Bullinger and Pellican.

I confine all sacraments within the limits of obsignation [sealing]: he adds exhibition, but in the sense that what is heavenly in the sacraments is received only by the godly, [their] faith having been carried up into heaven. Here I assent and confess that, our minds [*animis*] having been drawn up into heaven by faith, we receive there through the Holy Spirit the true communion of the body and blood of Christ after the fashion of a sacrament, that is, by the method of obsignation. So far have we advanced: nor do I doubt but that the matter will succeed in other points, especially since Luther is no more....

But it is evident from this letter that à Lasco failed to grasp the particulars of Bucer's theory, or in general to appreciate the fundamental and irreconcileable difference between Suvermerian and Sacramentarian doctrine—the fact that the Suvermerians believed the consecrated elements to be *signa exhibitiva*, signs that exhibited Christ present, whereas the Sacramentarians believed them to be *signa representativa*, signs that represented Christ absent.

À Lasco's own predilections led him inevitably to the latter view. 'I have always loved your simplicity,' he wrote to Bullinger (Aug. 31, 1544), 'because, in view of the present diversity of sects and opinions, this seems to be extremely necessary for the preservation of the purity of sound doctrine': and this irresistible attraction soon drew him, as it drew all doubters, towards the lodestone rock of Zurich. In April 1545 he wrote, again in the form of a letter to a friend, another statement of his sacramental doctrine. This statement superseded his first *Epistola ad amicum quendam* with its ingenious but somewhat strained interpretation of the words of administration, which I conjecture to be that doctrine '*quam in Frisia reliqui*' to which he ultimately succeeded in converting Bucer: a fact which proves, incidentally, that he had laid aside that theory rather than abandoned it. (The internal evidence of Cranmer's *Answer* suggests that he also was somewhat influenced by this theory.)

Though written in April 1545, this letter was not published until April 1551, when it was printed as a preface to à Lasco's reprint (dedicated to the Princess Elizabeth) of Bullinger's *Absoluta de Christi Domini et catholicae ejus ecclesiae Sacramentis tractatio*[1]. The occasion was appropriate, for, in every respect except the name, the doctrine of this letter was pure Zwinglianism. The emphasis is still on the metaphor of obsignation—'by the

---

[1] ' I send you a little book on the sacraments which I have published here, to which is annexed an old letter of mine, which you knew, on the same matter.' (*À Lasco to Hardenberg*, May 31, 1551.) It was published under the title '*Epistola Joannis à Lasco ante Quinquennium ad amicum quendam scripta, continens in se summam controversiae Coenae Domini breviter explicatam.*'

use of the Supper our communion with Christ is sealed after the fashion of a sacrament'—and three doctrines are definitely rejected,

>...the Popish transformation,...[and] the local (as they call it) and natural inclusion of the body and blood of Christ in the bread, or under the bread and wine, because neither of these can be established without manifest idolatry—and the doctrine of those who teach that all sacraments are bare signs, and count them among things indifferent, and wish them to be known merely of their human use, [as things] by which we are separated from the Jews and all heathen.. . .

But, unlike the stricter Zwinglians of Zurich, à Lasco was prepared to tolerate other conceptions of the Presence, provided only that their advocates did not carry the controversy into the market-place and so destroy the peace and tranquillity of the Churches. (It is recorded that when he was in Bremen at the beginning of 1550, he received the sacrament from the hands of a strict Lutheran pastor.)

Apart, however, from this unusual tolerance, à Lasco may be reckoned as a Zwinglian from the year 1545. In the summer of that year he had intended visiting Zurich (and, it must be admitted, Strassburg also), but was prevented by other engagements. Yet he remained in frequent correspondence with Bullinger and Pellican, and continued to maintain their doctrine: for in 1555 he stated to the King of Poland that his sacramental doctrine remained the same as that expounded in this letter ten years before. It was, therefore, as a Zwinglian and unshakeable in his belief, that à Lasco came to England: and his residence there had no effect upon his doctrine.

Cranmer, who was then engaged in organising his great Protestant Council, invited him over in the early summer of 1548. It seems that à Lasco accepted the invitation, but 'the sudden intervention of some other engagement' compelled him to postpone his visit: however, Cranmer sent him a third letter (dated July 4) in which he explained his project, urged à Lasco to come as soon as he might, and prayed him, if possible, to bring Melanchthon with him. À Lasco was persuaded, obtained leave of absence from the Countess, and sailed for England at the beginning of September. He was reluctant to leave East Friesland at that time, for three days before his departure an Imperial envoy arrived to compel the Countess to submit to the Interim, which she had hitherto defied. The storm-clouds of persecution were gathering over the duchy: à Lasco could but exhort his clergy to be steadfast in the faith and of a good courage, and promise to return to them as soon as he might.

Many of his acquaintances were already in England. Dryander had just been appointed Greek Reader at Cambridge: Martyr had already been at Oxford almost a year: Jan Utenhove, whose half-brother, Karel, à Lasco had known at Basel, was living at Canterbury: and Dr William Turner, author of *The huntyng and fyndyng out of the Romyshe foxe* and other pamphlets, who had been living in exile at Emden, was now physician to Protector Somerset, and was also plaguing Cecil to procure him some high and lucrative office in the Church.

Of the events of à Lasco's visit little is known. On September 21 he was at Lambeth, rather uncertainly awaiting the arrival of Cranmer, who was expected in a week's time. On December 14 he wrote to Calvin from Windsor, mentioning that he was convalescent from a serious illness. But most of the time he spent in the Archbishop's palace, as appears from Cranmer's last desperate appeal to Melanchthon, dated February 10, 1549, of which he was the bearer: and it is evident from the report of the Debate in the House of Lords that he very considerably upset the Archbishop's views upon the sacramental question. Seeing, however, that the Conference could not meet, he returned home, and was back in Emden on March 19.

There he found the Countess on the point of submitting to the Interim: resistance could not be much further prolonged. Accordingly, he entered the diplomatic service of the Duke of Prussia, and went to Dantzig and Konigsberg, where he endeavoured, though unsuccessfully, to obtain permission from the King of Poland to return to his own country. He was recalled by an urgent summons from Emden: the Countess had accepted the Interim, but all except the Lutheran pastors refused to submit. The churches were closed, but services were held in the churchyards, and the Coetus continued to meet. À Lasco was the soul of the resistance. But it was useless: the Emperor demanded his extradition, and the Countess implored him to depart. Leaving his family behind him, he returned to the service of the Duke of Prussia, who in May 1550 sent him to London as his diplomatic agent there. For a short time he stayed with Cranmer again: then he moved into a house in Bow Lane, where he was joined by his wife and his four children. The whole family were naturalised on June 27: this time à Lasco had come to stay.

On July 24 he was appointed Superintendent of the Strangers' Church in London.

Besides the foreign theologians and students at the University, many humbler refugees, craftsmen and artisans for the most part, found refuge from persecution in this country. It is true that there were not as many refugees here under Edward VI as under Elizabeth, for the years 1567 (the arrival of Alva in the Netherlands), 1572 (the Massacre of St Bartholomew), and 1585 (the Sack of Antwerp) were each followed by a considerable influx, while even before 1570 there were colonies of the Strangers—

French, Flemings, and Walloons for the most part—in London, Norwich, Yarmouth, Maidstone, Canterbury, Sandwich, Southampton, Winchelsea and Rye. Yet even under Henry VIII a number of Huguenots had taken refuge in England—no less than 47 Frenchmen were naturalised in the year 1535-6—and Francis I vainly demanded their extradition: moreover it was a matter of considerable significance that the accession of Edward VI coincided almost exactly with that of Henry II of France, a persecuting bigot, and was shortly followed by the publication of the Interim by the Emperor Charles V. It seems that a French Church was formed at Canterbury at the end of December 1548: its founder appears to have been Jan Utenhove, who was then living there, and its pastors François Perroussel (or Pérussel), called la Rivière —a renegade monk, a Bachelor of Theology and former Master of the Novices at the Sorbonne, who had lately been a minister in the French (Protestant) Church at Strassburg—and also perhaps a certain Claudius Colinaeus, who married Utenhove's maid[1]. About the same time a French Church was formed in London, of which Richard Vauville, a quondam Augustinian monk from Berry, was pastor. An attempt was also made to obtain a pastor for the Germans (i.e. Flemings) there. On December 23,

---

[1] 'Salutant te D. Franciscus ac D. Claudius, cui dedi ancillam meam nuptui. Is [i.e. Franciscus] aliquando est concionatus in nostra Gallica Ecclesia. Nescio an alioqui de facie tibi sit notus; hoc tamen scio quod religione ac fide tibi sit conjunctissime.' (*Utenhove to Fagius*, Canterbury, Nov. 20, 1548.) De Schickler makes a curious mistake (i. 9): 'Cette toute première congrégation, Utenhove l'avait appelée, dans sa lettre à Fagius du 20 novembre 1548, "*Nostra Ecclesia Gallica*": elle est française.' But the reference is clearly to the French Church at Strassburg. Martyr's letter of congratulation to Utenhove— 'Quod autem uos et conciones inter parietes habeatis, et conuentus piorum quandoque sint non possum non uehementer gaudere....Nil difficilius in mundo esse uideo quam ecclesiam fundare'—is dated January 15, 1549, and it is improbable that the French Church at Canterbury was founded long before that date.

1548, Ochino, having induced Cranmer to let him invite
Musculus to England—he had just been driven to leave
Augsburg—told him that there were 'more than five
thousand Germans in London,' to whom he might preach
and administer the sacraments; or he could have a lecture-
ship at Cambridge, if he preferred it. (Musculus, however,
would not think of coming unless there should not be
afforded him an opportunity of serving Christ in Germany,
and when he was offered a Professorship at Bern, accepted
that.) A more definite attempt was made in the following
summer. When Bucer was at Lambeth, a deputation of
'Germans' resident in London waited on him, and begged
him to help them: accordingly, he wrote to Hardenberg
(Aug. 14, 1549),

> There are 600 to 800 Germans here, godly men and very
> ravenous for the word of God. They asked me and my [friend]
> Fagius to procure for them some faithful preacher in the
> language of Brabant, to which most of them belong. We indeed
> have at home [at Strassburg] Martin Faber[1], a well-tried
> brother, whom you knew, and with a very small and, as things
> now are, uncertain stipend: I had thought of summoning him;
> but his voice is so feeble, that I dare not expect that he would
> give satisfaction in this situation. And so I have turned to you;
> if perchance you know somebody to whom this office could
> safely be entrusted....The brethren will bear the expenses of
> the journey, and provide honourably [for him]....

But this church was not formed until the return of à Lasco.

'Dr John à Lasco,' wrote Micronius to Bullinger (May
20, 1550),

> arrived in England on May 13th. His coming was greatly to
> the delight of all godly persons. He has determined to remain

---

[1] Faber visited London in June 1550, and stayed with Cranmer at
Lambeth: he and Alexander called on à Lasco, and were shocked at
his Sacramentarianism. After this short visit, Faber went away to
Saxony, where he had been given a post. (*Faber to Bucer*, London,
June 9, 1550.)

in London, and to establish a German church, of which he himself may be appointed superintendent. And indeed it is a matter of the first importance that the word of God should be preached here in German for the averting of the heresies which are introduced by our countrymen. There are several Arians, Marcionists, Libertines, Donatists, and similar monsters. A few days ago, namely May 2, a certain woman [Joan Bocher] was burned alive for denying the incarnation of Christ.

At that time Jan Utenhove was also in London—'where I am now bringing up a family,' he wrote to Bullinger (Jan. 20, 1550)—living with Hooper, for whom he expressed the warmest admiration. Jan Utenhove, who has already been mentioned in these pages, came of a noble family at Ghent: he had fled from his native country to escape persecution in 1544, and, after a period of wandering, settled at Strassburg: thence he came to Canterbury in 1548, but returned to Strassburg in the following spring to study theology. But when he was on his way, on April 11, 1549, at Cologne, he met Hooper, who was journeying home to England. Hooper, who appears to have known him previously, persuaded him to go to Zurich instead, and gave him a letter of introduction to Bullinger.

...When he comes to you, receive him with your ancient kindness, which Switzerland has long been accustomed to show to all foreigners. He is a man of illustrious birth and character, very pure in the true religion....His eminent virtues and remarkable learning will sufficiently commend him to all godly and learned men: he is coming to you by our persuasion, in order that he may hear holy sermons and theological lectures, and observe the use of the holy Supper which as it is most simple among you, so it is most pure. He will lodge with Mr Butler the Englishman, his old friend. How much he has suffered from the Emperor for the sake of Christ's gospel, it is irrelevant to my present [purpose] to write....

Burcher, whom he met in Strassburg on June 1, gave him
another letter to Bullinger: 'He does not disapprove of
our religion, being a man of learning and godly judgment....He is a disciple of the French church, which is
not opposed to your religion.' At Zurich, Bullinger formed
a great opinion of him: 'That nobleman of Ghent, van
Utenhove,' he wrote to Burcher (June 28), 'has far
surpassed your commendation of him: he is an incom-
parable man; and I thank you, because by your instrumentality and our [friend] Hooper's I have formed a
friendship with a man so distinguished in every respect.'
The admiration was mutual: 'If you knew how often he
has thanked me for sending him to Zurich, you would
marvel,' wrote Hooper to Bullinger (March 27, 1550).
But he stayed there barely a month, for he was in Strassburg again on July 7 (1549): there he found à Lasco, who
was on his master's business, and travelled back with him
up the Rhine. (À Lasco must have known of Jan Utenhove
from his half-brother Karel, who had been a fellow-boarder
at Erasmus' house in Basel in 1524–5: and who, it may
be mentioned, seems to have visited Cambridge in the
autumn of 1550[1].) Jan Utenhove himself returned straight
to England, and, after visiting Cambridge, settled down
in London with Hooper.

Utenhove's friendship with Hooper had extremely
important consequences. In the first place, it was largely
through Hooper's influence that the Strangers' Church
was founded. Since his arrival in May 1549, he had
quickly made his mark as a leader of the Puritan party in
the Church, and had secured the patronage of Somerset,
who at that time was toying with Calvinism on the one
hand, and necromancy on the other. Very soon after his

---

[1] *Bucer to Jan Utenhove*, Cambridge, September 18, 1550. But
this letter is almost illegible: cf. the very different readings given by
Pijper (App., Ep. vi) and by Hessels (No. 11).

arrival, he began (apparently without any authority) to preach in London: 'I also,' he wrote to Bullinger (June 25), 'having compassion on the ignorance of my brethren, read a public lecture twice in the day to so numerous an audience that the church cannot contain them': and these Scripture readings, and more particularly, perhaps, the heckling that he received from the Anabaptists, earned him a considerable popular notoriety. Lampoons were written against him, and fixed on the doors of St Paul's and St Magnus': but Edward Underhill, the Hot Gospeller, constituted himself 'Hooper's champion.' Hitherto, however, Cranmer had not regarded him very favourably: but at the beginning of September he and Latimer laid information to the Council against Bishop Bonner, who had been commanded, as a test of his orthodoxy, to preach a sermon at St Paul's Cross on September 1 denouncing the rebels against the Prayer Book of 1549, but instead, like Balaam, had blessed them altogether. Hooper was therefore one of the most important witnesses against Bonner in his trial (Sept. 13, 16, 18) before Cranmer and the other Commissioners, which ended in Bonner's deprivation: and after that, the Archbishop became 'more friendly to him.' The Council also were grateful for this service, and Somerset invited him not infrequently to preach at Court: nor did the fall of his patron long distress him, for he soon found another in the Marquis of Dorset, Warwick's friend. On February 5, 1550, Cranmer sent for him, and ordered him, in the name of the King and Council, to preach a course of sermons before the King every Wednesday during Lent.

I shall choose (I think) an extremely suitable subject, which will touch beautifully upon the duties of individuals, namely the Prophet Jonah. Do you, my reverend friend [Bullinger], write back as soon as possible and admonish me diligently [as to] what you think suitable to be said in such a crowded auditory. It is certain to be great when before the King: for in the city there is such a crowd at my lectures that very often the church does not contain them.

But Hooper was wise in his generation, and touched so lightly upon the duties of his noble hearers, and so heavily upon the shortcomings of the bishops and clergy, who 'unquiet the ship of this realm two manner ways; one by the neglecting of their true duty, the other by a defence of a false and damnable superstition,' that Warwick found him a man after his own heart, and an agreeable change after Latimer: with the result that upon the conclusion of these sermons, on April 7 Hooper was offered the bishopric of Gloucester, which was granted him by the Council on May 15. In the meanwhile, before his consecration, he went to visit his parents in Somerset, and on his return (c. June 15) was sent by the Council to preach to the rebels in Essex, 'quae est regio Angliae plena periculi,' and to the Anabaptists in Kent. Though Hooper lacked charity, he did not lack courage.

Meanwhile à Lasco, who had left Lambeth at the end of June, and had taken a house in Bow Lane, was finding difficulty in organising a Strangers' Church in London or in obtaining a place of worship for their use, owing to lack of influence at Court. (Presumably Cranmer did not altogether favour the project.) Consequently, on Hooper's return to London (c. July 12), he was appealed to: à Lasco and the designate ministers and elders of the Church met at Utenhove's house at eight in the morning to discuss their plans, and then Hooper joined them for lunch, and after lunch had their difficulties laid before him[1]. At this time Hooper's influence with the Council was very strong:

[1] *À Lasco to Utenhove*. Kuyper dates this letter 'm. Iunii 1550,' that is, c. June 15, following Hooper's return from Somerset. But I think that it was written after Hooper's return from his mission to Kent and Essex. Up to June 25 at least à Lasco was staying with Cranmer at Lambeth.

he represented to them that it was important that the Strangers should have an organised Church, 'for avoiding of all sects of anabaptists and such-like' (as the King recorded in his Diary): and it is therefore not surprising to find that on July 24 they were assigned, by letters patent, the old church of the Austin Friars, which had been despoiled and abandoned since the Dissolution.

Volumus praeterea—so ran the royal license[1]—quod Johannes a Lasco natione Polonus, homo propter integritatem et innocentiam vitae ac morum et singularem eruditionem valde celebris, sit primus et modernus superintendens dictae ecclesiae, et quod Gualterus Deboemis [Deloenus], Martinus Flandrus, Franciscus Riverius, Ridulphus [Ricardus] Gallus, sint quatuor primi et moderni ministri.

The two former were the ministers of the Flemish and German congregation, the two latter of the French and Walloon. 'Franciscus Riverius' (Rivius) was that François Perroussel (la Rivière) who had been a minister in the French church at Canterbury: 'Ridulphus Gallus' was Richard Vauville, who was already pastor of the French church in London, which was now incorporated in the German congregation. He had lately (June 2) married 'Joanna, mistress Hooper's maidservant.' 'Gualterus Deloenus' (Wouter Deleen) was a native of Alkmaar: he had been resident in London for some time, and had published there a revised Latin Testament, dedicated to Henry VIII: à Lasco speaks of him as 'formerly the late king's librarian,' and certainly there is an entry in King Edward VI's Household Book of *Quarter Wages* paid in 1547 to 'Gualterus de Lenus of 'cxvj^s viij^d'[2]. 'Martinus Flandrus,' better known as Martin Micronius (de Cleyne), was, like Utenhove, a native of Ghent: he had been trained as a physician, but, having embraced the Reformation,

[1] Burnet, v. 305–11 (No. LI).
[2] *Trevelyan Papers* (Camden Soc.) I. 197.

fled to Germany with Utenhove in 1544, and after some years of wandering settled down in Basel. There, in March 1549, he and his wife joined Hooper, who was returning to England from Zurich. Since May 16, when they had arrived in London, he had been living there, probably with Hooper.—At the beginning of the following year (1551) an Italian congregation was also organised, under à Lasco's superintendence, and permitted the use of this church, which had been renamed the Jesus Temple: their pastor was Michael Angelo Florio, who later gave a great deal of trouble and almost created a schism in the Strangers' Church.

We command and straitly enjoin the mayor, sheriffs and aldermen of our city of London, the Bishop of London and his successors, with all other archbishops, bishops, justices, and ministers of ours whatsoever, that they permit the aforesaid, the superintendent and ministers and their successors, freely and peacefully to enjoy, use and exercise their own rites and ceremonies and their own peculiar ecclesiastical discipline, notwithstanding that they do not agree with the rites and ceremonies customary in our kingdom, without impeachment, molestation or disturbance of them, or of any one of them, by any statute, act, proclamation, injunction, restraint or use to the contrary previously made, issued, or promulgated to the contrary notwithstanding....

Ridley was furious. He was as stout a Protestant as any of the bishops, but the erection of this autonomous church in the heart of his own diocese constituted an intolerable breach of ecclesiastical discipline. The notions of the Middle Ages were but slowly discarded: they went first in the sphere of commercial morality: and the old idea of one Church outside which there is no salvation—*extra Ecclesiam nulla salus*—died extremely hard, if indeed it is dead yet. The men who had dared, under the pressure of necessity, to rend the seamless robe of Christ, were not prepared to have it torn to ribbons. This dominant theory explains the reluctance of the Elizabethan Puritans to leave the Church to whose principles they could not subscribe, and of the Church to expel the traitors whom she could not subdue. In 1550 the idea of Nonconformity in the religious sphere was as remote as that of resignation in the political. This patent of self-government granted to the Strangers' Church anticipated it by more than a century: for this was a revolutionary experiment: the Council had, no doubt unconsciously, abused their authority, and their action was fiercely resented by the bishops.

Their protest was not ineffective. First, the Strangers found that the restoration and redecoration of the Jesus Temple (at the King's expense) was being deliberately protracted. Growing impatient, at the end of August à Lasco asked the Lord Treasurer if they might have the key, 'in order that we might be able to have sermons there on Sundays at least,' but was told that this was impossible, because the Temple was a royal gift, and could not be handed over till it was finished. The Lord Treasurer also asked why they wished to have their own ceremonies, since the English ceremonies were not repugnant to the word of God: and, after some argument, concluded by saying that the foreigners ought either to adopt the English ceremonies, or to condemn them by the word of God. The work dragged on meanwhile into the winter: but 'by the singular goodness of God,' wrote Micronius to Bullinger (Oct. 13), 'a certain church has been made over to us Germans by the favour of some citizens of London, in which we are allowed to have sermons until the other is finished.... We began to preach in this church of ours on September 21; and now so large a congregation of Germans attends that the church does not hold them.' It was next decided to draw up a constitution: and so on

October 5 four Elders (of whom Utenhove was one), and on the 12th four Deacons were ordained 'according to the apostolic ordinance... with public prayer and the laying-on of hands'; the former were to assist the ministers in 'the preservation of doctrine and morals in the church,' the latter 'to take charge of the poor and exiled for Christ's sake.'

But the reasonable malevolence of Ridley and the other bishops pursued them. On October 20 Micronius added a postscript to this letter: 'By canvassing and persuasion the bishops have effected with the King's Council, that the free use of the sacraments is not to be permitted to us, but we must be fettered by the English ceremonies, which are intolerable to all lovers of godliness. This occasions the greatest distress to our Dr John à Lasco and to all godly persons.' In the following summer à Lasco was still 'diligently exerting himself among the bishops on behalf of his office, in order that we may be permitted to enjoy the liberty granted [by the royal license]; but much as he tries, he effects nothing': Calvin himself, who had been informed of all this by Utenhove, addressed a remonstrance to Edward VI: 'Quant à l'usaige des sacrements et ce qui concerne l'ordre spirituel qu'il vous a pleu leur en faire aura son effect.' Eventually— probably in the autumn of 1551—the King himself interposed his own royal authority, and insisted that the Strangers should be permitted to enjoy the liberties which he had granted to them[1].

Nevertheless, the Church grew and flourished, although, as Micronius wrote, 'We feel indeed sometimes that we

---

[1] 'Etsi enim id in Senatu Regio omnibus propemodum placerèt, ipséque Cantuariensis Archiepiscopus rem modis omnibus promoueret: non deerant tamen qui id molestè ferrent, adeoque & reluctaturi fuerint huic instituto Regio, nisi Rex ipse, non tantum autoritate sua restitisset: sed productis etiam instituti huius rationibus conatus eorum repressisset.' (*Forma ac Ratio*, p. $\beta3^b$–4^a: Kuyper II. 10–11.)

are assailed by Satan through the enemies of Christ, the hypocrites, the bishops, and the heretics.' The last serious trouble with Ridley occurred in November 1552. A proclamation had been issued, compelling all citizens to attend their parish churches regularly: upon this pretext, the ecclesiastical authorities arrested some of the foreigners, members of à Lasco's congregation, living in Lesser Southwark. À Lasco promptly appealed to the Lord Chancellor, who referred him to Cecil, who brought the matter before the Council: and they, understanding well enough who was at the root of the trouble, issued an order 'To the Bishop of London to conferre with Joannes Alasco, and betwene them to devise summe good meanes for the appeasing of a disquiet lately happened in the Straungers' Churche in London uppon thexecution of the Statute for the comming to churche.' Presumably 'summe good meanes' were devised, for no further attempts were made to interfere with the liberties of the Strangers.

In this age of indifference, a modern Churchman may be disposed to judge harshly of Ridley's conduct. 'All this mischief,' wrote Micronius, 'is stirred up against us by the bishops, and especially by London, who does us the more harm in proportion as he seems the more vigorously to favour the word of God.' Micronius evidently thought him a hypocrite. But, judged by the standards of his age, it was Ridley who was in the right of the matter. He was fighting for the authority of the Church of England against Dissent, for tradition against innovation, for unity against secession. The privileges granted to the Strangers' Church by the royal license had constituted a serious invasion of his jurisdiction. Nor was his wrath mitigated by the fact that à Lasco had presumed to interfere in the domestic policy of the Church of England—even Strype and Burnet, writing more than a century later, did not

regard that matter lightly—and had instigated Hooper in
his resistance to the established order in the most violent
controversy of this period: the Vestiarian Controversy
of 1550–1.

On April 7, 1550, Hooper was offered the vacant
bishopric of Gloucester by the Lord Chancellor, on behalf
of the Council. He declined, however, to accept it unless
it were granted him 'without any superstitious ceremonies.' The Council summoned him before them on
April 10, to explain his objections. He said that he
objected to the form of the Oath of the King's Supremacy
in the new Ordinal—'So help me GOD, *all saints and the
holy Evangelists*'—and to the use of vestments. He had
raised both these points before, in his *Third Sermon upon
Jonas* (March 5), in which he had condemned the new
Ordinal on these grounds: the form of the oath he had
dismissed as a printer's error, but as to the vestments he
had said:

Yet do I much marvel that in the same book it is appointed,
that he that will be admitted to the ministry of God's word
or his sacraments, must come in white vestments; which
seemeth to repugn plainly with the former doctrine, that
confessed the only word of God to be sufficient [for man's
salvation]. And sure I am, they have not in the word of God,
that thus a minister should be apparelled, nor yet in the primitive
and best church. It is rather the habit and vesture of Aaron
and the gentiles, than [of] the ministers of Christ.

These views were strongly opposed by the bishops: but
a majority on the Council, led by Somerset (for Warwick
was absent through illness), overruled their objections,
and appointed Hooper to the bishopric on May 15, as is
recorded in the Council Book. (The letters patent of his
appointment are dated July 3.)

It seemed that Hooper had gained the victory. He

himself went down to Somersetshire to see his parents, and then, in June, accepted a mission from the Council to preach in the seditious and heretical districts of Kent and Essex. He intended to go down to his diocese on his return, and invited Utenhove to accompany him. Meanwhile on June 29 he wrote to Bullinger:

At last, for the glory of God, the result of our disputation was what I and all godly persons hoped, but not through myself alone, but through the grace of God and the promptitude of the councillors and their love for God and for the purity and candour of the rising church. 'But,' you will say, 'I have not yet heard the result.' It was such, that they will set me free from all defilement of superstition and from the imposition [*impostura*] of the oath. On this condition I accepted the charge committed me. Aid wretched me with your prayers, lest that little flock should perish, for which Christ died....

His friends were jubilant: Christopher Hales, for example, wrote to Gualter (May 24), 'Hooper was made bishop of Gloucester two [*sic*] days ago, but under godly conditions: for he refuses to be called Rabbi or *my lord*, as we are wont to say: he refuses to be tonsured[1], he refuses to be made a magpie,'—an obvious gibe at the vestments—'he refuses to be consecrated and anointed in the usual way, with many other things which you may learn from other sources. From his bishopric he has 2000 crowns per annum. God grant he may so govern his flock as to be a godly example to the other shepherds.' So ended the first round.

But the triumph of the Zwinglians was premature. On Hooper's return from Kent, he found that the bishops refused to consecrate him under those conditions: the battle had to be fought all over again. In the matter of the oath, however, he won an initial victory. On July 20

---

[1] This was only customary: it was not prescribed by the new Ordinal.

he appeared before the King in the presence of the
Council, and stated his objections. Micronius and ab
Ulmis relate the pretty story (which Fox must have
somehow overlooked) of the pious young King striking
out the offensive words with his own pen, and exclaiming,
'What wickedness is here, Hooper? Are these offices
ordained in the name of the saints, or of God?' Since he
noted in his Diary under this date, 'Houper was made
bishop of Glocestre,' the story may well be true. But
though the King was on his side, and the Council had
evidently granted him the dispensations he demanded,
Hooper was far from being made bishop of Gloucester
yet. However, Warwick sent him to Cranmer with the
following somewhat peremptory note:

After my most harty commendatiōs to your grace, these may
be to desire the same, that in such reasonable things, wherein
this bearer my L. elect of Glocester, craueth to be borne
withall at your hands, you would withsafe to shew him your
graces fauour the rather at this my instaunce: which thyng
partly, I haue taken in hand by the kynges Maiesties owne
motion. The matter is wayed by his highnes, none other but
that your grace may facily condescend unto. The principal
cause is, that you would not charge the said bearer with an
oth burdenous to his conscience. And so for lacke of tyme
I commit your grace to the tuition of almighty God. From
Westm. the 23. of Iuly, 1550.

Your graces most assured louing friend. I. WARWIKE.

Apparently Cranmer allowed the dispensation in the
matter of the oath—indeed, he could hardly refuse it now:
but for the rest he referred Hooper to Ridley, who, being
applied to, refused to use any other form of consecration
than that prescribed by Parliament. ('Thus the bishops
mutually endeavour that none of their glory may depart.')
Hooper went back to the Council, who gave him another
letter to Cranmer and the bishops (Aug. 5), giving them

leave to 'omit and let pass certain rites and ceremonies, offensive to his conscience,' and exempting them from the guilt of praemunire incurred by so doing. Ridley, on being shown this letter, told him that he would reply to him or to the Council shortly: but, while Hooper awaited his answer, he hastened to the palace and laid his views before the Council in person, pointing out that the vestments were ἀδιαφόρα—things indifferent—which the Church deemed it advisable, from motives of policy, to retain; that for private individuals to set their judgment against that of the Church, and to be granted exemptions whenever they demanded them, would be fatal to the authority of the Church; and that Hooper, by refusing to admit that the vestments were things indifferent, was being extremely unreasonable, and his conduct was likely to cause scandal in the Church.

He so far persuaded many, that afterwards they would hardly listen to Hooper's defence, when he came into the palace a little after; Hooper therefore asked that if they would not hear him speak, they would at least hear and read his defence in writing. This Hooper obtained: wherefore he has delivered to the king's councillors in writing [his views] about abolishing the use of vestments and similar trifles. And if the bishop cannot satisfy him [the King] with other reasons, Hooper will win. We are daily expecting the end of this controversy, which is only conducted between individuals either by conference or by letter, lest any tumult should be excited among the ignorant. You see in what a state the affairs of the church would be, if they were left in the hands of the bishops, even of the best of them.

Hooper contended 'that a christian man, having been instructed about the impiety of the use of vestments... could not use them with a clear conscience in the ministry of the church; both because they bring with them an opinion of merit, hypocrisy, a thousand kinds of superstitions and stumbling-blocks, and also because they truly obscure the priesthood of Christ too much.' In short, he refused to admit that they were things indifferent, because they were definitely Romish. And so ended the second round.

At this point à Lasco intervened in the dispute. The Strangers' Church stood solid at Hooper's back: they regarded his conduct with admiration—'I do not doubt,' Micronius had written to Pellican, 'but that he will be the Zwingli of England': moreover they were the more anxious for his victory, since his cause was so closely related to their own. They also were anxious to be allowed to discard the vestments in their Church and other Romish superstitions (such as kneeling to receive Communion), and to be allowed to enjoy the complete immunity that had originally been granted to them by the royal license. Further, they were under an obligation to Hooper which they were anxious to repay. Probably in October of this year[1], à Lasco addressed to Cranmer a lengthy statement of his opinions: the first part, which argues for the abolition of kneeling at the Communion, may be considered later: the second part, which argues for the abolition of vestments, is of more immediate importance.

Now as to the refusal of the vestments, the whole question seems to turn on this: whether [*num*] to the public worship [*cultus*], instituted by God himself in his Church with prescribed ceremonies, anything ought to be added, about which God himself gave no command....

[1] This letter bears neither name nor date. It was clearly addressed to Cranmer: but the date is less certain. Simler dates it '*circa finem Maji* 1550, *post suum ex Polonia reditum*': Kuyper (on the strength of a very doubtful reference to the Sweating Sickness) August 1551. I conjecture that it was written between August 5, 1550, and about the middle of November of the same year, when Hooper wrote to Bullinger, 'Solus D. a Lasco ex omnibus peregrinis, qui aliqua autoritate valent, a meis partibus stetit'; and probably in October.

À Lasco was right: the controversy could be reduced to this one issue—whether, as the Germans held, all things might be tolerated that were not condemned by holy Scripture, or, as the Swiss maintained, all things must be condemned that were not specifically commanded by it. To à Lasco, tradition was a snare: but Cranmer was more in sympathy with the former view, which has been nobly expressed by Hooker: 'Where the Scripture is silent, the Church is my text; where that speaks, 'tis but my comment.' However, à Lasco supported his argument with a string of texts, which are only convincing if you grant the major premiss. They may be briefly cited:

(*a*) 'Of the tree of the knowledge of good and evil, thou shalt not eat of it: for in the day thou eatest thereof thou shalt surely die.' (Gen. ii. 17.) *Ergo*, God demands *obedience* above all. Cf. 'To obey is better than sacrifice.' (1 Sam. xv. 22.)

(*b*) 'What thing soever I command you, observe to do it: thou shalt not add thereto, nor diminish from it.' (Deut. xii. 32.)

(*c*) 'But the prophet, which shall presume to speak a word in my name, which I have not commanded him to speak,... that prophet shall die.' (Deut. xviii. 20.)

(*d*) 'Hearken not unto the words of the prophets that prophesy unto you:...they speak a vision of their own heart, and not out of the mouth of the Lord.' (Jerem. xxiii. 16.)

(*e*) 'And look that thou make them after their pattern, which was shewed thee in the mount.' (Exod. xxv. 40: cf. Acts vii. 44: Heb. viii. 5.)

(*f*) 'How can ye believe, which receive honour one of another, and seek not the honour that cometh from God only?[1]...He that speaketh of himself seeketh his own glory: but he that seeketh his glory that sent him, the same is true, and no unrighteousness is in him.' (John v. 44, vii. 18.)

---

[1] Cf. *Utenhove to Bullinger*, London, April 9, 1551: 'The bishops... being, doubtless, far more solicitous for their own glory than for Christ's....'

As arguments against the use of vestments, these do not seem entirely conclusive.

Meanwhile Warwick and the Council were growing impatient. Hooper's stubbornness placed them in a difficult and humiliating position. By giving him the bishopric, they had gone too far to withdraw: on the other hand, as the bishops contended, the vestments were things indifferent, and, in the second place, they were prescribed by the King's authority, with whom rested the appointment or removal in the Church of things indifferent. As Martyr observed, 'it is very offensive to the king's councillors and to many other men, nobles and commoners alike, that a decree publicly received, and confirmed by the authority of the kingdom, should be torn up as impious, and condemned as repugnant to the holy scriptures.' Warwick, as Hooper's patron, had done all he could for him, and naturally expected him to be content with that. Instead of that, Hooper continued to send him long statements of his objections, in which Warwick was not interested, but otherwise remained intractable. Warwick, turning theologian himself, told him 'that the king must be obeyed in matters of indifference, that one must avoid placing a stumbling-block [in the way of] the weak, after the example of St Paul when he had a vow, to be shorn, and when he circumcised Timothy.' But Hooper refused to admit that vestments were things indifferent, and on October 3 submitted a long statement to the Council, of which a fragment has been preserved.

The doctrine of Paul is this (Gal. iii.), that whosoever recalls things abrogated in Christ transgresses the Lord's will. And he manifestly teaches (Heb. vii., viii., ix., x.) that the priesthood of Aaron has been abolished in the priesthood of Christ, with all its rites, vestments, unctions, consecrations, and the like. If therefore those shadows of the Aaronic priesthood cannot consist with the priesthood of Christ, [how] much less that popish priesthood, which even by the testimony of their own books has been derived either from Aaron or from the Gentiles. Nor truly does [the priesthood of Christ] lack its own mystery because our Saviour Jesus Christ hung naked upon the cross. For the Aaronic priests used vestments in their ministry, because the truth of their priesthood, Christ himself, had not yet come: but Christ, when he himself was to be sacrificed, was stripped of all vestments, showing by this the priesthood which, since it was the truth itself, had no longer need of veils or shadows.

Finding Hooper thus obdurate, the Council tried to make Ridley give way. On October 6, 'because they would in no wise the stirring up of controversies betwixt men of one profession, [they] did send for him, willing him to cease the occasions hereof.' Ridley begged to be allowed to put his case in writing, and on October 19 he came and presented it to the Council. Unfortunately Hooper happened to come there too, a few minutes later, and a most violent scene occurred. Hooper demanded a copy of Ridley's answer: Ridley hotly told the Council not to give it him. Both men lost their tempers, and heaped insults on each other. The occasion was not very edifying, but it served to show the Council that there was no hope of their agreement under present conditions.

Why Hooper came to the Council on that day was probably to inform them that two days earlier (Oct. 17) he had written to Bucer and to Martyr enclosing a summary of his opinions, and asking them both to give him their views on the controversy. 'I am striving[1] that the dispute may be composed by the judgment of godly men,' he wrote to Bullinger. This step was probably taken on the advice of à Lasco, who, it will be remembered, had recently visited both Martyr and Bucer. However, the

[1] 'Contendo' ap. Simler (73. 134): the Parker Soc. edtn has 'Consentio.'

replies that Hooper received from them were not what he had hoped.

Martyr's reply is dated November 4. It is extremely long, but may be summarised somewhat as follows:

Reverend and most beloved in Christ Jesus,—I have studied your MS. as well as I could, though I could only keep it one night, because your messenger took it to Cambridge early next morning. At first I took no small pleasure in your singular and ardent zeal, whereby you endeavour to bring Christianity back to chaste and simple purity, and to cut off everything that cannot be turned to solid edification and is therefore considered superfluous by the godly. 'Verilie to saie, as touching mine owne selfe, I take it grieuouslie to bee plucked awaie from that plaine and pure custome, which you knowe all we used a great while together at *Argentine* [Strassburg], where the varietie of garments about holie seruices were taken awaie'[1]. So I agree with you: I hope that the diversity of vestments may be abolished, because by ceasing to use them we should follow the Apostolic Church more closely, and because 'I perceiue the Popes followers indeuour still by these reliques to renew at the least wise some shewe of the Masse: and doe more cleaue unto these things than the nature of things indifferent can require.'

But I cannot allow that they are not things indifferent, or that they are in their own nature contrary to the word of God. I am not ignorant that things indifferent sometimes may be

[1] Martyr's conduct in this controversy was not very creditable. To Thomas Sampson (whom, in another letter—February 1, 1560— he advised that he might wear vestments in preaching or in celebrating the Holy Communion, provided that he continued 'speaking and teaching against the use of them') he wrote, November 4, 1559, 'Ego cum essem Oxonii vestibus illis albis in choro nunquam uti volui, quamvis essem canonicus: mei facti ratio mihi constabat' ('When I was at Oxford, I would never wear a surplice in the choir, although I was a canon: I was satisfied that I had good reason'). Moreover on April 25, 1551, when the controversy was ended, he wrote to Gualter, 'That Hooper is delivered from all his troubles, I think you understand from others. I never failed him, and I always hoped well of his cause': which was very far from the truth.

used, and sometimes not. But the use of vestments is a harmless and necessary concession to the infirmity of the times. By contending for its abolition 'more bitterly than behooueth,' we may hinder the advancement of the Gospel. 'For if we would first suffer the Gospell to be spreade abroad and to take deepe roote, perhaps men woulde better and more easilie be perswaded to remooue awaie these outward attires. While a man is sick and is somewhat uppon the mending hande, he grieuouslie suffereth certaine light and unfit things to be remooued from him aswel in meate as in drinke: but yet the very same man hauing recouered health, doeth euen of himself reiect them as things unacceptable and unprofitable. If *England* were first wel and diligently instructed, and confirmed in the chief and most necessarie points of Religion: so farre as methinkes I see, it wil not at the length take in ill part, that these things in some sort should bee remooued. But nowe when there is brought in a change in yᵉ chiefe & necessarie points of religion, and that with so great disquietnesse, if wee shoulde also declare those things to bee wicked which be things indifferent, al mens mindes in a manner would be so alienated from us, as they woulde no more shewe themselues to be attentiue and pacient hearers of sounde doctrine and necessarie Sermons.' England is greatly indebted to your zeal: 'onelie beware of this, least by unseasonable and ouer sharpe Sermons [*intempestivis nimisque acerbis concionibus*] you be a let unto your owne selfe.'—Secondly, to condemn the use of vestments is to condemn many Churches which are not alien from the Gospel and others of time-honoured reputation.

'You say that the Priesthood of *Aaron*, whereunto this diuersitie of garments seemeth to belong, must not be restored. For since we haue Christ for the Priest, the ceremonies of *Aaron* are abrogated, neither ought they with the sàfetie of godlinesse [to] bee called againe.' Of the sacraments of the Promise, that is true: but many useful customs of the Aaronic priesthood can be, and have been, retained without offence: e.g. the Apostles' command to the Gentiles to abstain from things strangled and from blood; tithes; psalm- and hymn-singing; prophesying; commemorative feasts. Should all these things be abolished, because they are traces of the old law? We may indeed retain such things indifferent, provided that they are harmless, and that we are prepared to discard them when they appear less profitable.

Secondly you say that vestments are not lawful because they are the inventions of the Antichrist of Rome. But, even if that were true, I fail to see why we may use nothing that is customary in the Roman Church[1]. The early Christians turned pagan temples into Christian churches, and used their revenues for the stipends of the clergy, &c.: cf. Tertullian, *De Corona Militari*. As a matter of fact, this diversity of vestments was not originated by the Pope. St John at Ephesus wore the *Petalum* or Pontifical Plate [Euseb. *Hist. Eccl.* III. xxi, v. xxiv]; Pontius records that when Cyprian was to be beheaded, he gave his robe to the executioners, his Dalmatic vestment to the deacons, and stood in his linen garments; Chrysostom mentions the white vestments of the clergy; cf. Tertullian, *De Pallio*; and what of the Chrisom robe given at baptism? Thus it appears that there were some distinctions of vestments in the Church earlier than the papal tyranny. 'But admitte that these things were inuented by the Pope, yet do I not perswade my selfe that the impiety of the popedome is such, that whatsoeuer it toucheth it doth altogether defile and pollute it, whereby godlie men may not be allowed to put it to a holie use.'

You yourself admit that all human inventions are not forthwith to be condemned. Such, e.g. is morning Communion. The Church must have some liberty in the ordering of public worship. '*Vnto the cleane all things are cleane...Euerie creature of God is good:* And it is not necessarilie required that we shoulde haue in the holy Scriptures an expresse mention of the particular thinges which we use. This generallie is enough to knowe by faith, that thinges indifferent cannot defile them which liue with a pure and syncere minde and conscience.'

[1] Cf. Jeremy Collier (ed. Lathbury) v. 397: 'To quit antiquity in any custom, because it is continued in the Church of Rome, has neither reason nor charity in it.'

'These things haue I shortly abridged, as touching the
controuersie which you propounded unto me out of which
I wish with all my heart that you maie happilie unwinde your
selfe. And those thinges which I haue written I praie you to
take in good part.'...

Bucer's reply, which, though not dated, is apparently of
the same date (for it was delivered to Martyr, to read and
to forward, on November 5), is on the same lines. It also is
extremely long.

Reverend Sir—I have studied your MS. carefully. I would
have given anything to prevent this controversy, since it places
such an impediment in the way of the ministry of yourself
and others. I think you cannot doubt that I should greatly
rejoice if all external matters were restored to Apostolic
simplicity, for I have always taught that no peculiar vestment
should be used in the administration of the Sacraments, and,
observing the abuse of vestments in many places here, I would
give much to secure their abolition. But this abuse is only a
symptom of the underlying disease of Antichristianity. [Here
follows a valuable digression on the appalling state of the
Church of England.] If we united against these evils and
eradicated the disease, then the symptoms (e.g. the abuse of
vestments) would vanish: but there is no use in trying to cure
the symptoms without first curing the disease. We must first
provide faithful pastors for every parish, and dismiss the
unfaithful without delay, and thus restore the whole communion and discipline of Christ.

No rite should be retained or added unless it conduces to
edification. If the Churches would listen to me, they would
certainly not retain the vestments used by the Papists: and
thus they would proclaim their repudiation of Rome, confess
that they acknowledged complete liberty in externals, and
leave no ground for contention among the weaker brethren.
But I should hesitate to affirm that these vestments abused
by Antichrist have become so contaminated that they cannot
be allowed in any Christian Church. Every creature of God
is good: none is of itself either Aaronical or Popish, save in

the minds of those who abuse it by attaching to it an impious symbolism.

Moreover who can deny that God has left a wide discretion to his Church? 'It is evident that our Lord Jesus Christ, as regards the ministry, the Word, and the Sacraments, has prescribed to us in his own words only the substance; and has left his Church at liberty to order everything else which appertains to the decent and useful administration of his mysteries. Hence we celebrate the Holy Supper neither in the evening, nor in a private house, nor recumbent, nor among men only....Some reckon among the things which are left free to the free ordering of the Churches, to celebrate the Lord's Supper once only, twice, thrice, four times, or oftener in the year; and to stand [as a spectator merely] at the Supper, without participating of the Sacraments. And yet it is evident that each of these [customs] is truly Popish.' Provided, then, that the Churches use such rites and ceremonies as they may appoint to illustrate, and not to obscure, the Gospel of Christ, and for the commendation and adornment of his ministry, they do not transgress the will of God. God knows, I would give much to have the vestments abolished, seeing how widely the abuse of them prevails: but I do not find anywhere in Scripture the use of them condemned. 'As to all those passages of Scripture which you have adduced against the traditions of man, you know well that they are all only to be understood of those things in which men desire to establish a worship of God from their own [imaginations], making of no account the commandments of God. Even you yourself prefer to take food with washed rather than unwashed hands.'

'If these [observations]...satisfy your charity, I shall rejoice in the Lord: if otherwise, I entreat you to point out to me briefly those passages of Scripture in which I may see that this opinion of mine concerning liberty in those matters is inconsistent with the word of God.'...

Apparently Hooper asked à Lasco to reply to this letter for him: but Bucer's letter to à Lasco (Strype, *Mem.* IV. 444-55) is to the same purpose. 'I have, according to my gift, weighed your reasons; and yet I can perceive no other, but that the use of al external things, as wel in holy ceremonies as in private matters, ought to be left free to the churches of God.'

It also occurred to Cranmer to consult Bucer, and probably Martyr too. Bucer had sent his observations on the controversy to Peter Alexander, who gave them to the Archbishop to read: and so, on December 2, Cranmer wrote to him, asking for an answer to the following questions:

Whether, without offence to God, it is lawful for the ministers of the Church of England to use those vestments which at this time they wear, and are so prescribed by the Government?

Whether he that shall affirm that it is unlawful, or shall refuse to wear this apparel, offendeth against God, for that he sayeth that thing to be unclean, that God hath sanctified; and offendeth against the Government, for that he disturbeth the public order?

Bucer in his reply (dated Dec. 8) declared his reluctance to intervene in the controversy: but he answered both questions in the affirmative, though with the reservation, in the case of the first, that the ministers should explain to the people that the white surplice is a symbol of heavenly purity, to which it should draw the minds of the worshippers, and that it has no connection with the Church of Rome. The second affirmative he gave without any qualification: but added that 'since undoubtedly at this day these vestments are to some an occasion for superstition, to others for pernicious contention, it is better to abolish them'—only, however, after the whole Church has been thoroughly reformed, purged of all sacrileges, false doctrines, superstitious rites, and defended from simony and spoliation. With this exordium the letter concludes.

Martyr was staying at Lambeth at the time, and he also seems to have been pressed to give his opinion, and to have replied 'that he was ardently desirous of simplicity above all in the sacred ministry; and therefore recommended that the distinctions of dress be abolished, and that as soon as it could be decreed by public authority; but meanwhile he could not admit that their use was impious or condemned by Scripture; yet because that diversity of vesture has little or nothing of edification, and many superstitiously abuse it, he therefore judged that it ought to be removed.'

Meanwhile Warwick and the Council had come to regard Hooper as an unmitigated nuisance: the more so, since he had actually involved himself in a subsidiary controversy, hardly less bitter, upon the question of Divorce. Ridley, to show that he did genuinely regard the vestments as things indifferent, had made Hooper an extraordinarily generous offer (though it is possible that Cranmer would not have sanctioned it): 'Let him revoke his errors, and agree and subscribe to the doctrine, and not condemn that for sin, that God never forbade, ungodly adding unto God's word, and I shall not, for any necessity that I put in these vestments, let to lay my hands upon him and to admit him bishop, although he come as he useth to ride in a merchant's cloak, having the king's majesty's dispensation for the act, and my lord archbishop's commission orderly to do the thing.' But Hooper would not yield an inch. In desperation, the Council commanded him 'to keep his house: unless it were to go to the Archbishop of Canterbury, or the Bishops of Ely, London, or Lincoln, for counsel and satisfaction of his conscience; and neither to preach nor read [i.e. expound the Scriptures] till he had further license from the council.'

At this point Hooper lost his head and his case. Not only did he fail to keep his house, but also did an extremely

characteristic thing: he rushed into print with an Apology
—*A godly Confession and protestacion of the christian faith,
made and set furth by Jhon Hooper*, of which the Dedication
to the King is dated December 20, and which instantly
ran to two editions before the year was out. It is true that
Hooper showed a certain degree of caution: he denounced
sedition and heresy, and did not touch directly upon the
use of vestments: but he condemned the whole system
of Episcopacy ('I am sorry with all my heart to see the
Church of Christ degenerated into a civil policy') and
thereby challenged the authority of the bishops. This
pamphlet, ill-judged and inopportune, did exactly what
the bishops and the Council had been most anxious to
avoid: it took the controversy into the market-place. That
was unpardonable. 'Martyr has reported it for a most
certain fact, that [Hooper] has lost all influence with
almost all the nobility, and especially with Warwick,'
wrote John ab Ulmis, who made it his business to know
these things. Martyr himself wrote to Bucer,

His cause lies in such a state, that it cannot be approved
by good and pious men. I am grieved, I am grieved exceedingly,
that such things should happen among professors of the Gospel.
During all this time, while he is forbidden to preach, he
cannot, it seems, keep quiet: he has published a confession of
his faith by which he has again excited bitter feelings in the
minds of many. He complains moreover of the Council, and
perhaps, what is not told me, of us. May God give a happy
issue to unhappy acts.

On January 13 the Council committed him to Cranmer's
custody, 'to be reformed, or further punished, as the
obstinacy of his case requireth.' There, at Lambeth,
Martyr had three conferences with him, 'and exerted
every effort to break down his determination.'

And, certainly, at our first meeting, I entertained some hope
of softening him, although I had not clearly gained his assent;

and he requested me to return to him after dinner. In the meantime, another person had access to him—the actor-manager [*fabulae* χοραγός]—as both you and I well know. The result of his advice was, that he was rendered far more obstinate, as I afterwards learnt, than ever before. Therefore, seeing that nothing could be done, I left him sufficiently admonished, if he would but have listened, of the dangers which hung over him.

It is not difficult to guess the identity of the 'fabulae χοραγός.' It was à Lasco.

But the struggle was drawing to a close. The Council, by now completely alienated from Hooper, met at Greenwich on January 27, and 'upon a lettre from tharchebusshop of Canterbury, that Mr Hooper can not be brought to any conformytie, but rather persevering in his obstinacie coveteth to prescribe orders and necessarie lawes of his heade, it was agreed he shulde be committed to the Fleete': moreover the Warden of the Fleet was instructed 'to kepe him from conference of any person saving the ministres of that howse.'

This drastic treatment at last brought Hooper to a more reasonable frame of mind. He tendered his submission to the Council, but it did not satisfy them: and so on February 15 he addressed to Cranmer a humble, but not undignified letter of surrender. 'I now acknowledge the liberty of the sons of God in all external things: which I affirm and believe neither that they are impious in themselves, nor that any use of them is impious in itself; only the abuse, which can be pernicious to all, of those who use them superstitiously or otherwise evilly do I blame, together with Dr Bucer, Dr Martyr, and all godly and learned men.' He had come, he said, to distrust his own judgment, and to submit humbly to that of the Archbishop. He prayed him to use his influence with the rest of the Council, 'that they may be content in the name of Christ': and called God to witness that he was not making this surrender in dissimulation, nor from fear, nor for any cause but that of the Church.

Either by the generosity of his opponents or by the influence of the King, a compromise was allowed him: 'he was to be attired in the vestments prescribed when he was consecrated, and when he preached before the king, or in his cathedral, or in any public place; but he was dispensed with upon other occasions.' He was consecrated at Lambeth on March 8. A fortnight earlier (Feb. 24) Bullinger had written Cranmer one of his insolent, pontifical letters, bidding him put an end to the controversy in Hooper's favour. Cranmer did not reply.

With Hooper's surrender the controversy ended: although à Lasco, it is true, tried to revive it, and in the autumn composed a paper (dated Sept. 6) replying to Martyr's arguments. A general reconciliation followed: Cranmer, Ridley, and Warwick received back Hooper into favour: only the ministers of the Strangers' Church, who had stood by him to the end, regretted his submission, and Bullinger, who never trusted Warwick again. 'I read with interest, but not without grief,' he replied to a confidential letter from Utenhove, 'what you relate concerning our [friend] H. You seem however to judge rightly in thinking that this has not happened to him without the singular providence of God. Humbled by his fall, Peter learned to trust less in himself and to reverence God more ardently. And this will, I hope, be the result with Dr Hop. also, whom I hear to be laborious, indefatigable, and marvellously diligent in his office. God grant he may continue so, and for many years be faithful to the Church of God.'

Hooper himself was conscious of a certain embarrassment in his relations with Bullinger, and in his next letter, dated from Gloucester, August 1, 1551—he had not

written to him since November 1550—tried to pass over
his offence. 'Because the Lord has put an end to this
controversy, I do not think it is worth while to violate the
sepulchre of this unhappy tragedy.' It is unfortunate for
the peace of the Church of England that that sepulchre
should have been so soon, and since then so frequently,
re-opened.

The defeat of Hooper baffled the efforts of the Strangers'
Church to secure the freedom of worship that had been
granted to them. Moreover they had their full share of
internal troubles. Soon after they had received the Jesus
Temple, the French congregation, which was the senior,
quarrelled with the German congregation, which was the
larger, over their share in it: and the dispute was not
composed until the King, appealed to by à Lasco, granted
them also the chapel of St Anthony's hospital in Threadneedle Street, which was allotted to the French on strict
business terms. Throughout they were plagued by
heretics, Flemings for the most part, as it appears:
'besides the old errors concerning pædobaptism, Christ's
incarnation, the authority of the magistrate, the [lawful-
ness of an] oath, property and community of goods, and
the like, new ones are springing up every day, with which
we have to contend. There are moreover especially the
enemies of Christ's divinity, the Arians, who are now
beginning to shake our churches with greater violence than
ever they have done, denying the conception of Christ by
a virgin....' From this, too, the intervention of the State
afforded them some relief. A bill was introduced in the
Lords, 'For the Preservation of the King's Majesty's
Subjects from such Heresies as may happen by strangers
dwelling among them: quae commissa est Episcopis
London. Norwicen. Gloucestren. et Exon. [Ridley,
Thirlby, Hooper, and Coverdale]': and the findings of

this committee were such that Micronius wrote (Feb. 18, 1553), 'Now no foreigner can obtain [the privilege of] English citizenship, unless he first make some confession of his faith to the ministers of the strangers' churches. And if this lasts for some years, this kingdom will be delivered from great and various errors, which are usually introduced by foreign sectaries.' However one of the ministers, Wouter Deleen, had himself become infected with heresy: he reproved the use of god-parents in baptism, denounced from the pulpit as idolatrous all Churches that did not use the simplest Communion rite, and as 'surgeons of Antichrist' all who in any way tolerated genuflexion at that service, and condemned the Article on the Descent of Christ into Hell. But he was persuaded of his errors and recanted (*À Lasco to Bullinger*, June 7, 1553).

There was more serious trouble with Michael Angelo Florio, the pastor of the Italian congregation. In January 1553 he was found guilty of fornication, and deposed from his office. On January 23 he wrote to Cecil, imploring his clemency and favour, reminding him of human frailty and of the recovery of good men who had fallen, and praying the Council not to banish him. Then, thirsting for revenge, he began to stir up the controversy on predestination, and, since à Lasco himself was too powerful to be attacked, incited some of the Italian congregation to accuse one[1] of the other ministers before the Coetus of teaching a different doctrine from that of Calvin. Calvin was in friendly correspondence with à Lasco, who had congratulated him (with slight verbal reservations, which enabled à Lasco to feel that he retained his independence) on the *Consensus Tigurinus*: he took a fatherly interest in the Strangers' Church, and gave them occasional advice—for example, that it was undesirable in their services to pray

[1] Probably La Rivière.

for the salvation of the Bishop of Rome, even by way of
a joke. But the Strangers' Church was not professedly
Calvinist. Calvin himself apologised to them (Sept. 27,
1552) for the conduct of some of his followers in their
congregation, against whom it had been 'reproachfully
alleged, that they wished to make an idol of *me*, and a
Jerusalem of *Geneva*.' Florio's attack was therefore easily
frustrated: à Lasco himself intervened to defend his
colleague: declaring his admiration for Calvin, he yet
asserted that he had written 'too hardly' upon predestination, and refused to condemn anyone who taught a more
moderate doctrine.

Two other foreign congregations were also founded in
England in this reign. The more notable was the colony
of Flemish weavers at Glastonbury, who were settled
there by Somerset, who had seized the Abbey after its
Dissolution, in 1551. He appointed as their Superintendent Valérand Poullain, of Lille. Poullain had been
Calvin's successor in the ministry of the French Church
at Strassburg (1547–8), and had then come to England,
where he tried to secure a post at Oxford through Martyr's
influence. None was forthcoming, and in May 1549 he
went back to Strassburg on a brief visit: on his return to
London, in August, Martyr procured him an appointment
as tutor to the son of the Earl of Derby ('Comes d'Ar-
biensis'). Probably it was this post that brought him under
Somerset's notice. The little colony had a hard struggle,
in spite of the favour of the Court: the housing accommodation was inadequate, only six houses being habitable
when they arrived (although 26 others could be made
habitable, but at the present they had neither roofs, doors,
nor windows), for the accommodation of 34 families and
6 widows (who were supposed capable of living three in
a house, and therefore counted as two families)—a number
which the arrival of 10 more families brought up to 46:

moreover their overseer, Somerset's bailiff, Cornish, 'proved very deceitful and false to them,' and the natives were hostile, 'it being the temper of the common sort,' as Strype remarks, 'to be jealous of strangers, and rude to them': further they were dragged heavily into debt. But they had certain privileges: they were allowed to use their own Liturgy, a copy of which was sent up to the Council and approved: they received loans from the Government: in December 1552, seventy of them, including Poullain, received free patents of denization: and they were also given the privileges of an English guild. The Council Book generally refers to them as 'worsted-makers,' but according to their own account they made worsteds and '*sayes*,' which Chambers defines as 'a kind of serge, or a very light crossed stuff, much used abroad for linings and by the religious for shirts, and, with us, by the Quakers, for aprons, for which purpose it is usually dyed green.' It was also used for bed-hangings.

The other Strangers' Church was at Southampton, where an old church near the harbour was allotted for the use of the Walloons and Channel Islanders: but there is no more definite evidence of its foundation than a petition addressed by the foreigners to the Mayor and Aldermen during the reign of Elizabeth, requesting that they might have a church assigned to them and be permitted to use sermons and sacraments as under Edward VI.

In spite of their disagreement, Cranmer's relations with à Lasco continued friendly. In July 1551, when the Sweating Sickness was raging in London, à Lasco and his wife caught the infection, and their lives were despaired of: whereupon Cranmer invited them both to come to stay with him at his country house at Croydon, where à Lasco recovered, though his wife died. (He married again on January 29, 1553, for the sake of his children.) Then on

October 6, 1551, he was appointed on the Commission of 32 for the revision of the Ecclesiastical Laws, though not on the sub-committee of eight who prepared the materials for revision. But he no longer had any influence over the Archbishop. Burnet and Strype allege that he was one of the protagonists on the Puritan side in the controversy on kneeling at the Communion (Sept.–Oct. 1552): but this is doubtful, although his views were certainly those of Knox.

His work in England was already drawing to its close. On June 7, 1553, he wrote to Bullinger, 'Our King has lately been in a very weak state of health: but now (thanks be to our Lord God) he is convalescent.' A month later, the King was dead. On August 3 Mary arrived in London, while Northumberland's rebellion was petering out in the Eastern Midlands. By the beginning of September it was evident that the foreign Protestants could not safely remain in England. À Lasco called a meeting of the ministers, elders and deacons at his house in Bow Lane: a decision was taken for immediate flight to Denmark. Two Danish ships, the *Mohr* and the *Kleine islandishe Krähe*, happened to be lying off Gravesend, and on these 175 exiles, including a few English and Scots, embarked on September 15. Among their number were à Lasco, Utenhove, Micronius, and Vauville. Deleen and his son Peter and la Rivière remained, 'to comfort the rest of the brethren of the Belgian Church who had remained in London.' Those who were remaining, both men and women, escorted the emigrants as far as Gravesend: there, 'montant sur la falaise, ils suivirent des yeux les deux voiles, les accompagnaient encore à travers les flots par le chant du psaume favori d'à Lasco, le deuxième[1], et terminaient par la prière et la collecte pour les pauvres ce

---

[1] 'Hoe rasen so die Heydenen te hoop? En die volcken betrachten ydel dinghen,' &c.

culte du désert qui déjà annonçait la persécution im-
minente'[1].

Poullain also remained for some months, and took part
in the Disputation on the Eucharist held in Convocation
at Westminster (Oct. 1553): then he fled with his congregation (from Glastonbury) to Frankfort: it seems that
la Rivière went with him. He 'obtained a churche there /
in the name of all suche as shuld come owte off Englande
for the Gospell / but Especially from Glassenbury whiche
were all french men'[1]: and on April 20 (as Anne Hooper,
who had also fled there, wrote to Bullinger) opened his
ministry sensationally by baptising his son in the Rhine.
Vauville later became a minister in this church, and died
there in 1580.

Meanwhile misfortune and privations had dogged the
steps of à Lasco, Micronius and Utenhove. On the voyage,
the two ships were separated by a storm, and when at last,
on October 29, the parties re-united at Helseborg—the
party from the larger ship had been compelled to march
through Norway on foot—they found the Danes, who
were strongly Lutheran, unwilling to give them shelter.
A long time was spent in weary and fruitless disputations
with the King's Chaplain, Paulus Novimagus: Utenhove
preserved a record of them, but they throw little further
light on the sacramental doctrine of the Strangers' Church,
for, verbose as they are, the arguments of the exiles consist
of little more than an interminable series of guarded but
indignant negatives. Permission to stay in Denmark was
refused them. It is said that the main body found shelter
at Danzig: but à Lasco and his companions wandered
across North Germany, holding disputations as they went,
in Copenhagen, Wismar, Lübeck and Hamburg: finally
they arrived in Emden in April 1554. À Lasco stayed
there almost a year, by grace of the Countess, and then

[1] De Schickler, I. 69.   [2] *Troubles at Franckford*, p. 5.

went on to Frankfort: thence, in December 1556, he went
to Poland with Utenhove to carry the Reformation into
his native land. The King received them with favour, and
appointed à Lasco to be Superintendent of the churches
in Little Poland, where he laboured for Protestant reunion, paving the way for the ultimate compromise of
Sandomir. He died, after a long illness, at Calish in
Poland on January 8, 1560, leaving his widow in great
poverty.

Meanwhile the small remnant of the Strangers' Church
that had remained in England fell upon evil days. Queen
Mary and the Council were anxious for their extradition.
In March 1554 all who had not received letters of denization were ordered to leave the country within twenty-four
days. Wouter and Peter Deleen fled to Hamburg, with about
thirty others. From his vicarage at Emden the Norman poet,
Pierre du Val, addressed to his old companions the famous
Consolateur (*Petit Dialogue d'un consolateur consolant l'Église
en ses afflictions, tiré du Psaume CXXIX*). In February
1558 bills were actually before Parliament 'To make void
Letters Patent made to Frenchmen to be denizens' and
'To expulse French denizens and other french Persons
out of the Realme.' But these were never carried: the
death of Mary saved the refugees from this last attack: and
the reign of Elizabeth opened for them with renewed hope.

Utenhove and Deleen returned to England in September
1559: the Church of the Austin Friars and St Anthony's
in Threadneedle Street were granted back to the Strangers:
but Elizabeth, wiser than her brother, would no longer
permit them the privilege of being a *corpus corporatum
politicum*, and appointed the Bishop of London, Grindal,
as their Superintendent. So a new Strangers' Church
arose out of the ruins of the old: but of the former
ministers and elders under Edward VI, only Peter Deleen
and Jan Utenhove remained.

CHAPTER SEVEN

THE REVISION OF
THE PRAYER BOOK

Non parum conatibus nostris obstat,
quod forma, quam senatus vel parla-
mentum (ut vulgo dicimus) toto regno
praescripsit, sit tam manca ac dubia,
etiam aliqua in parte plane impia.....
Tantum eo libro offendor, nec sine gravi
causa, ut si non corrigatur, nec possum
nec volo cum ecclesia in usu coenae fieri
particeps.

Hooper to Bullinger, London, March 27,
1550.

Deinde scis non ita unius Angliae haberi
abs te rationem, quin orbi simul universo
consulas.

Calvin to Cranmer, Geneva [April? 1552].

THE REVISION OF THE PRAYER BOOK

HAVING considered the doctrinal standpoint of Cranmer, of Hooper, and of the foreign theologians, we may now attempt to evaluate the influence of each upon the Revision of the Prayer Book of 1549.

The first alteration was in the form of an addition. The Prayer Book of 1549 had contained no Ordinal. It is true that on September 9, 1548, Cranmer, assisted by Holbeach and Ridley, had consecrated Farrar Bishop of St David's after a manner that differed considerably from the Roman ritual, but this was irregular, and the consecration was held privately in the Archbishop's house at Chertsey: and in the following year Cranmer, assisted by Ridley, held an ordination in St Paul's, which Strype says 'was celebrated after that order that was soon established.' It was obvious that the old Pontificale, so happily described by Canon Dixon[1], with all its immoderate wealth of ceremonial, must be discarded. A bill for the provision of a new Ordinal was designed by Cranmer to be passed in Parliament's November session, but it was not introduced in the Lords until January 8, and did not pass its first reading until January 23: and when it was finally carried two days later, 13 bishops were absent, and for the 9 who voted for it—Cranmer, Goodrich, Barlow, Holbeach, Ridley, Farrar, Wharton, Skip and Sampson—5 (Tunstall, Heath, Day, Aldrich and Thirlby) voted against.

This Act enjoined that a new Ordinal should be 'devised' before April 1 by a committee of six bishops and six other men of this realm learned in God's laws, 'by the King's majesty to be appointed and assigned.' They were appointed by the Council on February 2, and although their names have not been preserved, it is probable that they were the same as the members of the

[1] III. 189 ff.

Windsor Commission who had prepared the Prayer Book of 1549, with one exception: in the place of Day of Chichester, who had refused to subscribe to the completed liturgy, Heath of Worcester, also a champion of the Old Learning, was appointed, but proved no more compliant. The new Ordinal was published by Grafton at least a month before the date prescribed (April 1): and it is almost certain that the function of the Commission was not to 'devise' a new Ordinal, but to accept or suggest improvements to one that had already been drawn up, presumably by Cranmer and Ridley, on the basis of a draft made by Martin Bucer.

Bucer's draft is published in his *Scripta Anglicana* under the title *De ordinatione legitima ministrorum ecclesiae revocanda*[1]. It was probably written while he was at Croydon (May–June 1549), and we may suspect that his visit to Goodrich at Ely in July was paid in connection with it. Between this draft and the Ordinal of 1550 there is, however, one important difference, which is, indeed, the key to Bucer's project. He recognised only two distinct orders in the Church, and his object was to provide one single form of ordination that would be suitable to both. In the preface to his draft, he wrote:

The ministries of the Church are of two kinds, according to the institution of the Holy Spirit. In one is contained the administration of the Word, of the Sacraments, and of the discipline of Christ, which belongs properly to Bishops and priests. In the other the care of the poor, which was committed to those whom they called Deacons. But in numerous Churches more ministers have been constituted, who subserved either ministry or both, as were Readers, Acolytes, Exorcists, Door-keepers, Subdeacons, &c.

[1] For a careful comparison of Bucer's draft with the Ordinal of 1550, see the Appendix to Canon R. T. Smith's *We ought not to alter the Ordinal* (pamphlet, 1872).

It is true that at the end of his draft he inserted a paragraph in which the distinction he draws is rather between the higher and the two lower orders of clergy, but this was probably a concession to the custom of the English Church.

But since there are three orders of priests and managers [*curatores*] of the Church, the order of Bishops: then of priests, whom the ancients called Cardinals, who administer the principal government of the Church in places where there are no Bishops: and their priests, who are for an assistance to these, and are called among us Deacons, or assistants. So let ordination be attempered to each: so that when any Superintendent, that is Bishop, is ordained, everything may be somewhat more [fully?] and more gravely done and finished [*aliquanto pluribus & grauius gerantur & perficiantur*] than when a priest of the second or third order is ordained. So also let some distinction be made between the ordination of a priest of the second and of the third order.

But precisely what form this distinction was to take was left to the imagination: though, since Bucer proposed only one form of ordination for all three orders, it is clear that he did not contemplate any alteration in the form of words to be used.

This had an important consequence. 'Nothing,' says Canon Smith, 'can be more weak or colourless, or less expressive of an actual gift of grace,' than 'the words which Bucer suggested to be said during the laying on of hands.' These—which were to be used for a bishop as for a priest or deacon—were as follows:

The hand of Almighty God, the Father, the Son, and the Holy Spirit, be upon you, protect and govern you, that ye may go and bring forth much fruit by your ministry, and may it remain [with you] unto life eternal. Amen.

Compare with these the words prescribed by the Ordinal of 1550:

The Fourme and maner of Orderinge of Deacons	*The Fourme of Orderyng Priestes*	*The Fourme of Consecrating of an Archebisshoppe or Bysshoppe*
Take thou aucthoritie to execute the office of a Deacon in the Churche of God committed unto thee: in the name of the father, the sonne, and the holy ghost. Amen.	Receiue the holy gost: whose sinnes thou doest forgeue, they are forgeuen: and whose synnes thou doest retayne, they are retayned: and bee thou a faithful dispensor of the worde of god, and of his holy Sacramentes. In the name of the father, and of the sonne, and of the holy gost. Amen.	Take the holy goste, and remember that thou stirre up the grace of God, which is in thee, by imposicion of handes: for god hath not geuen us the spirite of feare, but of powere, and loue, and of sobernesse.

But in almost every other respect, *The Fourme of Orderyng Priestes* is closely modelled upon Bucer's Ordinal. A few prayers are shortened, the three Psalms are made alternative, the Oath of Supremacy is inserted, the collect 'Most mercifull father' is added at the end of the service: but otherwise the form of 1550 is a faithful translation of Bucer's *De Ordinatione Legitima*; even the order of the service is unchanged. Moreover even the other two forms of ordination, so far as they bear any resemblance to the *Fourme of Orderyng Priestes*, owe it to the same model, although their separate existence is a denial of the principles of Bucer's plan. Bucer had also supplied a Questionnaire on 30 points of doctrine to be addressed to the ordinand 'in the presence of the Coetus,' as a preliminary to his ordination ('sicut...in Authentica Iustiniani, Quomodo oporteat Episcopos. Et in ea quae titulum habet, De sanctissimis Episcopis '): this was not published in the English Ordinal, although the previous examination of candidates is directly implied.

It may be noted that the Act for the publication of an Ordinal provided for the ordination of 'other ministers of the Church' below the rank of deacons: but this liberty was not exercised.

The Ordinal of 1550, although it returned to primitive

antiquity and preserved the difference of the clerical degrees and authority of the episcopal office, yet abrogated almost all the ceremonies of the mediæval Pontificale. Heath of Worcester refused to subscribe to it: he was summoned before the Council on February 8, and committed to the Fleet a month later, where he remained until the end of the reign. (His imprisonment and deprivation may be not unconnected with his reluctance to give up his episcopal estates to the New Nobility.) To John Hooper it was also intolerable, but for very different reasons. Preaching before the King on March 5, he denounced the form of the Oath of Supremacy and the 'playne Albe' (for a deacon or priest), the 'Surples and Cope' (for a bishop), which were still enjoined by the rubrics—the slender relics of the elaborate vestments of the Pontificale. For this sermon Cranmer had him summoned before the Council four days later, and spoke against him 'with great severity': but Hooper related that the rest of the Council took his side against the bishops, and so 'the issue was to the glory of God.' This was the prelude to the Vestiarian Controversy. In the end, Hooper was victorious. In the matter of the oath, he won his victory on July 20, the form being altered to 'so helpe me God, through Jesus Christ': in the matter of the vestments, although he himself suffered a resounding defeat, yet in the Ordinal of 1552 the rubrics prescribing vestments were omitted.

But scarcely had the addition of the Ordinal been made, before a thorough Revision of the Prayer Book of 1549 became necessary. The two influences making for revision are indicated in the Act of Uniformity of 1552:

And because there hath arisen in the use and exercise of the foresaid common service in the Church heretofore set forth, divers doubts for the fashion and manner of the ministration of the same, rather *by the curiosity of the minister and mistakers*, than of any worthy cause: therefore as well for the more plain and manifest explanation hereof, as *for the more perfection of the said order of common service, in some places where it is necessary to make the same prayer and fashion of service more earnest and fit to stir christian people to the true honouring of Almighty God*: The king's most excellent majesty, with the assent of the lords and commons in this present Parliament assembled, and by the authority of the same, hath caused the foresaid order of common service, entitled, *The book of common prayer*, to be faithfully and godly perused, explained,.and made fully perfect.

'The curiosity of the minister and mistakers' refers not, of course, to the influence of the foreign Puritans in England (as Cosin and Wheatley held), but to the policy of the Papists, who continued, even in Ridley's own cathedral, to celebrate the Communion as though it were the Roman Mass, and either in practice or in theory 'followed the policy hitherto pursued by the Catholic party in the episcopate, whether rightly or wrongly, of contesting every inch of ground with the innovators and putting a Catholic, even if a strained interpretation upon what had been imposed on the church by the law'[1]. In the opposite camp stood those who demanded 'the more perfection of the said order,' greater simplicity of ritual and doctrine, a clearer repudiation of the Church of Rome, and grudged Cranmer even the admission that the Book of 1549 was 'a very Godly order...agreeable to the word of God, and the primitive Church.' Hooper, for instance, described the book to Bullinger as 'inadequate and ambiguous, in some parts even manifestly impious': 'I am so offended with that book,' he declared, 'nor without grave reason, that if it be not corrected I neither can nor will participate with the Church in the use of the Supper.' Fortunately for the Puritans, the policy of the

---

[1] Gasquet and Bishop, p. 279.

Papists empowered them to demand a drastic revision. They could point out that because the Prayer Book had spoken of 'the Holy Communion, commonly called the Masse,' the parish priests were everywhere celebrating the Mass and commonly calling it the Holy Communion. Thus the First Prayer Book of Edward VI paid the penalty of ambiguity. The Puritans refused it because it was not definitely Protestant: the Papists disliked it because it was implicitly Protestant, and expended a great deal of ingenuity in pretending that it was not.

The most brilliant exponent of this policy was Gardiner, Bishop of Winchester. At his trial at Lambeth on January 8, 1551, he delivered to Cranmer in open court a long manuscript which he had written in prison in the Tower, entitled *An Explication and Assertion of the true Catholic Faith touching the Blessed Sacrament of the Altar, with confutation of a book written against the same*—that is, of Cranmer's *Defence of the True and Catholic Doctrine and Use of the Lord's Supper*, published about six months earlier. Gardiner's answer (which was published in France in 1551 without name of printer or place) was a diabolically ingenious attempt to prove Cranmer's sacramental theology unorthodox by the criterion of his own prayer book, and incidentally to provide a theoretical basis for the practice of the Catholic parish priests: he affected to think it incredible that Cranmer could have written his own book, because it was so clearly irreconcilable with the doctrine implicit in the Prayer Book, and therefore throughout he referred darkly to 'this author,' as though the book were a forgery: which infuriated Cranmer to the highest degree. His object was to prove that *The Booke of the Common Prayer and Administracion of the Sacramentes, and other Rites and Ceremonies of the Churche after the use of the Churche of England* was, in respect of this holy mystery, 'well termed not distant from the catholic faith, in my judgment': and he supported his contention by five illustrations.

I. The words of administration, 'The body of our Lorde Jesus Christe whiche was geuen for thee, preserue thy bodye and soule unto euerlastyng lyfe,' 'The bloud of our Lorde Jesus Christe which was shed for thee, preserue thy bodye and soule unto euerlastyng lyfe,' imply the Catholic doctrine of transubstantiation.

II. The rubric on the 'sort and fashion' of the Communion bread prescribes that it is to be 'unleauened, and rounde, as it was afore, but without all maner of printe, and somethyng more larger and thicker than it was, so that it may be aptly deuided in diuers pieces: and euery one shall be deuided in two pieces, at the leaste, or more, by the discrecion of the minister, and so distributed. And menne muste not thynke lesse to be receyued in parte then in the whole, but in eache of them the whole body of our sauiour Jesu Christ.' The last sentence is truly 'agreeable to the Catholic doctrine.'

III. The prayer of consecration—'with thy holy spirite and worde, vouchsafe to bl†esse and sanc†tifie these thy gyftes, and creatures of bread and wyne, that they maie be unto us the bodye and bloude of thy moste derely beloued sonne Jesus Christe'—also implies transubstantiation.

IV. The petition for the dead in the prayer, *Almightie and euerliuyng GOD*—'We commend unto thy mercye (O Lorde) all other thy seruauntes, which are departed hence from us, with the signe of faith, and nowe do reste in the slepe of peace: Graūt unto them, we beseche thee, thy mercy, and euerlasting peace...'—supports the Catholic conception of the Mass as a propitiatory sacrifice.

V. The prayer of humble access is a prayer of adoration.

On two other occasions Gardiner appealed to the Prayer Book in support of his own views. Both these may be noted here.

VI. In his examination before the Privy Council he insisted (according to Fox's account) 'that although the elevation [of the host] was taken away, yet the alteration, in one special place, was indeed reserved: and showed it to them, adding it must needs be so.' The reference is, apparently, to the third of the *Certayne Notes* at the end of the Prayer Book, 'As touching kneeling, crossing, *holding up of handes*, knocking upon the brest, and other gestures: they may be used or left, as euery mans deuocion serueth, without blame': it might apply to the two rubrics in the prayer of consecration, 'Here the prieste must take the bread into his hādes,' 'Here the priest shall take the Cuppe into his hādes,' but that that prayer is followed by the rubric, 'These wordes before rehersed are to be saied...without any eleuacion, or shewing the Sacrament to the people.'

VII. In defence of altars, he had written: 'This altar is a table before our Lord, and in the book of Common Prayer it is well called by both names.'—The allusions to it in the rubrics of the Communion office are, indeed, as follows: *the lordes table, the Lordes table, the Altar, Goddes borde, the Alter, the Altar, the Altar, gods boord, the Altar.*—'But if these be only a table as Mr Hooper would have...[let] there be not any controversy in the matter, but as it were good fellowship, without either standing or kneeling...wherein the book of Common Prayer lately set forth in this realm giveth a good lesson to avoid Mr Hooper's fancy, which is that some ceremonies there must needs be, and then such as be old and may be well used.'

Gardiner's 'crafty and sophisticall cauillation' was, as it happened, presented to the Archbishop after Revision had already been agreed on, and at the moment when the bishops were actually met at Lambeth to discuss it. In view of this meeting, Goodrich, bishop of Ely, had requested Bucer to write a criticism, or *Censura*, of the Book of 1549, and Cranmer, strongly approving, had invited Martyr to do the same. Bucer, however, had one advantage over his colleague: alone of all the foreign theologians in England, he had taken the trouble to learn

English, and so was able to study the original[1]: whereas Martyr had to do the best he could with a partial translation by Cheke.

The *Censura Martini Buceri super libros sacrorum, seu ordinationis Ecclesiae atque ministerii ecclesiastici in regno Angliae*[2] was finished on January 5, 1551, and sent to Goodrich, who presented it to Cranmer. Like almost all that Bucer wrote, it is exceedingly long. He began, quite characteristically, by declaring his general satisfaction with the Prayer Book of 1549:

When first I came to this kingdom, in order that I might see what doctrines and what ceremonies had been received in the Church, and whether I could sincerely join my ministry to them, I studied that Prayer Book diligently, so far as I could, through an interpreter: and having done so, I gave thanks to God, that he had given you to reform these ceremonies to that pitch of purity, nor did I blame anything aptly received therein which was not taken from the word of God, or at least was not contrary to it. For there are not lacking certain minor points [*paucula quaedam*] which, if anyone did not candidly interpret them, might seem not sufficiently to agree with the word of God.

Of these the most important refer to the Communion office, to which nine of the thirty-nine chapters of the *Censura* are devoted: but he criticised all the other offices as minutely. A general warning against superfluity of ceremonies, and a caution that such as may properly be retained should be carefully explained to the people, is the general tenour of his observations. *Non omnia vetusta*

[1] In the *Scripta Anglicana*, his *Censura* is printed together with Aless' garbled Latin translation of the Prayer Book: but Bucer had not used Aless' version. Cf. Dixon, III. 293–4.

[2] The editor of the *Scripta*, Conrad Hubert, adds '*ad petitionem R. Archiepiscopi Cantuariensis, Thoma Cranmeri, conscripta.*' But it was written for Goodrich: cf. G. and B. p. 288, *n.* 1. It may be noted that the title of the *Censura* as published was composed not by Bucer, but by Hubert: hence its resemblance to the title of Aless' version.

signa hodie aedificant: for many ceremonies, originally edifying, have become polluted by their association with the Romish Antichrists[1].

His criticisms on the Communion office require to be considered in greater detail. Again they are preceded by a general encomium:

'Concerning this [office] I give the utmost thanks to God, who has given it to be drawn up so pure, and so scrupulously faithful to the word of God, especially at [considering?] the time at which this was done. For excepting a very few words and signs I perceive nothing in it at all which may not be drawn out of the Holy Scriptures: if only everything were worthily exhibited and explained to the people of Christ. But what I could wish to be more fully explained, perfected, or corrected in this office, are these.'

(1) *The four introductory rubrics*. The first three are admirable. The fourth, directing that 'the Priest that shal execute the holy ministery, shall put upon hym the vesture appoincted for that ministracion, that is to saye: a white Albe plain, with a vestement or Cope,' should be omitted: not because vestments are so impious *per se* that pious men cannot use them piously, but because too many regard their

---

[1] Thus he condemned the use of the Chrisom, or christening robe, in Baptism, though he approved of signing with the cross: in the same office he condemned the benediction of the water, and the rite of exorcism, which implies that all unbaptised persons are demoniacs, and so invalidates many of the miracles of Christ and of the Apostles. He allowed the ring in marriage: he approved of reservation for the sick, though he condemned extreme unction: he disallowed the prayer for the soul of the departed in the Burial Service. He admired the Commination Service, and wished to have it read more frequently: he was urgent for the restoration of the whole penitential discipline of the Church, and for frequent and general catechising: and he condemned several miscellaneous abuses, such as bell-ringing at other times than before public worship, the excess of saints' days and holy days (which, he suggested, should be reduced in number, and kept only in the afternoon, thus perhaps inventing the half-holyday), and the abuse of the interior of the church during the week as a convenient rendezvous, a place for the transaction of business, and a playground for children. (Cf. Dixon, III. 288 ff.)

use as superstition, because they are a source of contention, because we ought to strive after Apostolic simplicity in all external things, and because by abolishing them we should testify that we have nothing in common with Rome, and that we defend and follow Christian liberty.

(2) *The seven concluding rubrics.* (*a*) The first rubric directs that the English Litany shall be said or sung on Wednesdays and Fridays, and that after the Litany, 'though there be none to cōmunicate with the Prieste,' yet he shall put on the Communion vestments and recite the Communion office 'untill after the offertory,' and then conclude with one or two of the collects (at his discretion) and the blessing. 'And the same order shall be used all other dayes whensoeuer the people be customably assembled to pray in the churche, and none disposed to communicate with the Priest.' This is a counterfeiting of the Mass: and I have heard on good authority that there are titled women who request the priests to say 'memories' (masses for the departed) when there are no communicants, and that there are priests who do this. (*b*) The second rubric, which implies the celebration of the Communion in side chapels or in private houses, is also open to grave abuse. (*c*) The third rubric, about the 'sort and fashion of the bread,' is wise, but for the last sentence, 'And menne muste not thynke lesse to be receyued in parte then in the whole, but in eache of them the whole body of our sauiour Jesu Christ': which Gardiner (II) had noted with approval. (*d*) The fourth rubric, commanding that a collection be taken, I approve. (*e*) The fifth rubric, which enjoins that in all churches 'there shal alwaies some Communicate with the Prieste that ministreth,' adds, of necessity, 'Some one at the least of that house in euery Parishe to whome by course...it apperteyneth to offer for the charges of the Communiō, or some other whom they shall prouide to offer for them, shall receiue the holy Communion with the Prieste.' This leads to grave abuse. [Cf. the report of the Venetian envoy, Daniele Barbaro, to his government (May 1551), 'They choose one person in every family to communicate every Sunday, so certain merchants treat it as a joke and are in the habit of sending one of their

servants; and the parish priests do this to obtain alms': or Article XII of Bishop Hooper's Injunctions of 1551[1].] (*f*) The sixth rubric, which compels 'euery man and womā...to communicate once in the yeare at the least,' is shocking to me: for who could partake worthily at the Lord's table who only comes there under legal compulsion, and then only once a year?[2] (*g*) The seventh rubric is as follows: 'And although it bee redde in the aunciente writers, that the people many yeares past receiued at the priestes hādes the Sacrament of the body of Christ in theyr owne handes, and no commaunde-mēt of Christ to the contrary: Yet forasmuch as they many tymes conueyghed the same secretely awaye, kept it with them, and diuersly abused it to supersticion and wickednes: lest any suche thynge hereafter should be attempted, and that an uniformitie might be used, throughoute the whole Realme: it is thought conuenient the people commōly receiue the Sacra-mēt of Christes body, in their mouthes, at the Priestes hande.' The precaution is unnecessary, for the priest can easily see whether the communicant eats the bread or not: whereas this rubric is contrary to the Apostolic use, and suggests the exaltation of the priest above the people, after the manner of the Church of Rome.

(3) *The four rubrics following the Offertory Sentences.* (*b*) The second rubric, which enjoins that 'whyles the Clerkes do syng the Offertory, so many as are disposed, shall offer unto the poore mennes boxe euery one accordynge to his habilitie and charitable mynde,' I approve so strongly that I wish measures might be taken to make it more effectual. The proper office of a Deacon is to collect alms and distribute them

---

[1] 'Item, that the parsons, vicars and curates shall diligently exhort the multitude of their parishioners to use the communion and sacrament of Christ's precious body and blood, and not to permit in any wise one neighbour to receive for another, as it is commonly used in this diocese; for when he that should receive it himself, by the order of the king's law, is not disposed to receive, he desireth his neighbour to receive for him, which is contrary to God's word.' (II. *Hooper* [P.S.] p. 133.)

[2] His own view was that Christians ought to communicate every Sunday. (Cap. XXII. *S.A.* p. 489.)

to the poor. (*c*) I do not think it desirable that the men should have to sit on one side of the choir, and the women on the other. (*d*) I fear that the direction in the fourth rubric, 'Than shall the minister take so muche Bread and Wine, as shall suffice for the persons appoynted to receiue the holy Communion,' may promote superstition.

(4) *The* Certayne notes for the more playne explicacion and decent ministracion of thinges, conteined in thys booke, *at the end of the Prayer Book.* [(*a, b*) The first two rubrics refer to vestments, on which Bucer had already given his opinion.] (*c*) The third rubric—'As touching kneeling, crossing, holding up of handes, knocking upon the brest, and other gestures: they may be used or left, as euery mans deuocion serueth without blame'—cannot be allowed. 'That license of popish gestures'—of those 'gestures of the never-sufficiently-to-be-execrated Mass'—'which this rubric seems to allow, must be withdrawn forthwith.'

With the Communion office itself Bucer was better satisfied than with its rubrics.

(5) *The Homilies.* The reading of a Homily before the celebration (after the Creed) is admirable. I venture to suggest 18 subjects for further Homilies. [Most of these are connected with the Communion, but others are of more general application, e.g. on alms-giving, the provision of grammar schools, usury, fraud, extravagance in dress and food, and so forth.]

(6) The *Sanctus* and *Agnus Dei* should not be sung until the minister has finished the preceding prayers: for this is an abuse frequently committed by 'clerks impatient of delay.'

(7) *The prayer for the Church.* This prayer ('*Almightie and euerliuyng God*') contains a petition for the souls of the departed, which is superstitious and should be struck out. The phrase, 'which...nowe do reste in the slepe of peace,' is particularly misleading, and encourages the heresy that the souls of the departed are not raised until the day of judgment.

(8) *The prayer of consecration.* In this prayer ('*O God heauenly father*'), for the words, 'Heare us (o merciful father) we beseech thee; and with thy holy spirite and worde, vouchsafe

to bl†esse and sanc†tifie these thy gyftes, and creatures of
bread and wyne, that they maie be unto us the bodye and
bloude of thy moste derely beloued sonne Jesus Christe,'
something after this manner should be substituted: 'Hear us,
O merciful Father, and bless us, and sanctify us by thy Holy
Spirit and word, that by true faith we may perceive in these
mysteries the body and blood of thy Son [given] by his own
hand to be the food and drink of eternal life.' I cannot approve
the benediction of inanimate things: the less so in this case,
'For thence comes ἀρτολατρεία, because the bread is adored
instead of Christ.'—The rubrics directing the priest to take
the bread into his hands at the words, 'Take, eate,' and the
cup at the words 'drynk ye all of this,' are liable to abuse,
because 'some say these [words] so bowing themselves to the
bread and wine, and breathing on them: as if indeed they
ought to be said to the bread and wine, and not to the men
present: or [as if] something ought to be changed in these
elements by the pronunciation of these words.'

(9) *The prayer of oblation.* In this prayer ('*Wherfore, O
Lorde and heauenly father*'), for the words 'and commaunde
these our prayers and supplicacions, by the Ministry of thy
holy Angels, to be brought up into thy holy Tabernacle before
the syght of thy dyuine maiestie,' should be substituted (since
'Christ, not an angel, is our mediator') the words, 'and
graciously receive these our prayers and supplications for the
sake of thy Son our Mediator.'

(10) *The prayer of humble access.* Let this prayer ('*We do
not presume*') stand as it is: above all, do not alter the words,
'Graunt us therefore (gracious lorde) so to eate the fleshe of
thy dere sonne Jesus Christ, and to drynke his bloud in these
holy Misteries, that we may continuallye dwell in hym, and
he in us, that our synfull bodyes may bee made cleane by his
body, and our soules washed through hys most precious
bloud': 'for these words are exceedingly pure and agreeable
to the words of the Holy Spirit.'

As an afterthought, he added in chapter XXVI (which
relates to the final admonition *Of Ceremonies, why some be*

abolished and some retayned) a further warning against the priests who counterfeited the Mass 'with vestments, lights, genuflections, crucifixes, washing the chalice, and other Mass gestures, breathing on the bread and chalice of the Eucharist, transferring the book on the table from the right to the left side of the table, placing the table in the same place where the altar used to stand, showing the bread and chalice of the Eucharist to the old men and other superstitious persons who adore it, but do not partake of the sacraments.' The *Censura* concludes with an appeal for more pastors, stricter discipline, more generous care for the poor, an end to alienation and spoliation of Church property, and the compilation of a Confession of the faith of the Church of England upon all Christian doctrines, particularly those in dispute.

A copy was sent to Martyr (then at Lambeth) who received it probably on January 8 (1551). In his letter of thanks, he stated that his own *Censura* covered far less ground, because he had not had a complete translation of the Prayer Book to work on: unfortunately, he had presented it to Cranmer two or three days earlier, but he had since drawn up some short supplementary articles, based on Bucer's manuscript, which he gave to Cranmer probably on January 10, and certainly not later. He agreed with Bucer on every point except one: he did not approve of the rubric in the order of the Communion of the Sick,

And yf the same daye there be a celebracion of the holy comunion in the churche, then shall the priest reserue (at the open communion) so muche of the sacrament of the body and bloud, as shall serue the sicke person, and so many as shall communicate with hym (yf there be any). And so soone as he conueniently may, after the open communion ended in the church, shall goe and minister the same...

and expressed his surprise that Bucer had not condemned it. The bread and wine should clearly be consecrated in the presence of the sick person, 'since I consider, as you also think, that the words of the Supper belong more to the man than to the bread, or to the wine.... And it is really amazing how they dislike saying those words in the presence of the sick man, to whom they are especially profitable, when they are willing to repeat the same [words] uselessly when during communion in the church the wine happens to run short in the cup—[uselessly,] since the persons who are present and receive the sacraments have already heard them.'

Before investigating the actual history of the revision, it is well to know how far the Book of 1552 was affected by these criticisms.

(1, 2, 3, 4) All the rubrics to which Bucer had objected were omitted, including the *Certayne Notes*.

(7, IV) The prayer for the Church was moved from its position before the prayer of consecration, and placed immediately following the offertory sentences. The subject of this prayer was changed from 'the whole state of Christes churche' to 'the whole state of Christes Church *militant here in earth*,' and the petition for the souls of the departed was struck out, and with it the preliminary thanksgiving for the lives of the Virgin and the saints, to which Bucer had not objected.

(8, III) The prayer of consecration was altered: yet the words substituted were not those that Bucer had suggested, but these: 'Heare us O mercyefull father wee beeseche thee; and graunt that wee, receyuing these thy creatures of bread and wyne, accordinge to thy sonne our Sauioure Jesus Christ's holy institucion, in remembraunce of his death and passion, may be partakers of his most blessed body and bloud.'

(9) In the prayer of oblation, the words implying the mediation of angels were omitted, without any substitution: the prayer was much shortened, and was now placed after the administration.

It will be noted that these three prayers, which in the 1549

Book had been continuous, following the arrangement of the Canon of the Mass[1], were now separated.

(10, V) The prayer of humble access was left unchanged, as Bucer had desired: but in order that it should not be misconstrued into an act of adoration, it was placed before the prayer of consecration, instead of after it.

(I) The words of administration were expunged, and in their place were substituted, 'Take and eate this, in remembraunce that Christ dyed for thee, and feede on him in thy hearte by faythe, with thankesgeuing,' and 'Drinke this in remembraunce that Christ's bloude was shed for thee, and be thankefull.' (In the Prayer Book of 1559, the words of 1549 and of 1552 were combined, as in the present Book.)

(VII) The word 'altar' was everywhere removed, and 'table' or 'God's board' substituted.

The vestments were much reduced.

In the Communion of the Sick, reservation was no longer allowed, in accordance with Martyr's suggestion.

Finally, as a further precaution against superstition, the Communion Office was no longer entitled ' *The Supper of the Lorde and the Holy Communion, commonly called the Masse,*' but ' *The Order for the Administracion of the Lordes Supper, or Holye Communion*': and, in the title of the Prayer Book itself, for the words ' *...and other Rites and Ceremonies of the Churche after the use of the Churche of England,*' were substituted, in order to mark the breach with Rome, the words ' *...and other Rites and Ceremonies in the Churche of England.*'

These were the principal changes made in the Book of 1552. They constitute a remarkable concession to the Sacramentarians, but not a complete surrender.

The causes and results of this revision are, however, far clearer than its history. There is no record of the names

[1] Cf. Maskell's *Ancient Liturgy of the Church of England according to the Uses of Sarum, Bangor, York, and Hereford, and the modern Roman Liturgy, arranged in parallel columns* (1844), p. 36 ff.

of those to whom the task was committed. Cardwell suggests (*Two Lit.* xx) that the commissioners who drew up the Ordinal of 1550 were employed upon it: Dixon that the revision was entrusted to the members of the commission for the reform of ecclesiastical laws (III. 250), who were probably also consulted about the Forty-two Articles (III. 382).

It is certain that revision was already contemplated in the late autumn of 1550, when Goodrich asked Bucer to write a *Censura* upon the Book of 1549. It is also certain that a meeting of bishops was held at Lambeth in January 1551, in order to discuss it. On January 10 Martyr wrote to Bucer from Lambeth:

I thank God who has given an ample opportunity that the Bishops should be admonished through us about all these things. It has already been decided in this conference of theirs, as the Most Reverend [Cranmer] tells me, that many things are to be changed. But which those things are, that they have agreed must be amended, he did not explain to me, not did I dare ask him. But in truth this refreshes me not a little, which Dr Cheke has told me; if they are unwilling, he says, themselves to make the necessary changes, the King will do it himself; and when Parliament meets, he will interpose his own Royal authority.

Martyr returned to Oxford the same day: whence, about four weeks later, he wrote to Bucer again:

Concerning the Reformation of the Rituals, I cannot write anything further as to what will be [done], except that the Bishops have agreed among themselves on many emendations and corrections in the published Book. Indeed, I have seen the alterations on which they have decided, noted in their places; but, as I am ignorant of English, and could not understand them, so I am unable to give you any certain information about them. However, I do not think they have gone so far as to decide to adopt the whole of your and my suggestions.

To our [Archbishop], indeed, I said more than once that, having undertaken this correction of the Rituals, they ought to look well to it that the restoration they make should be so simple, chaste, and pure, that there may be no further need for emendation: for, if frequent changes should take place in these matters, it might at length easily come to pass that they would fall into general contempt. And I am persuaded that if the business had been committed to his individual hand, purity of ceremonies would without difficulty have been attained by him: but he has colleagues who offer resolute opposition. Cheke is the only person there, who openly and earnestly favours simplicity. But this is a matter of the deepest concern—that while they are entirely occupied with those subjects of minor importance, those things in the Church which ought to be considered as the prow and the stern, remain neglected! For, as to establishing order in the parishes, and [providing] that doctrine and discipline may be ministered everywhere among the people—not a syllable ($o\dot{v}\delta\grave{\epsilon}$ $\gamma\rho\dot{v}$)! For my own part, I expect little fruit; because I cannot perceive, in [any] other way, among those who ought to govern the Church, [any] interchange of counsels and deliberations.

Who were these bishops? I think it probable that they were the four bishops who had been appointed among Gardiner's judges: Cranmer, Ridley, Goodrich, and Holbeach. The trial was being conducted at Lambeth at this very time. It may be noted that all these four had been members of the Windsor Commission, and had presumably been engaged in preparing the recent Ordinal. Others of their colleagues may have assisted in this conference: we only know definitely that Hooper did not, for this was the period of his disgrace. Cheke seems to have been present, as a representative of the Court: perhaps Cox also, the King's Almoner, for Bullinger wrote to him some 'sound and wholesome counsel respecting the reformation of the church of God,' to which he replied (May 5, 1551) that he agreed that simplicity was desirable,

'But in this Church of ours what can I do, being weak both in learning and in authority? [I can] only try to persuade our bishops [*praesules*] to embrace the same opinion and doctrine as myself, and meanwhile commit to God the care and issue of his business.'

But undoubtedly Martyr was wrong in his estimate of Cranmer's attitude. The Archbishop hated the necessity for revision: he was alarmed by the portent of Hooper's fight against the vestments, and by the favour in which the Puritans were held at Court. In spite of Cheke's threat, that the Church had nine months to set her house in order, and if she did not do it in that time it would be done by Parliament (which was to meet at Michaelmas), he temporised for as long as possible. He set himself to write a reply to Gardiner's *Explication*, which might even remove the necessity for revision. It did not: but fortune favoured him. In the summer of this year occurred the fifth and last epidemic of the Sweating Sickness in this country. Of all known plagues, this was the most remarkable. It attacked the rich rather than the poor, men in the prime of life rather than old men, women and children, healthy persons rather than delicate, and clean towns rather than dirty[1]. This epidemic broke out at

---

[1] The previous epidemics occurred in 1485, 1508, 1517, and in 1528 (when the Sweat travelled over to the mainland of Europe, where it ravaged Germany from the Rhine to the Oder, and from the Baltic to the Alps, breaking up the Colloquy between Luther and Zwingli at Marburg, though it entirely avoided France and Italy). The virus was a soil-poison, and its periodic activity was conditioned by fluctuations in the level of the sub-soil water: outbreaks of the plague followed either unusual drought or excessive rainfall, and generally occurred in the autumn. The virus was brought over to England by Henry Tudor's Norman mercenaries, who were enlisted in the neighbourhood of Rouen, where the Sweat, in a modified form, made its appearance as an endemic malady 230 years later. The symptoms were described by Dr Forestier in 1485: 'And this sickness cometh with a grete swetyng and stynkyng, with rednesse of the face and of all the body, and a contynual thurst, with a grete hete and

Shrewsbury on March 22, and 'posted from town to town thorow England and was named Sto[o]p-gallant, for it spared none. For there were some dauncing in the Court at nine o'clock that were dead at eleven'[1]. It reached London on July 7; on July 10 the King 'repaired to Hampton Court with a small company.' It raged in London for about three weeks, carrying off about 900 persons: it then travelled north and east, and ceased everywhere before the end of September. But the meeting of Parliament was postponed until January 23, 1552.

Nevertheless, the Court reminded Cranmer of their warning. On November 29 a debate on the real presence in the Eucharist was held in Cecil's house, in the presence of the Earl of Bedford and six other members of the Court, between Cecil, Cheke, Horne, Whitehead, and Grindal on the one side, and Feckenham (Bonner's chaplain) and Young upon the other: and it was continued on December 3 in the house of Sir Richard Morrison,

hedache because of the fumes and venoms.' Attacks were not always fatal, but when they were, death followed very suddenly. The Sweat was nicknamed 'New Acquaintance, alias Stoupe! Knave and know thy Master,' or Stoop-gallant. It was pre-eminently a *morbus procerum*. The epidemic of 1551 was regarded as 'a most signal token of divine vengeance' (*Hooper to Bullinger*, Aug. 1, 1551): 'You know I pro- phesied truly to you before the Sweat came,' wrote John Bradford, the martyr, in his *Farewell to Cambridge*, 'what would come if you repented not your carnal gospelling.' Hooper and most of his house- hold were attacked by it at the end of July: à Lasco very nearly died of it: Martyr escaped it, for Oxford was more lightly attacked than Cambridge, where 200 are said to have died, including Traheron's pupils, the Duke of Suffolk and his brother, the last of their line. (Warwick conferred the title on the Marquis of Dorset, his principal supporter.) The Court fled from London, and Parliament was prorogued till January. For further details, see Dr Creighton's *History of Epidemics in Britain* (1891), vol. 1. ch. v. pp. 237–81: cf. *Rerum Anglicarum Henrico VIII. Edwardo VI. et Maria Regnantibus, Annales*, by F. H. (1628), pp. 178–9: also Sir William Osler's *Principles and Practice of Medicine*, 10th edtn (1925), p. 373.

[1] Narration of Thomas Hancock, vicar of Poole, in Dorset. (Strype, *Mem.* v. 111–12.)

when the Earl of Rutland and the Marquis of North-ampton joined the audience, and Watson the disputants on the Papists' side. It is said to have been renewed at the Earl of Bedford's house, and again at Cheke's: and finally this edifying entertainment was taken on a pro-vincial tour, when Hooper confronted Feckenham at Pershore and in his own cathedral church at Worcester.

Meanwhile on October 6 a Commission of Thirty-two was appointed to reform the canon laws: (*Bishops*) Cranmer, Ridley, Ponet, Goodrich, Coverdale, Hooper, Barlow, Scory; (*Divines*) J. Taylor, Cox, Parker, Latimer, Sir Ant. Cooke, Martyr, Cheke, à Lasco; (*Civilians*) Petre, Cecil, Sir T. Smith, R. Taylor, May, Traheron, Lyell, Skinner; (*Lawyers*) Hales, Bromley, Gooderick, Gosnold, Stamford, Carel, Lucas, Brock. Of these, the Council directed that eight should 'rough hew' the material for revision: these were nominated on October 22—Cranmer, Ridley, Cox, Martyr, R. Taylor, Traheron, Gosnold, Lucas—but the list was revised on November 11, when Goodrich, May, and Gooderick were substituted for Ridley, Traheron, and Gosnold. The Thirty-two had their commission renewed by Parliament on February 2, 1552, when Rede, Coke, and Gawdy were substituted for Latimer, Lyell, and Brock. It may easily be established that all Edward's Commissions were composed of much the same people, apart from the steady weeding-out of Papists: for example, six of these commissioners had served on the Commission that drew up the Order of the Communion of 1548, fourteen on the Heresy Commission of Twenty-five in 1549, and seven on the Commission of Ten that tried Gardiner: three of them (Cranmer, Goodrich, and Ridley) having served on all three Com-missions, and five others on two. From this it is more than probable that a majority at least of the Thirty-two had a hand in the Revision of the Prayer Book: as is, indeed, suggested (though not very clearly) in the letters of ab Ulmis, and by a letter of Martyr to Conrad Hubert, dated October 28, in which he wrote that all would yet be well with the state of religion in England, if they had only time. But this Commission does not seem to have met until the opening of Parliament: for which Martyr, remembering Cheke's words, was eagerly waiting.

In a very important letter (Simler MS. 76. 93) addressed to Otto Heinrich, the Count Palatine, and dated from Oxford, November 23, 1551, Martyr, after giving a critical summary of the state of the Reformation in England and of its present defects, concludes as follows:

We were trusting that all these things and others like them would be somewhat further reformed in this Parliament [*Comitia*], which had been appointed for this month of November, and there was hope that a decision would also be pronounced concerning the doctrine of the holy eucharist. But that assembly has for some reason been postponed to next January; we all pray that God will deign to provide for it the desired commencement and a happy issue.

Parliament met on January 23, and Convocation, as usual, on the following day. The records of this Convocation have been lost, but Heylyn makes the following statement[1] with regard to it:

In the Convocation, which began in the former year, *An.* 1550[2], the first Debate among the Prelats was of such Doubts, as had arisen about some things contained in the *Common-Prayer-Book*, and more particularly touching such Feasts, as were retained, and such, as had been abrogated by the Rules thereof; the Form of Words used at the giving of the Bread, and the different Manner of Administring the Holy Sacrament. Which being signified unto the *Prolocutour*, and the rest of

[1] Heylyn's *Ecclesia Restaurata: or, the History of the Reformation of the Church of England* (1661), p. 107.

[2] Not 1550, but 1552. This is decisively proved by Gasquet and Bishop, p. 286 *n.*

the Clergy, who had received somewhat in Charge about it the day before; Answer was made, that they had not yet sufficiently considered of the Points proposed, but that they would give their Lordships some account thereof in the following Session.

But Parliament paid little deference to the opinions of Convocation. The Council had already decided to take the law into their own hands. Upon the first day of the session, a bill to enforce attendance at church was introduced in the House of Lords, where it passed its third reading on January 26, when it was entrusted to Rede and Godsalve to be taken to the Commons, where it was read for the first time the same day. On March 9 a bill of Uniformity was read for the first time in the Lords. It stated that, for the two reasons already noted,

the King's most excellent Majesty, with the assent of the Lords and Commons in this present Parliament assembled, and by the authority of the same, hath caused the aforesaid Order of common service, entitled The Book of Common Prayer, to be faithfully and godly perused, explained, and made fully perfect: and by the foresaid authority hath annexed and joined it, so explained and perfected, to this present Statute: adding also a form and manner of making and consecrating Archbishops, Bishops, Priests and Deacons, to be of like force, authority and value as the same like foresaid Book....

The latter clauses were perhaps anticipatory. Three weeks later, the bill for church attendance was superseded by another: the Commons joined this to the bill of Uniformity, which had passed its third reading in the Lords on April 6 (the Earl of Derby, Lord Stourton, and Lord Windsor, and the Bishops of Carlisle and Norwich voting against it), and on the same day was sent to the Commons, together with 'a Book of the said service, drawn out by certain persons appointed by the King's Majesty for that purpose.' The bill became law on April 14.

The entries in the Lords' Journals prove that the

revision was completed by April 6, if not by March 9. Still the references to those who performed this task are vague, although the wording of the bill may be thought to indicate the Commission of Thirty-two. The only definite statement that we possess occurs in a letter from Cranmer to the Council dated October 7, 1552, in which he writes, with regard to the question of kneeling at Communion, 'I trust that we [i.e. himself, Ridley, and Martyr] with just balance weighed this at the making of the Book, and not only we but a great many bishops, and other of the best learned within this realm, and appointed for that purpose': the words, '*a great many*,' again suggest the Thirty-two. It may also be noted that Hooper was staying at Lambeth throughout the parliamentary session: he, too, was a member of that Commission. An attempt seems indeed to have been made to take the sense of Convocation upon the questions in dispute (which were debated in the Upper House, although the Lower House delayed giving their answer until it could no longer be of any use): but there is no evidence to show that the Book of 1552 was ever submitted to Convocation, or that it had any synodical authority. It may be assumed that the basis of the revision was the draft prepared by the bishops in January 1551, while the internal evidence of the Second Prayer Book, read in conjunction with Cranmer's letter to the Council of October 7, suggests a determined resistance to the Puritan demands, and very skilful management on the part of Cranmer. It is true that the Archbishop allowed very substantial concessions to the Zwinglians: but that was partly for another reason, and in any case the doctrine of the Prayer Book remained essentially Suvermerian. Beyond these guarded statements it would be unsafe to go, until further evidence has been discovered.

It is very remarkable that the Second Act of Uniformity allowed so long an interval before it came into operation, for it was not until All Saints' Day (Nov. 1) that the new Prayer Book was appointed to come into use. This was probably done for two reasons: partly, in order that the new Articles of Religion, whose preparation seems to have occupied the Commission when the liturgy was finished, might be published at the same time: partly, in order that the Protestant General Council, Cranmer's favourite project, might first be assembled in this country, and that, in deference to its resolutions, certain emendations might, if necessary, be made.

The alliance between Zurich and Geneva, the *Consensus Tigurinus* of 1549, seemed to supply the nucleus of Protestant Reunion: and for that very reason Cranmer had permitted the Suvermerian doctrine of the Book of 1552 to assume such a sacramentarian colour. Now, on March 20, 1552, he wrote to Bullinger and to Calvin (who, it may be noted, would probably have been invited in 1548, but that he was a Frenchman, and our relations with France were then so strained that war was imminent[1]): he invited both of them to attend a 'godly synod,' whose deliberations might serve as a counterblast to the decrees of the Council of Trent, which had reassembled in May 1551. But, in order to counterbalance their influence, he invited Melanchthon once more, urging him to come.

Only Calvin's answer has survived. He declared his enthusiasm for the project: 'As far as I am concerned, if it appears that I can be of any service, I shall not shrink from crossing ten seas, if need be, for that object. If helping the kingdom of England were the only object, that of itself would be a sufficient reason for me. Now when what is sought is a weighty agreement of learned men rightly framed according to the standard of Scripture,

---

[1] 'Heri rursum ex Anglia literas accepi…Bucerus exspectatur, Franciscus noster Dryander iam adest, et de Calvino mussatur, nisi quod Gallus est.' (*A Lasco to Hardenberg*, [Emden], July 28, 1548.)

by which churches that would otherwise be far separated from each other may coalesce; I think that it is wrong to spare myself any labours or difficulties. But,' he added, 'I hope my insignificance will cause me to be excused. If I follow with my prayers what shall be begun by others, I shall have done my part.... Would that my ability corresponded to the ardour of my zeal!' It is probable, however, that this was merely a conventional expression of modesty, and that, if he had been pressed to come by a second invitation, he would have accepted. Bullinger's answer has been lost. He was at this time in feeble health: his *Diarium* contains the entry, 'Diser zit hat ich ein badenfart zu Urdorff uff 3 wuchen,' while a letter of Stumphius records that he returned from taking the waters towards the end of May: yet, though there is no mention of this invitation in the *Diarium*, it is probable that he would have sent Gualter or some other colleague to represent him. But from Melanchthon there came nothing but a painful and forbidding silence.

So Cranmer's most cherished project was again abortive: and again the principal cause of its failure was Melanchthon. But the project was worthy of its author: and it is from this aspect, rather than from the narrower standpoint of Anglican theology, that the statesmanship of the Second Prayer Book must be judged. It is interesting to speculate whether it could indeed have supplied a basis for Protestant Reunion. It is improbable, for Bullinger, when he read it, condemned it strongly:

Maister Whittingham...(in his journey) passed by Zurik to knowe off Maister Bullinger what he thought off the booke off Englande for that he (who had raported to maister Williams / Whittingham, Gilbie and others / that Cranmer Bishop off Canterbury had drawen up a booke off praier an hundredth tymes more perfect then this that we nowe haue / the same could not take place / for that he was matched with such a

wicked clergie and conuocation / with other enymies) Euen he /
I saie / yet stood in this that maister Bullinger did like well
off thinglishe order / and had it in his study. But when
Whittingham had demaunded that question / Bullinger tolde
him / that indede Maister H [Horne?] and Maister C. [Cham-
bers?] asked his judgemente concerninge certaine pointes off
that booke / as Surples / priuate baptisme. Churching off
wemen / the ring in mariage / with suche like[1] whiche (as he
saied) he allowed not / and that he nether coulde yff he woulde /
nether woulde yff he might / use the same in his churche / what
so euer had beyn reported.

(This passage from the *Brieff discours off the troubles
begonne at Franckford* (p. 1.) has an additional importance,
because on a careless reading of it was ascribed to Bullinger
the statement that the Second Book was not intended by
Cranmer to be final. It will be seen that the person who
reported this was not Bullinger, as Strype (*Cran.* 1. 381–2)
and Neal (1. 68) declared, but one of the English exiles,
whose testimony, moreover, was not very reliable: yet
although this error was corrected by Jenkyns in the
Preface (p. liv) to his edition of Cranmer's writings (1833)
and by Cardwell (*Two Lit.* 1841, p. xxxv *n.*), it was
repeated by Gasquet and Bishop (*Edward VI and the Book
of Common Prayer*, 1890, p. 287 *n.*), and even Canon
Dixon in his review of that work (*History of the Church
of England*, 2nd edtn, 1893, vol. III. App. p. 559) ques-
tioned only the probability of the report. The author of
the original rumour may have referred to the lost Fifty-
four Articles of 1553 'for an uniform order to be observed
in every church within this realm,' mentioned in the

---

[1] Bullinger also refused to allow any form of Communion of the
Sick or private communion: 'Verily, St Paul requireth a public
assembly of the church and a general meeting for the due celebration
of the supper.' (*Fifth Decade* [P.S.], p. 428.) Dr Cox, when the
revised Prayer Book was about to come into use, was very much
worried by this passage. (*Cox to Bullinger*, Oct. 5, 1552.)

King's 'Warrant Book' under May 24, 1553. The Fifty-four Articles concerned rites and ceremonies, as the Forty-two concerned doctrine: but it is probable that they merely enforced uniformity on the lines of the Book of 1552, and not beyond them. However, these Articles have entirely disappeared, leaving no trace.)

Calvin also pronounced his judgment that the Second Prayer Book was not entirely satisfactory:

> In the liturgie off Englande / I se that there were manye tollerable foolishe thinges / by theis wordes I meane / that there was not that puritie whiche was to be desired. Theis vices / thoughe they coulde not at the firste daie be amended / yet / seinge there was no manifeste impietie / they were for a season to be tollerated. Therfore / it was lawfull to begin off suche rudimentes or absedaries / but so / that it behoued the lerned / graue / and godly ministers off Christe to enterprise farther / and to set foorthe some thinge more filed from ruste / and purer. Yf godly Religion had florished till this daie [1555] in Englande / there ought to haue bin a thinge better corrected and manie thinges cleane taken awaie[1].

As to the Forty-two Articles, if it had been intended to publish them with the new Prayer Book, the intention was not realised. It is evident from Martyr's letter to Bullinger of June 14 that after the Prayer Book was finished, and 'everything removed from it which could nourish superstition,' the Commission set themselves to draw up the Articles: but in these the desired reform could not be thoroughly accomplished ('*non potuit ad umbilicum perduci*') for, although there was no longer any controversy upon transubstantiation or upon the real presence, yet upon the questions whether grace is conferred through the sacraments, and whether infants were justified or regenerate before baptism, the Commission was divided.

---

[1] *Troubles at Franckford*, p. xxxv.

'The men cannot be pulled away from the merit of works, and, what is more to be lamented, they are unwilling to confess it': a complete deadlock seems to have been reached when Parliament was dissolved (April 15) and the Commission was adjourned. It appears that the Commission had before them a draft which Cranmer had made in the previous year, probably at the meeting of bishops at Lambeth in January 1551, and of which he sent copies to certain of the bishops with a view to its emendation or adoption. It is impossible to say what alterations or additions were made by the Commission: especially since the corrected draft was carefully revised by Cranmer during the summer before it was presented to the King (probably at the beginning of October), and not only that, for on September 19 it was offered to Cecil and Cheke for a last inspection. The spirit of the Articles that were finally submitted was tolerant and comprehensive: the controversy upon faith and works was cautiously evaded: only in the articles on the sacraments did the Puritans appear to have secured some measure of success. In the article, *Of the Sacraments*, it was declared that 'the Sacramentes were not ordeined of Christe to be gased upon, or to be caried about, but that we shoulde rightlie use them'; 'in soche onelie, as worthelie receive the same, thei have an wholesome effecte and operacione,' yet not *ex opere operato*—a phrase which was now condemned as unscriptural and superstitious. Further, the sacraments are 'not onelie Badges and tokens of Christien mennes professione, but rather...certeine sure witnesses and effectuall signes of grace and Goddes good will towarde us, by the whiche he dothe worke invisiblie in us, and dothe not onlie quicken, but also strengthen and confirme our faith in him.' As *Baptism* is not only a sign of our profession, but also a sign and seal of our new birth, so *the Lord's Supper* is not only a sign of the mutual love of Christians toward each other, but rather 'a sacrament of our redemption by Christes death, insomoche that to soche as rightlie woorthelie, and with faieth receive the same, the breade which we breake, is a communion of the bodie of Christe. Likewise the cuppe of blessing is a communion of the bloude of Christe.' But transubstantiation 'cannot bee proved by holie writte, but is repugnaunt to the plaine woordes of Scripture, and hath given occasion to many supersticions.' Further, since a body 'cannot be at one time in diverse places,' and since Christ is in heaven, therefore we ought not to believe 'the reall and bodilie presence (as thei terme it) of Christes fleshe and bloude in the Sacramente of the Lordes supper.' Finally, 'the Sacramente of the Lordes supper was not commaunded by Christes ordinaunce to be kepte [i.e. reserved], caried about, lifted up, nor worshipped.'

Almost every one of these clauses (as Dixon has noted[1]) was a direct rebuttal of some decree recently promulgated at Trent, and it is known that Cranmer was greatly perturbed about that Council: yet it is not unreasonable to conclude that these articles exhibit the influence of the Puritan element in the Commission. The coincidence that Martyr's letter of June 14 contains the actual phrase, 'realem praesentiam (ut ita loquar),' when the Latin draft of the Articles has 'Realem et Corporalem (ut loquuntur) praesentiam,' is in itself suspicious. But the triumph of the Puritans was not so complete here as it was in the unpublished *Reformatio Legum Ecclesiasticarum*, where, in the article on the sacraments, they inserted the following amazing clause: 'The Eucharist is a sacrament in which they who sit as guests at the Lord's holy table receive food from the bread, and drink from the wine.'

Having perused the Latin draft of the Articles, the Council submitted it, on October 21, to the inspection of

[1] III. 523–6 n.

the Royal chaplains (Harley, Bill, Horne, Grindal, Perne, and Knox), who added their signatures for an *imprimatur*, although Knox and perhaps some other lodged a separate protest against the article *Of the Book of ceremonies of the English Church*. The manuscript, together with this protest, was then (Nov. 20) returned to Cranmer, who made an alteration in the article in question, and returned the draft to the Council (Nov. 24) with a brief summary of his opinions, and a request 'that the bishops may have authority from him [the King] to cause...all their clergy to subscribe to the said articles. And then I trust that such a concord and quietness in religion shall shortly follow thereof, as else is not to be looked for many years.' But Cranmer's request for immediate publication was not granted: the order for subscription was not issued until June 9, 1553, nor did the King sign the Articles until June 12, though they were already in Grafton's press in May: when, with complete lack of scruple, the Council caused to be added to their title the statement that they had been 'agreed upon by the bishops and other learned men in the synod at London, in the year of our Lord God MDLII,' i.e. 1553 (March) after modern reckoning. The title was designed to imply that the Articles had been passed by Convocation, which was untrue: Cranmer protested to the Council, and was told 'that the Book was so entitled because it was set forth in the time of Convocation,' which was not true either: but there the matter rested, and the Articles continued to profess a synodical authority to which they had no claim[1].

But the delay procured before the coming into force of the new Prayer Book subjected it to a last attack by the extremists. In the course of the summer Northumberland,

[1] Dixon goes into this complicated problem very thoroughly, III. 513–17 *nn*.

as Warden General of the Marches, had visited the North, and (for private reasons) had brought back with him in his train John Knox, a licensed preacher, who had preached before him at Newcastle. It appears that in the diocese of Durham the order prescribed by the First Prayer Book had not been strictly enforced: Knox himself had followed the custom of using common bread at the Communion, and of administering the sacrament to the receivers sitting, and seems even to have substituted a form of service of his own for that prescribed in the Book of 1549. The Court was at Windsor when Northumberland rejoined it at the end of September 1552, and the King shortly intimated his desire that Knox should preach before him. Knox seized the opportunity to denounce the custom of kneeling to receive the sacrament. Coming when it did, upon the eve of the publication of the revised Prayer Book which retained that custom, the sermon created a sensation: the King was alarmed that any vestige of idolatry had been permitted to remain: and the Council hastily despatched a letter (Sept. 27) to Grafton, the printer,

to stay in any wyse from uttering any of the bookes of the Newe Service, and yf he have distributed any of them emongst his company [i.e. retail dealers], that then he gyve straight commaundement to every one of them not to put any of them abrode untill certaine faultes therein be corrected.

It was the occasion rather than the substance of Knox's sermon that made his attack so formidable. There was nothing new in his arguments. Gardiner had pointed out that, logically, the next step after turning the altar into a table was to turn the Eucharist into a supper: if you are to have a table, why not sit at it? But the edge of his sarcasm was blunted by the fact that Hooper had already advocated in earnest what he suggested in ridicule. In Hooper's fourth sermon before the King (March 12, 1550) he had urged on the attack on altars in which Ridley, the new bishop of London, was the leader: in his sixth sermon (March 27) he had pleaded that it should be pressed to its logical conclusion.

The outward behaviour and gesture of the receiver should want all kind of suspicion, shew, or inclination of idolatry. Wherefore, seeing kneeling is a shew and external sign of honouring and worshipping, and heretofore hath grievous and damnable idolatry been committed by the honouring of the sacrament, I would wish it were commanded by the magistrates, that the communicators and receivers should do it standing or sitting. But sitting, in mine opinion, were best, for many considerations. The Paschal lamb was eaten standing, which signified Christ not yet to be come, that should give rest, peace, and quietness. Christ with his apostles used this sacrament, at the first, sitting; declaring that he was come that should quiet and put at rest both body and soul; and that the figure of the passover from thenceforth should be no more necessary; nor that men should travel no more to Jerusalem once in the year, to seek and use a sacrament of the Lamb to come, that should take away the sins of the world.

Further, the first part of à Lasco's letter to Cranmer [Oct.? 1550] recited his objections to kneeling, viz.,—it is undeniable that the Last Supper was partaken by the apostles sitting; by sitting to receive the sacrament we declare our abhorrence of popish idolatry, and symbolise our rest in Christ.

This same proposal was brought up—probably by Hooper and à Lasco—before the Commission while the revision was in progress, and was decisively rejected. Being unable to carry it by constitutional methods, à Lasco resolved to confound his opponents by publishing his *Forma ac ratio tota Ecclesiastici Ministerii, in peregrinorum Ecclesia*, an expository edition of the liturgy of the Strangers' Church: in this he rehearsed at greater length the same arguments in favour of sitting to receive the sacraments, and explained why that use was followed by his congregations[1].

A few weeks later this was followed by Knox's sermon, delivered quite independently, it seems, of these previous declarations. He was fighting in defence of a practice that had been introduced by certain of those extremists, not only in the North but even in London[2], because it had not been expressly forbidden in the First Prayer Book. The new Book contained a new rubric directing the minister to deliver the sacrament to the people '*kneling*': for certain congregations this would involve a definite retrogression towards the old Roman use. Moreover uniformity was now enforced by heavy penalties. The Council saw the force of his arguments, and wrote to Cranmer bidding him reconsider his decision with Ridley and Peter Martyr.

Cranmer's reply to the Council (Oct. 7), written in haste before he had seen Ridley, was masterly in the extreme. He pointed out that the same arguments had been raised and rejected during the revision, and continued:

I know your Lordships' wisdom to be such that I trust ye will not be moved by these [vain]glorious and unquiet spirits which can like nothing but that is after their own fancy, and cease not to make trouble and disquietness when things be most quiet and in good order. If such men should be heard,

---

[1] 'Habeo nunc prae manibus ceremonias nostrae Ecclesiae omnemque illius in nostro ministerio gubernationem. Prodibit spero sub hyemem. Scribo autem non sine Theseo, nostro inquam Micronio, quem nostrae hic Ecclesiae valde gratulor.' (*A Lasco to Bullinger*, June 7, 1553.) But, owing to the King's death, the *Forma ac Ratio* was not published till 1555, and then at Frankfort.

[2] 'O how oft have I seen in England, at the ministration of the holy communion, people sitting at the Lord's table after they have heard the sermon, or the godly exhortation set forth in the book of common prayer read unto them by the minister, bitterly weep, heartily repent....' (Becon's *Displaying of the Popish Mass* (1555): III. *Bec.* [P.S.], p. 256. Becon was rector of St Stephen's, Walbrook.)

although the Book were made every year anew, yet should it not lack faults in their opinion.

But, say they, it is not commanded in the Scripture to kneel, and whatsoever is not commanded in the Scripture is against the Scripture, and utterly unlawful and ungodly. But this saying is the chief foundation of the error of the Anabaptists and of divers other sects. This saying is a subversion of all order as well in religion as in common policy. If this saying be true, take away the whole Book of Service. For what should men travail to set an order in the form of service, if no order can be set but that is already prescribed by the Scripture? And because I will not trouble your Lordships with reciting of many Scriptures or proofs in this matter, whosoever teacheth any such doctrine (if your Lordships will give me leave) I will set my foot by his to be tried by fire, that his doctrine is untrue, and not only untrue, but also seditious, and perilous to be heard of any subjects, as a thing breaking the bridle of obedience and loosing them from the bond of all princes' laws.

My good Lordships, I pray you to consider that there be two prayers which go before the receiving of the Sacrament, and two immediately follow, all which time the people, praying and giving thanks, do kneel, and what inconvenience there is, that it may not be thus ordered, I know not. If the kneeling of the people should be discontinued at the receiving of the Sacrament, so that at the receipt thereof they should rise up and stand or sit, and then immediately kneel down again, it should rather import a contemptuous than a reverent receiving of the Sacrament.

But it is not expressly contained in the Scripture, say they, that Christ ministered the Sacrament to his Apostles kneeling. Nor they find it not expressly in Scripture that he ministered it [to them] standing or sitting; but if we will follow the plain words of Scripture, we shall rather receive it lying down on the ground, as the custom of the world [was] at that time almost everywhere, and as the Tartars and Turks use yet at this day to eat their meat lying upon the ground. And the words of the Evangelist import the same, which be ἀνάκειμαι and ἀναπίπτω, which signify properly to lie down upon the floor or ground, and not to sit upon a form or stool. And the same speech use the Evangelists where they shew that Christ fed five thousand with five loaves, where it is plainly expressed that they sat upon the ground and not upon stools....

But what weighed most with the Council was Cranmer's argument that it was no light matter that 'the Book being read and approved by the whole state of the realm in the High Court of Parliament, and with the King's Majesty his royal assent,...should now be altered again without Parliament.' On receiving this letter, the Council wrote (Oct. 8) 'To tharchebusshop of Cauntorbury to stay his going in to Kent till Tewseday next, for that the Lordes wolde conferre with hym.' The Court returned to Westminster on October 10, and Cranmer, having conferred with Ridley and Martyr, attended the Council next day, and, being satisfied with the result, retired to his manor of Ford in Kent.

The next document in the controversy is a memorandum, in Cecil's handwriting, for the Council-meeting of October 21 :

> Mr Knocks—b. of Cat[rb]
> y[e] book in y[e] B. of Durh[m]
> a Briefe of the Dispute at Windsor, for the King.

From this it may be suspected that the King, with his almost superstitious terror of superstition, was dissatisfied with the decision of the Council, and supported Knox. At that meeting of the Council (Oct. 21) the new Articles were sent, as has been mentioned, to the six Royal chaplains for their inspection. Knox's protest against the Article *De Libro caeremoniarum Ecclesiae Anglicanae*, which stated that the new Prayer Book was agreeable to the Gospel in its doctrine and in its ceremonies, contains phrases which show very clearly that he had read Cranmer's letter to the Council—this is probably the explanation of Cecil's note, 'Mr Knocks—b. of Cat^{rb}'—and desired to reply to it. In this memorial he denied that the ceremonies (not the doctrine) of the new Book were not repugnant to the Scripture, rehearsing at great length his objections to kneeling at Communion: the custom originated from the idolatrous belief in the real presence; to retain it 'permytteth the idolatere to continue in his idolatrie'; though in itself the custom is a 'thynge indefferent,' yet 'among such varietie in opyniones' it 'edyfieth no man but offereth occasion of slaunder and offence to many,' for (1) idolatry is tolerated, (2) 'the consciences of weyke brethren are not a lyttel offended: ffor by vyolence of a law are they compelled to honore God (their conscience reclaimyng thereto) in suche sorte as in that action nether the example of Christ nor yet any express commandment of his sacred word assured them of [against] evel doing,' and (3) 'it is permitted to idolatours to tryumph over the Churche of God...; for albeit we crie never so lowde, that in that action no adoration ought to be given to no creature, yet whisper they, yea and plainlie do they speak— "crye what they list," saythe the Papists, "yet are the gospellers compelled to do the self-same thynge that we whom they call idolatours do in every gesture and be- haveyor"'; kneeling is the gesture of supplication and grief, rather than of joyful thanksgiving; sitting symbolises our rest in Christ.

When this memorial was presented we do not know. But on October 27, probably at the King's instance, the Council sent 'A lettre to the Lorde Chauncellour to cause to be joygned unto the Booke of Common Prayer lately set forth a certaine declaracion, signed by the Kinges Majestie and sent unto his Lordship, touching the kneling att the receyving of the Communion.' This declaration was the Black Rubric: which declared that kneeling was enjoined in the new Prayer Book 'for a sygnificacion of the humble and gratefull acknowledgyng of the benefites of Chryst,' and to ensure reverence and uniformity; but it was not to be understood as an act of adoration either of the sacramental bread and wine, which 'remayne styll in theyr verye naturall substaunces, and therefore may not be adored,' nor of the natural body and blood of Christ, which 'are in heauen and not here.' The extremists had been defeated, but they received, from the King's intervention, a greater measure of success than Cranmer could have approved: and further, in the final form of the Articles the clause declaring the ceremonies of the new Prayer Book agreeable to Scripture was cut out[1]. But Knox had to be consoled for his defeat: the Council at the same meeting (Oct. 27) issued 'a warrant to the foure gentlemen of the privie chamber to pay Mr Knokes, preacher in the north, in way of the King's Majesty's reward, the sum of xl. l.,' and on the same day Northumberland wrote to Cecil that he had decided to offer him the bishopric of Rochester. Knox took the bribe, though not the bishopric, and wrote to his old congregation in the North counselling submission, 'remembring alwayes, beloved bretherne, that dew obedience be given to magistrates reulars and princes, without tumult, grudge or seditioun.' Provided 'that the magistrates mak knowin, as that they have done if ministers were willing to do thair dewities, that knelyng is not reteyned in the Lordes Souper for maintenance of anye superstitioun, much less ...anye adoratioun...but onlye for uniforme order to be kept, and that for a tyme, in this Church of England'; 'that commone order clame not kneling in the Lordes Soupper as either necessarie or decent to Christis actioun, but onlye as a ceremonye thought goodely by man and not by Christ himself'; and 'that my fathers, whome

[1] See Hardwick's *History of the Articles*.

I feare and honor, and my brethren in labors and pro-
fessioun, whom I unfeynedlie luif, do not truble my
conscience imputing unto me anye foolish interprise' for
having tried to restore the original use of the Lord's
Supper;

'These things granted unto me, I nether will withstand
godlie magistrates, nether brak commone order nor yit
contend with my superiors or fallow preachers, but with
patience will I beare that one thing; daylie thirsting and calling
unto God for reformation of that and others'[1].

For the remainder of the reign, the Council pursued
Knox with offers of preferment: but he rejected them
with contumely, refusing to accept any office until kneeling
at the Communion was prohibited. *'Onlye for uniforme
order to be kept, and that for a tyme'*: the extremist faction,
having already come within an ace of victory, were waiting
with impatience and with confidence for their final
triumph: they enjoyed the favour of the King and the
support of Northumberland, and it was already doubtful
how long their great adversary, Cranmer, would be able
to restrain them.

[1] Knox's Epistle to the Congregation of Berwick-on-Tweed (Dec.?
1552) is printed by Lorimer, pp. 251–65.

CHAPTER EIGHT

NORTHUMBERLAND

Praeterea, si quid D. Biblander...vel
D. Gualterus...sint aliquid edituri,
dedicent etiam vel regi vel duci Somer-
sediae, avunculo regis, domino meo...,
vel marchioni de Dorcestria, vel comiti
de Warwick, fidelissimo ac intrepido
militi Christi.
Hooper to Bullinger, London, March 27,
1550.

Anglia non potest eo carere, ut verum
fatear: sanctissimum organum et auda-
cissimum est verbi Dei.
Hoôper to Bullinger, London, June 29,
1550.

Si Decades, quas a te pii multi singulis
nundinis exspectant, praesto paratas
habeas, rogo ut duci Northumbriae illas
dedices: te vehementer amat, et Christi
gloriam promovet diligenter.
Hooper to Bullinger, London, February
28, 1553.

Kepe that close which thou hast; the
world is daungerous. The great devell,
Dudley ruleth; (duke, I shuld have sayd);
wel, let that passe, seing it is owte, but
I truste he shall not longe.
The Epistle of Poor Pratte [July 1553].

CHAPTER EIGHT

NORTHUMBERLAND

SLOWLY, inexorably, the tangled threads of this perplexing period were being gathered up into the hands of a single individual—John Dudley, Duke of Northumberland.

It is not altogether easy to remember that the great leaders of the sixteenth century were essentially human. It is not easy to recognise historical characters as men ot like passions with ourselves. But we should appreciate that the leaders of the Edwardine Reformation were as human as the modern Bench, and confronted by even graver problems, in which, however, the general public took a no more intelligent interest than it does to-day: for it was not until the latter end of the sixteenth century that theology became the chief intellectual interest of the age—in spite of the Renaissance, few laymen in this period had any intellectual interests, and their attitude on religious questions was determined by either blind or calculating prejudice. Among the clergy, there were saints of God fighting for the Reformation, and saints of God fighting against it: but even these had very human weaknesses: they were too timid (though, it is true, the times were dangerous), or too harsh (yet their cause did not admit of moderation), or too obsequious (but, without the support of the nobility, they could effect nothing). Conditions were unprecedented: it was not easy to frame a policy: even in their worst blunders they acted for the best. It was not their fault that Fate had delivered them into the hands of the vilest gang of political adventurers in the history of this country.

The period of Somerset's domination had been brief To this day, his character remains somewhat of a mystery. It is, of course, as an aristocratic demagogue that he will be longest remembered: but historians have yet to decide whether he most resembles the elder or the younger Gracchus. Probably he was too much of a dilettante greatly to resemble either. He had no definite policy: he toyed with a number of projects during his brief tenure of power, but regarded none of them with much conviction. He lent his name to the Commission on Enclosures, and thereby alienated the Court: he despoiled the Church and patronised the Puritans, and thereby alienated the people. As a Calvinist he was probably sincere, for a time: in his private devotions he reminded the Almighty that he was one of his Elect[1], and the proclamation which he issued to parents 'to keep their children from the evil and pernicious games of dising, carding, bowlyng, tenys, coytes, closshes, and the like' was quite in the spirit of Genevan puritanism. Calvin had great hopes of him, but unfortunately overdid it: for Somerset soon grew tired of long admonitions upon his duty, and, as Knox recorded, 'became so cald in hering God's word, that the yeir before his last apprehension he wald gae visit his masonis, and wald not dingye himself to gae from his gallerie to his hall for hearing of a sermon.' 'He had grown so cold in the service of Christ,' wrote Francis Bourgoyne to Calvin after his execution, 'that there was hardly anything he had less to heart than the state of religion here. Nor in this respect did he retain anything praiseworthy except that in word alone, if any occasion demanded, he always professed himself a gospeller.' He was bored with Calvin, and far more interested in his new diversion, the building of Somerset House, for which he pulled down three bishops' houses, two churches, the cloister and charnelhouse of St Paul's, and would have pulled down Westminster Abbey if the Dean and Chapter had not bought him off at a price they could ill afford, and St Margaret's,

---

[1] '...[recorded in] the book of life...written with the very bloud of Jesus.' (Strype, *Mem.* IV. 311–12.)

Westminster, if the parishioners had not rioted against his
workmen. This did not make him popular in London.
He also amused himself with experiments in the finding
of stolen goods by necromancy, keeping a Welsh sorcerer
in his own household, and occasionally employing another
who used 'the chrystal stone' 'to invocate the sprat
Scariot [Judas Iscariot?] which he called divers times into
the crystal to have knowledge of things stolen.'

At Council meetings he was both weak and arrogant.
The nobility demanded a stronger leader. Things were
brought to a head in the summer of 1549 by the Peasants'
Revolt in the Eastern Counties. Somerset took no steps
to crush it, and it was rumoured that he was in sympathy
with the rebels: but the rising was ruthlessly repressed
by the first English captain of his time, John Dudley, Earl
of Warwick. In September, Somerset fell.

The cause of his overthrow is clear enough after the
event. Paget had warned him of the risk he ran by playing
the demagogue, which the New Nobility hated the more
because they never knew what it might not lead to next.
('What seeth your Grace? Marry, the King's subjects all
out of discipline, out of obedience, caring neither for
Protector nor King. What is the matter? Marry, sir, that
which I said to your Grace in the gallery [outside King
Henry's death-chamber]. Liberty! Liberty! and your
Grace's too much gentleness, your softness, your opinion
to be good to the poor—the opinion of such as saith to
your Grace, "Oh, sir, there was never man that had the
hearts of the poor as you have."') There lay the real cause
of Somerset's downfall. But this was not clear at the time,
for Warwick carefully staged the plot to look like a Counter-
Reformation. The ostensible ringleaders were Lords
Arundel and Southampton, Sir Richard Southwell, and
other members of the Catholic aristocracy: Warwick
himself lurked in the background. The general impression

was confirmed by the fact that Somerset, during the crisis, scattered hand-bills about London, accusing the Council of conspiracy to assassinate him and the King, and 'to plant again the devil and the antichrist of Rome.' Nothing could have served the conspirators better. The situation was critical: Gardiner had lately petitioned to be released from the Tower, and Bonner had just appealed against his sentence of deprivation. When a proclamation was published forbidding all preaching, the Protestants thought that all was lost. Hooper expected 'to be restored to his country and his Father in heaven': there were Catholic riots in Oxford (where the Mass was openly celebrated) terminating, according to Stumphius, in drunken orgies: in Switzerland it was rumoured that Ochino and Bucer had been arrested together with the Protector, and that the Reformation had collapsed.

But immediately the crisis was over and Somerset had fallen, Warwick thrust his dupes aside. Southwell was thrown into the Tower on a mysterious charge of sowing seditious pamphlets: Southampton was dismissed from the Council, and confined to his house, where he died of chagrin: Arundel was also confined to his house, but survived to endure a fine of £12000: while Gardiner and Bonner continued to languish in the Tower. Further to demonstrate his power, Warwick released his defeated rival, restored him to the Council-table, and performed several other ostentatious acts of clemency towards him: but Somerset's wings were clipped, and Warwick watched carefully lest they should grow again. In the winter of 1551, when he showed signs of becoming troublesome and talked vaguely of raising the London 'prentices and of recovering his Protectorate, he was removed by a quick and secret palace revolution and hurried to the block. His career is closed by the laconic entry in his nephew's Journal:

Jan. 22, 1552. The Duke of Somerset had his head cut off

upon Tower-hill, between eight and nine o'clock in the morning.

The London mob knew that they had lost a friend, but the Protestants were not disturbed. They had found a new and no less powerful patron. Hooper's sermons before the King had produced a most favourable impression on the Court: writing on February 5, 1550, he was able to assure Bullinger that 'the Marquis of Dorset, the Earl of Warwick, and the majority of the king's councillors assist as much as they can the cause of Christ.' But in that interesting discovery he was anticipated, of course, by John ab Ulmis.

That Warwick—who by this time had seized the earldom of Northumberland, and raised it to a Duchy—should have embraced the cause of Zwinglianism with such enthusiasm while he remained a secret Papist was puzzling, no doubt, to his contemporaries. But the explanation is not difficult to find. Like the Zwinglians, he made it his object to reduce the Church of England to primitive simplicity. The estates of the Church, for example, were a vast mediæval accretion. The monastic revenues had already been disposed of, but the bishoprics were as yet untouched. Henry VIII had been approached on the subject, but, being a sincerely religious man, had shown himself more inclined to endow new bishoprics than to disendow old ones: he did actually create six new bishoprics[1] and endowed·them with monastic lands, and had in hand a scheme to create nine more. It was therefore not until the son of Henry VII's notorious tax-collector assumed the reins of power that the New Nobility could have their way[2]. But it need not be assumed that all those who

[1] Westminster, Chester, Gloucester, Peterborough, Bristol and Oxford.

[2] The spoliation was begun by Somerset. An interesting memorandum, dated February 15, 1547, upon 'the names of those to be raised to dignity, and lands to be given them,' contains the following entry, under the name of 'My lord of Hertford': 'with his dukedom

planned the spoliation of the bishoprics were actuated by the basest motives. Sir Philip Hoby, for instance, wished to confiscate part of the episcopal revenues for the maintenance of a crack cavalry regiment. The Puritans were perfectly disinterested: they disliked episcopacy, many of them had suffered from the vigilance of individual bishops, and they regarded the wealth of the prelates as a stumbling-block to the advancement of Christ's gospel. Thus 'Roderyck Mors'[1]—'a man banysshed his natyue contry, only by the cruelty of the forkyd cappes of Ingland for speakyng Gods truth'—admonished the Members of Parliament as follows:

> Ye must fyrst downe with all your vayne chantrys, all your prowd colledgys of canons, and specyally your forkyd wolffys the bysshoppes; leaue them no tēporal possessyons, but only a competent lyuyng. An hundreth pownd for a bysshop, his

[of Somerset]...£800 lands a year'; to which Somerset has added, in his own hand, 'and £200 of the next bishop's lands.' (G. and B. p. 46.) Further, at the trial of the Protector's brother, Lord Seymour of Sudely, in 1549, a servant of his, one William Wightman, gave the following evidence for the prosecution: 'Well, well, said he [Lord Seymour] they are at this point now that there can neither Bishoprick, Deanery, nor Prebend fall void, but one or other of them will have a *fleece* of it. Indeed I did, at this point, both grant his saying to be true, and aggravate the matter, to confirm his opinion, with naming the Deanery of Wells, the Bishoprick of Lincoln, and others, which I told him had been *sore plucked at.*—It maketh no matter, said he; it will come in again when the King cometh to his years, as he beginneth to grow lustily. By God's precious soul! said he, I would not be in *some of their coats* for five marks when he shall hear of these matters....' (Tytler, I. 170.) But under Dudley the pace of spoliation was redoubled.

1 'Roderyck Mors' was somewhat prejudiced against bishops. 'What a cockatryse syght was it,' he remarks in one place, 'to se such an abhomynable sort of pompos bisshops in lordly parlament robys, as went before the King at Westmyster the xvi. day of January in the yere .1541. euyn to the nōber of .xviij. whereas .iij. were inowe to poyson an whole world. What godly redresse to set forth the Christen relygon, or reformacyon of thinges for the comon welth, can be hoped for, where such a sort of vypers be?'

wife, and chyldern, is inowgh. If he be an honest man, and preach Christ sincerely, he cannot lacke besyde; if he do not, it is to moch.

But 'for the Lordes sake,' he added, 'take no example at the distribucyon of the abbay goodys and lādys': rather let the episcopal revenues be turned to charitable uses, such as poor relief, national education, endowment of motherhood, and so forth. Above all, let them not be

dyuyded...among the princys, lordes, and rych men, that had no neede theroff; but...to the vse of the comon welth, and vnto the prouysyon for the pore, accordyng to the doctryne of the Scrypture....For all men are geuen to seke their own pryuate welth only, & the pore are nothing prouyded for.

Others, like Hooper, holding much the same views, were prepared, with perfect sincerity of purpose, to sell the episcopal lands to the nobility in return for their support in forcing the doctrine and ritual of Zurich upon the English Church. Hooper was prepared to sacrifice everything except his principles. He fought so stubbornly against the people who wished to compel him to wear vestments that he was prepared to make the nobility a gift of all the episcopal revenues in the country if they would allow him to prohibit the use of vestments altogether. His motives were perfectly honourable. And thus was concluded the alliance between the English Puritans and the unscrupulous adventurer whom Hooper described to Bullinger (March 27, 1550) as 'that most faithful and intrepid soldier of Christ, the earl of Warwick.'

The character of the Father of Nonconformity exhibits many unpleasant traits. He was ungracious and immoderately severe. He was always prepared to believe, and to spread, any scandal about his theological opponents, although, as Calvin wrote to Bucer—the pious solicitude of Beza has suppressed Hooper's name, but the context admits no doubt of his identity—'not so much impelled by malice, as carried away by a blind impulse. You would hardly believe how atrociously he has sometimes wounded us, and the innocent, and his friends': on the other hand, he was prepared to tell Bullinger a string of barefaced lies in order to assure him that Zwinglianism was making headway in this country. On his arrival in England, he told Bullinger that 'the people lies oppressed by the amazing tyranny of the nobles,' but mature reflection convinced him that it would prejudice his cause if he became a 'Commonwealth' like Latimer, and his Lenten sermons before the King, in which he had first intended 'to touch freely on the duties of individuals,' contained nothing that could bring a blush to the cheek of the least hardened oppressor of the poor and plunderer of the Church. On the fall of his patron, Somerset, he transferred his loyalty without a qualm to Somerset's successful rival. It is true that in his struggle against vestments he refused to obey Warwick, and fell into disgrace: but they were reconciled as soon as Hooper submitted. For twelve months the new Bishop of Gloucester flung himself with untiring energy into the administration of his diocese, as though to expiate his submission. In 1552 he returned to London, and, while actually staying at Lambeth in Cranmer's palace, continued to intrigue with Northumberland against his colleagues. He, who had inveighed so bitterly against pluralities, received the see of Worcester in addition to his own, and handed over to the Crown the lands and revenues of Gloucester: in return for which Northumberland, with a sudden burst of generosity, let him be excused his first-fruits. Henceforward he stood high in his patron's favour. He received several little privileges from the Council[1]: on 'the xxjth of Aprill, 1553,'

---

[1] Cf. the entries in the Council Book under June 14, November 6, December 2, 1552, and April 16 and 21, 1553.

for instance, he was given, 'by way of rewarde, xx^{li} for his attendaunce here [at Greenwich] ever syns the Parliament by his Majesties commaundment'—a curiously suggestive entry. But if the Puritans were valuable for Northumberland's purpose, he was invaluable for theirs: and from the moment of Hooper's reconciliation with his patron, they leaned no longer upon the crozier of Canterbury, but upon the ragged staff of Warwick. Thus, by this infamous alliance, the Church of England was subjected to the last and most determined of all the Zwinglian assaults: and that assault was so far successful that Bullinger was able to write, seven years later, when he feared that England was about to become Lutheran, 'The Edwardine Reformation satisfies the godly. Much better is it than the Confession of Augsburg.'

But the acquisition of the estates of the bishopric of Gloucester was merely an incident in Northumberland's campaign of spoliation. It was the rich lands of the bishopric of Durham upon which he had set his heart: he intended to annex them to his spreading duchy of Northumberland. Tunstall, the saintly and venerable leader of the moderate party of the Old Learning, Knox's 'dreamy Duresme,' rested precariously upon his ancient throne. In the summer of 1550 one Ninian Menvile accused him of having 'consented to a conspiracy in the North for the raising of a rebellion'—apparently in defence of Somerset, at the time when the Protector was struggling desperately to retain his power. Menvile presented a written accusation: Tunstall rebutted it: and Menvile replied. The whole case rested upon a letter which was alleged to have been written to Menvile by Tunstall, but which unfortunately could not be produced. However, Dudley was determined to prove him guilty, and in the spring of 1551 the Council summoned him, together with his Dean and Chancellor, to London, where he was confined to his house. The three prisoners were frequently cited before the Council, but seem never to have been confronted with their accuser. The case, which was carried on by written interrogations and depositions, languished for lack of proof: when, at the beginning of November, the Dean fell ill, and died. On November 20 the deanery was given to Horne, one of the Puritan licensed preachers. On December 20 Tunstall was again summoned before the Council. The incriminating letter had been mysteriously found 'in a cask of the Duke of Somerset's after his apprehension': Tunstall admitted that it was his, but continued to deny that it was treasonable: but to the Council that 'seemed not a sufficient answer,' and they committed him to the Tower. However, the Council needed more conclusive evidence if they wished to attaint him of misprision of treason, and Dudley set himself to find it. It was supplied mysteriously by the new Dean of Durham, Horne.

Then, on March 28, 1552, a bill was introduced unconstitutionally into the Lords 'for the deprivation of the Bishop of Durham.' It was hurried through by Northumberland, passing its second reading on the 29th, and its third on the 31st. It was denounced by Cranmer[1]: but so strong was the pressure of the Court that only he and one temporal peer, Lord Stourton, cast their votes against it. In the Commons, however, the plot was less successful. There a bill for Tunstall's attainder was introduced on April 4, but the House refused to consider it unless the bishop were brought before them and confronted with his accusers. This, for many cogent reasons, Northumberland could not allow: he dropped the prosecution, and set himself to procure Tunstall's deprivation by the more ordinary and less public process of a commission. But he

---

[1] This was magnanimous, for in 1551 Tunstall had published an attack on Cranmer's *Defence of the true and Catholic Doctrine of the Sacrament*, entitled *De vera Corporis et Sanguinis Doctrina in Eucharistia*.

dissolved Parliament on April 15, and marked Cranmer down for vengeance.

'I have heard,' wrote Bishop Ridley, in his *Piteous Lamentation of the Miserable Estate of the Church*, 'that Cranmer, and another whom I will not name ['He meaneth himself,' *margin*], were both in high displeasure, the one for showing his conscience secretly, but plainly and fully, in the Duke of Somerset's cause, and both of late, but specially Cranmer, for repugning as they might against the late spoil of church goods, taken away only by commandment of the higher powers, without any law or order of justice, and without any request of consent of them to whom they did belong.' And Cranmer, in his letter to Queen Mary, written shortly after her accession, spoke of Northumberland as 'seeking long time my destruction.' By voting against the Chantries Bill on December 15, 1547, the Archbishop had flung down his gage: but until the prosecution of Tunstall Northumberland underestimated his resistance. Cranmer saw through the elaborate camouflage of justice: and, not content with defending Tunstall in the House of Lords, seems to have written to the Council exposing the real motives of the prosecution, for on April 26 Northumberland addressed to the Council the following reply:

After most hertie Commendacions to your good Lordships. ...As touching the Message receyved from your Lordships by my saied Lord Chanceler and Mr. Secretary *Cicell*, with Request by them to me in your Lordships behaulf, concerning Tharchbusshop of *Canterburye*, I trust my Aunswers unto them be suche, as the same may stand with your good Contentacions, referring it wholye to their Reporte. But my trust is, that neyther your Lordships, neyther they, do impute or esteeme the Matter to be myne, or for my Cause; for if the Contention had risen or growen upon any Cause of myne, I must neads judge and Condempne my self more worthie to be blamed than he, and no lesse worthie to be exempte; but the Matter touching, as I take it, dyvers Wayes most ernestlie, the King's Majestie, and the most waightie Affaires of his Highnes, which nowe you ar in Hand withall, my trust is, your Lordships will waye the Matter to be his, for whom I am not to good to beare Blame, Reproche, and Rebuke, whiche I know in this to have suffered verie moche; as to your Lordships good Wisdomes I do referre it, with Thorder also of any Thing, that herin may any wayes concerne me; so that, if any Reformation be to be had, or any other Order to your Wisdomes be taken, the Foundacion may be fetched from the originall Cause, as I do nothyng doubt your good Lordships. And so I leave to trouble the same any lenger at this Tyme, wishing to your Lordships all Things prosperous. This Morning the 26th of *Aprill*, 1552.

Your Lordshipps most assuredly,

NORTHUMBERLAND.

None the less, the Commission against Tunstall was not ordered to be held until September 21: and though Cranmer refused to have anything to do with it, his attitude excited less attention than it might have done six months earlier.

Meanwhile Northumberland pursued the Archbishop with vindictive hatred. Cranmer had practically ceased to attend the Council meetings since the fall of Somerset: but on May 2 the Council sent him a letter 'to sende hither tharticles that he delyvered the last yere to the Busshoppes, and to signifie whether the same were set forth by any publick authoritie or no.' Here Dudley had a strong case, for Cranmer had acted illegally in trying to issue his Articles without carrying them through Convocation, where they would probably have been defeated. (Who, it may be wondered, suggested this accusation to Northumberland? Can it have been Hooper?) However, the Council presumably recognised that there were exonerating circumstances, for the case was dropped, and Northumberland had to devise another. In July, he circulated a rumour that Cranmer was rich and covetous. The charge was one that was likely to fall gratefully upon the ears of the Court. But fortunately the Archbishop had a friend there in Cecil, who hated and feared Northumberland, and sent Cranmer intelligence of all thè intrigues that were proceeding against him. This one was easy to meet. 'But as for the saying of St Paul,' he wrote to Cecil (July 21),

'Qui volunt ditescere, incidunt in tentationem,' I fear it not half so much as I do stark beggary. For I took not half so much care for my living, when I was a scholar of Cambridge, as I do at this present. For although I have now much more revenue, yet I have much more to do withal; and have more care to live now as an archbishop, than I had at that time to live like a scholar....I pay double for everything that I buy. If a good auditor have this account, he shall find no great surplusage to wax rich upon.

And if I knew any bishop that were covetous, I would surely admonish him; but I know none, but all beggars, except it be one[1]; and yet I dare well say he is not very rich. If you know any, I beseech you to advertise me; for peradventure I may advertise him better than you. To be short, I am not so doted as to set my mind upon things here, which neither I can carry away with me, nor tarry long with them.

Then, in November, he was accused of having obstructed, or at least of not having diligently assisted the Commission of the Kentish magistrates for the recovery—that is, for the confiscation by the State—of church goods and plate that had been embezzled by private individuals. For this default he had, fortunately, an excellent excuse. But hardly was this charge cleared when one of the Duke's

---

[1] Holgate, Archbishop of York, who had enriched himself but impoverished his see. (J. S. Fletcher, *The Reformation in Northern England*, pp. 146–54.)

creatures, Sir Thomas Cheyney, Warden of the Cinque Ports, picked a quarrel with him, probably at Dudley's instigation: but of this nothing further is known. It is indeed possible that had Northumberland been more securely in power, Cranmer might shortly have suffered the fate of Becket, or might even conceivably have been martyred by the Puritans, instead of with them. But circumstances gave him a respite. In September 'the King did complaine of a continuall infirmity of body, yet rather as an indisposition in health then any set sicknesse. ...In *Ianuary*...his sicknesse did more apparantly shew it selfe, especially by the symptome of a tough strong streining cough'[1]. Throwing all other cares aside, Northumberland began to plot feverishly for the succession.

In the meanwhile, his designs upon the bishopric of Durham had not been proceeding smoothly. It was his intention to dissolve the original bishopric and to create two new sees, Durham and Newcastle, endowing each somewhat niggardly: the remaining estates were to be vested temporarily in the Crown, and, in due course, bestowed upon himself. In his capacity as Warden of the Scottish Marches, he had gone north in the summer to spy out the land of promise: where he heard in Newcastle a very outspoken sermon on Isaiah's vineyard from one of the Puritan licensed preachers, named John Knox. It occurred to him that it would be injudicious to leave this very vigilant and independent preacher in the diocese that he intended to despoil: so he brought Knox south with him in his train (with results that have been noted), and on October 28—Tunstall had been deprived a fortnight earlier, by a lay commission—suggested to Cecil that 'it might please the King's Majesty to appoint Mr Knocks' to the vacant bishopric of Rochester, for several irre-

---

[1] *The life and raigne of King Edward the sixt*, by Sir John Hayward (1630), pp. 167, 168.

proachable reasons: he would be 'a whetstone, to quicken and sharp the Bishop of Canterbury, whereof he hath need'; he would be 'a great confounder of the Anabaptists lately sprung up in Kent'; he would have to conform to the English use of the Lord's Supper; and his removal would put an end to the undesirable immigration of Scots who came to Newcastle 'chiefly for his fellowship.' 'Herein I pray you desire my Lord Chamberlain and Mr Vicechamberlain to help towards this good act, both for God's service and the King's.' Secondly, he suggested that the bishopric of Durham should be given to Horne, with 'one thousand marks more to that which he hath in his deanery—and the same house which he now hath, as well in the city as in the country, will serve him right honourably—so may his Majesty receive both the Castle, which hath a princely site, and the other stately houses which the Bishop had in the country': the stipend of the Chancellor should be assigned to the Dean, that of the Vice-Chancellor to the Chancellor: the Suffragan, 'who is placed without the King's Majesty's authority,' 'being neither preacher, learned, nor honest man,' should be deposed, and his living, 'with a little more to the value of it—a hundred marks, will serve to the erection of a Bishop within Newcastle.'

Thus may his Majesty place godly ministers in these offices as is aforesaid, and receive to his crown 2000^{ll} a year of the best lands within the north parts of his realm. Yea, I doubt not it will be iiii^m marks a year of as good revenues as any is within the realm; and all places better and more godly furnished than ever it was from the beginning to this day.

The scheme was beautifully simple. Unfortunately Knox declined the bishopric of Rochester with such comments that after the interview Northumberland wrote to Cecil (Dec. 7) in a rage, 'I love not to have to do with men which be neither grateful nor pleasable': and

Horne also, who had obviously expected a less niggardly reward for his services, had written to decline the mutilated bishopric, and had actually said in his letter 'that he cannot tell whether I be a dissembler in religion or not: but I have for twenty years stand [stood] to one kind of religion, in the same which I do now profess; and have, I thank the Lord, past no small dangers from it.' I have also thought good to remind you (the indignant Duke continued) of Horne's revelations about the Northern conspiracy: the matter should not be left to lie in hugger-mugger [secrecy], for perhaps it is more important than we think: let us investigate it, 'with all the circumstances and adherents,' while it is fresh in our memories, '*nisi forte, veniant Romani.*' *How*, for example, *did Horne find out about it?* How long did he know it before he uttered it to me? Who first told him of it, and under what circumstances? Let him be sent for, and made to give a written answer upon oath!—Alas,

I remember well your considerations concerning what might be judged by evil people of me, as though it might be imagined that I should be the procurer of the matter against the parties [i.e. Tunstall &c.] for displeasure, or for that I would be alone [in the North], or for to have some of his inheritance....For my own part, if I should have past more upon the speech of the people than upon the service of my master, or gone about to seek favour of them without respect to his Highness' surety, I needed not to have had so much obloquy of some kind of men; but the living God, that knoweth the hearts of all men, shall be my judge at the last day with what zeal, faith and truth I serve my master...seeking nothing but the true glory of God and his Highness' surety: so shall I most please God and have my conscience upright, and then not fear what man doth to me....

Fortified by these pious fruits of self-examination, Northumberland proceeded with his plan. 'For the love

of God,' he wrote to Cecil (Jan. 7), 'let not the see be so long destitute of some grave and good man: yea, rather a stout and honest man, that knoweth his duty to God and to his Sovereign lord, than one of these new obstinate doctors without humanity [i.e. manners] or honest conditions,' who are 'so sotted with their wives and children' that they neglect their office: 'and so they will do, so long as his Majesty shall suffer them to have so great possessions to maintain their idle lives.' Meanwhile God is forgotten in the North, and it is hard to govern where that is so. Thus he continued to importune Cecil: while in March he hurried through Parliament a bill dissolving the old bishopric of Durham and erecting two new sees, Durham and Newcastle, respectively endowed with 2000 and 1000 marks a year, and vesting the temporalities of the old bishopric in the King: by whom they were duly presented to his minister. But Northumberland was not fated to enjoy them long: for on July 6 the King was dead.

The death of Edward VI took place under mysterious circumstances. To the minds of the superstitious people it had been foreshadowed by the strange portents of the preceding year.

Item on Wytsone evyne it raynyd in dyvers places in London that it was sene lyynge in dyvers places on the erbbes [= cobbles] as redde as wyne.

Item the iiij. day of August betwenne x. and xj. at night was a woman in Oxfordshere at a place callyd Midylton-stone at the syne of the Eggylle viij. myle from Oxforde, and the good man's name was John Kenner, and she was delyveryd of a chyld with too heddes, iiij. hanndes, iiij. feete, and but one body, and the mydwyffe kersende them at home and was alowyd by the churche; and [they] lyffyd xv. days; and ette, and [one slept] wylle the other dyd wake, and lokyd with a mery chere whan anny persons lo[ked at] them. Item also in

that same cuntry was a henne hacchyd of a chekyn that had
ij. heddes and iiij. fette.

Item in the same month was tane at Bl[ack] wall and nere
abowte London was tane dyvers dolfyns[1].

Fuller, for some reason obscure, regarded the dolphins as
the most ominous. Under the title, *An ill Presage*, he
wrote: 'Six dolphins were taken in the Thames (three
near Queenborough, and three above Greenwich, where
the Thames is scarce tainted with brackishness) insomuch
that many grave men dispensed with their wisdom, and
beheld them with wonder, as not seen before on our shores;
a fish much loving man and music, swifter than all other
fishes and birds too; yea, than the swallow itself (if Pliny
say true).... Their coming up so far was beheld by
mariners as a presage of foul weather at sea; but by
statesmen, as a prodigious omen of some tempestuous
mutations in our land. And particularly, they suspected
the king's death....'

The 'tough strong streining cough' that attacked the
King in January 1552 defied the arts of his physicians.
Northumberland began to make desperate plans for the
succession: on January 19, writs were issued for a General
Election, and Parliament met in March. Northumberland
is alleged to have packed it[2]: if he had, the result was
singularly unsuccessful. After a stormy session this
Parliament was dissolved at the end of March, having
sat for less than a month. The session was notable chiefly
for a scene in the Upper House, when Northumberland,
still smarting under the rebuffs he had had from Horne

---

[1] *Grey Friars Chronicle* (Camden Soc.), pp. 74–5.

[2] Chiefly on the evidence of a query addressed by Renard to his
master, Charles V, on behalf of Mary, 'si le dict parlement' which
Mary was about to summon 'se doit faire général, ou y appellir
particuliers et notables du pays par representer le parlement selon
que le Duc de Northumberland l'a introduict': but Renard was not
in England in March 1553.

and Knox, made a savage personal attack on Cranmer, blaming him for the license with which preachers abused their betters, and recommending him to mind his own business if he valued his life. Meanwhile the King was growing worse. Hæmorrhage from the lungs occurred at the end of April: in May, 'his vitall parts were mortally stuffed, which brought him to a difficultie of speech and of breath, his legs swelled, his pulse failed, his skin changed colour, and many other horrid symptomes appeared'[1]. Northumberland's anxiety redoubled: he made desperate efforts to secure the alliance of either the Emperor or the King of France: on May 15 he brought about three marriages—Lady Jane Grey to Lord Guildford Dudley, Lady Catharine Grey to Lord Herbert, and Lady Catharine Dudley to Lord Hastings. The unhappy Cecil shammed sick, and absented himself from the Council from April 22 to June 11: whereupon the sympathetic Lord Audley wrote to him to 'be of good comfort, and pluck up a lusty merry heart, and thus shall you overcome all diseases,' and enclosed a prescription from his wife's book, 'proved upon herself and me both':

A good medicine for Weakness or Consumption

Take a sow-pig of nine days old, and flea him and quarter him, and put him in a stillatory with a handful of spearmint, a handful of red fennel, a handful of liverwort, half a handful of red nepe [= turnip], a handful of celery, nine dates clean picked and pared, a handful of great raisins, and pick out the stones, and a quarter of an ounce of mace, and two sticks of good cinnamon bruised in a mortar; and distil it together, with a fair fire; and put it in a glass and set it in the sun nine days; and drink nine spoonfuls of it at once while you list.

But what cured Cecil was the fact that on June 2 Cheke was sworn Secretary in his place. He returned on the

[1] Hayward, p. 178.

11th, though in mortal terror of assassination: to find Northumberland tampering with the King's will, holding the fleet and army in readiness, and making plans to seize the Princess Mary (then at Hunsdon House) immediately the King was dead. All these plots were hatched in deepest secrecy, but Scheyfne, the Emperor's Ambassador, contrived to gain information of every stage of the conspiracy and to pass it on to Mary. Meanwhile the tide of popular discontent was rising, and the Emperor was preparing to support his cousin's cause.

At the beginning of July it was already rumoured that the King was dead. In order that the people might assure themselves that he was still alive, Edward was carried to the window and shown to them, as his proud father had carried him to the window and shown him to the people thirteen years before: but, seeing the ghastly, pallid, shrunken features of the dying boy, the spectators believed that they had seen a corpse. On the evening of Thursday, July 6—the anniversary of the execution of Sir Thomas More—he died, at the age of fifteen years and eight months.

The body decomposed rapidly, even before death, and in a peculiarly revolting manner, lending colour to the popular rumour that he had been poisoned at Northumberland's orders. The charge was false; nothing could have been further from Northumberland's wishes than Edward's death: but the horrible disease from which he suffered, a disease unknown to medical science until 1862, naturally led to some such explanation. As a matter of fact, he actually died of pulmonary tuberculosis, inherited from his grandfather Henry VII, accompanied by Raynault's disease[1]. But Burcher communicated to Bullinger the common report from England:

A horrible and portentous crime has been committed by that

[1] Dr James Rae, in his invaluable book on *The Deaths of the Kings of England* (1913), supports this theory, though he suggests lung

monster truly rather than man, the duke of Northumberland. A trustworthy [informant] writes to me that our excellent king has been most shamefully carried off by poison. Before he was dead, his nails and his hair fell off, so that he had manifestly lost all his beauty, handsome as he was. The authors of the poisoning were ashamed to show to the people at his funeral the body of the dead king (as is the custom). Wherefore they buried him secretly in his paddock, adjoining the palace, and substituted in his place to be seen by the people a youth not unlike him, whom they had stabbed to death. This was confessed by one of the sons of the duke of Northumberland. The duke has been taken with his five sons and almost twenty nobles....

This story was generally believed. 'Some say he was powsynd,' wrote the author of the *Grey Friars Chronicle*, 'as it shal apere ar-after': 'he was poyssoned,' wrote Mr Machyn, the London undertaker, 'as evere body says, wher now, thanke be to God, ther be mony of the false trayters browt to ther end, and j trust in God that more shall folow as they may be spyd owt'[1]: as late as August 6,

---

syphilis as an alternative hypothesis. Dr C. MacLaurin in *Mere Mortals: Medico-Historical Essays* (1925) declines the syphilis theory on p. 61, but presses it hard in his essay on Edward VI (pp. 71-80). The chief evidence for it, as brought forward by both doctors, is (1) the 'weaknesse and faintnes of spirit' (Hayward, p. 168), as contrasted with the persistent cheerfulness of tuberculosis—the boy's last prayer was, 'Lord God, deliver me out of this miserable and wretched life' (Heylyn, p. 140)—and (2) the very curious entry in the King's Journal under April 2, 1552, 'I fell sick of the measels and small pox': the fact that two dissimilar eruptions came out at the same time suggests that there was some other toxin at work, probably syphilitic. On the other hand, lung syphilis is exceedingly rare, while Raynault's disease is quite enough to account for the depression of spirits. The theory that tuberculosis and Raynault's disease caused the King's death is on the whole the most satisfactory: but Raynault's disease does not by any means exclude the possibility that hereditary syphilis was present, though probably not in the lung.

[1] *The Diary of Henry Machyn, Citizen of London* (Camden Soc.), p. 35.

Simon Renard wrote to his master, the Emperor, 'que les artoix des piedz luy estoient tumbez et qu'il a estè empoissonnè.' The rumour was given credence by the fact that Northumberland concealed for two days the news of Edward's death, and then imparted it only to 'my Lord Mayor,...6 or 8 Aldermen, 6 Merchaunt Staplers, and 6 Merchant Adventurers' at the Court at Greenwich: 'which, opened unto them by the mouth of the Counsell, they were sworne to yt and to keepe yt secret'[1]. The same precaution was responsible for the persistent rumour (which so perturbed the Council that those who were arrested for spreading it were not pilloried, but secretly committed to separate prisons) 'that the late king should be yet on live,' and for the appearance of two Pretenders, one in 1555, the other in 1578[2]. But the king was dead indeed: and with him the hopes of Northumberland and of Hooper had perished also.

Northumberland's rising was foredoomed to faiiure. He had alienated in turn every party in the House of Lords: he had never held the affections of the people, and throughout his administration the tide of his unpopularity had steadily risen. His ambition was distrusted: there had been strange rumours current concerning the new coinage: 'Item the xvj. day [of Dec. 1551] was a proclamacion for the new qwyne [= coin] that no man [should speak ill] of it, for because that the pepulle sayd dyvers that ther was the ragyd staff [upon] it'[3]. The rumour that the King had been poisoned shattered the last vestige of his hopes. Even the Protestants mistrusted him now: the Hot Gospeller, Edward Underhill, was as forward as any to

---

[1] *Wriothesley's Chronicle* (Camden Soc.), p. 85. Cf. Hilles' letter to Bullinger, July 9, 1553: Hilles was a friend of the Lord Mayor, who seems to have disclosed the secret to him almost immediately.

[2] See an article in the *English Historical Review*, April 1908: 'A Legend concerning Edward VI,' by Margaret E. Cornford.

[3] *Grey Friars Chronicle*, p. 72.

serve the Queen, and the author of a contemporary pamphlet, *The Epistle of Poor Pratte*[1], evidently regarded Northumberland as a greater enemy to Protestantism than Mary:

> For we have had manye prophetes and true preachers, whiche did declare unto us, that oure kinge shal be taken awaye from us, and a tyrant shal reygne; the gospel shall be plucked awaye, the right heyre shalbe dispossessed, and al for our unthanck-fulnes. And thinkest thou not (Gilbard) the world is now come? Yea, truely. And what shal folow, yf we repent not in tymes. The same God wil take from us the vertuouse lady Mary, oure lawfull quene, and send such a cruel Pharao, as the ragged beare, to rule us; which shal pul us and pol us, spoyle us, and utterly destroy us, and bring us in great calamities and miseries. And this God wil send us; and al for our iniquities....

Had the conspirators succeeded in apprehending Mary, the rebellion might have been more dangerous. But, in spite of their precautions, Scheyfne was able to send her the news of the King's death, and when on the following morning (July 7) Lord Robert Dudley arrived at Hunsdon to arrest her with a company of horse, she had already fled, and was riding post-haste a hundred miles to seek the protection of the Howards in Norfolk. The loyalty of the Eastern Counties stood for a time in doubt: but the nation was rallying to her standard: and on July 20 Northumberland, betrayed on every hand by his fellow-plotters, threw up his cap and proclaimed Queen Mary in Cambridge market-place. On the following day he was arrested, and brought to London.

And on saynt James day at after-none at iiij. of cloke at after-none was browte unto London worshyppfully as he had

---

[1] *The copie of a pistel or letter sent to Gilbard Potter, in the tyme when he was in prison, for speakinge on our most true quenes part, the lady Mary, before he had his eares cut of. The xiij. of July* [1553]. Printed in *The Chronicle of Queen Jane and Queen Mary* (Camden Soc.), App. v. pp. 115–21.

deseruyd, and browte in at Byshoppes gatte by the erle of Arndelle, the wych browte hym unto the tower of London. And whan he came in at Byshoppes gate he was commandyd to put of hys atte, and soo dyd tylle he came to the tower; and after he came onsse to Shordych alle the pepulle revyled hym and callyd hym traytor and herytycke, and woulde not seyse for alle the ware spokyn unto for it. Wyth hys sones, as the erle of Warwyk, Ambrose Dudley, Henry Dudley, Androw Dudley, the erle of Huntyngtone, lorde Hastynges, sir John Gattes that was captayne of the garde, and sir Henry Gattes hys brother, sir Thomas Palmer, doctor Saunder[1]. Item here went the byshoppe of London [Ridley] that was goynge un-to the qwene to begge hys pardon, but he was tane at Ipsege, and there was put in warde[2].

On August 22 Northumberland was brought to the block. Upon the scaffold, whether in the hope of pardon in this world or in the next, he flung off the mask of Protestantism which had so long covered his rapacity. He warned the people 'to beware of these sediciouse preachers, and teachers of newe doctryne, whiche pretende to preache Gods worde, but in very deede they preache theyr own phansies, who were never able to explicate thēselues, they know not today what they wold haue to morowe, there is no stay in theyr teaching & doctryne, they open the boke, but they cannot shut it agayne': and declared his faith, that 'all the plagues that haue chaunced to this realme of late yeares'—war, famine, plague, sedition, privy conspiracy, and rebellion, and the spread of heresies—came from the wrath of God 'for that we haue deuyded our selfe from the rest of Christendome,...[and] forsakē the unitie of the catholyke Churche'[3]. This recantation lost

---

[1] Dr Sandys, Vice-Chancellor of Cambridge University.
[2] *Grey Friars Chronicle*, pp. 30–1. Cf. *Wriothesley's Chronicle*, pp. 90–1.
[3] *The sayinge of John late Duke of Northumberlande uppon the scaffolde, at the tyme of his execution. The .xxii. of August, A...1553* (pamphlet).

him his last apologists. The Puritans turned vindictively upon him, and outdid all their rivals in the defamation of his memory: for his apostasy had thrown them into unexpected confusion, and completed the ruin of their cause. The Church of England had lain almost at their mercy: but the prize had been snatched from them before the supremacy of Zurich could be definitively established, and never again was it to lie within their grasp. 'With good king Edward,' wrote Neal, in his *History of the Puritans; or, Protestant Nonconformists*, 'died all farther advances of the Reformation; for the alterations that were made afterward by queen Elizabeth hardly came up to his standard.' In the supreme crisis of her destiny two events occurred that saved the Church of England: the fall of Northumberland and the martyrdom of Cranmer.

EPILOGUE

EPILOGUE

THE inevitable epilogue to the history of the Edwardine Reformation is the narrative of Cranmer's martyrdom. By his death he conferred immortality upon his labours. In the most critical and formative period in the history of the English Church (the first years of Elizabeth alone excepted) he had laid down unalterably the lines of future progress, and had determined that Anglican theology should be neither Zwinglian nor Roman. The Elizabethan Reformation was based upon the precedents that he had established: he had touched nothing that he did not adorn[1]: he bequeathed to the Church whose course he had so long and faithfully guided, a spirit of tolerance and moderation rare in that age of bigotry and superstition, and a liturgy that is one of the most beautiful religious monuments of all time. It would be uncharitable to dwell upon the pitiful episode of his Recantations. They were, very largely, the fruit of his sincere erastianism, as has been noted: 'I am content,' he wrote, in his Third Recantation, 'to submit myself to the king and queen's majesties, and to all their laws and ordinances, as well concerning the pope's supremacy as others.' Moreover, the means by which they were extorted from him were nothing short of infamous. For two and a half years he had been kept in solitary confinement: he had been compelled to watch from the roof of his prison the dying agonies of Latimer and Ridley: and, having received that ghastly warning, he was subjected to the ingenious persuasions of two Jesuit friars, sent by Pole to convert him. In his noisome gaol he drew up four successive recantations: but they were too brief and non-committal to satisfy his judges. On February 16 he was formally degraded: on February 24

[1] 'Nihil enim quod non sit expolitum, acutum & elaboratum ex eo viro exspecto.' *Peter Martyr to 'a Certaine Friend,'* Zurich, March 15, 1557. (*Loc. Com.* p. 1118.)

a writ was issued to the mayor and bailiffs of Oxford for his burning, at some date not specified in the writ. On seeing this, he fell down in a dead faint[1]. The fear of death had laid hold upon him, and the strength of his fear made him ashamed and puzzled: yet the very candour with which he confessed it was a mitigation of his weakness. Old age is naturally greedy of life, but this was more than the normal *pavor mortis* that might be expected in a man of sixty-seven: nor was it merely the panic terror that might seize any man faced with such an agonising death. At this time Cranmer was actually suffering from some disease of the heart[2] which naturally aggravated very

[1] I admit that the anonymous author (Alan Cope?) of *Bishop Cranmers Recantacyons* says that this faint occurred 'ad quintum Calend. Februarii,' i.e. January 28, but I conjecture that it should be 'Martii,' for the sake of the coincidence. (This author's dates are not always accurate: e.g. he dates Cranmer's Sixth Recantation 'Martii die 9a.,' when it should be March 18.)

[2] This statement is based on the hostile evidence of the *Recantacyons*. The passage may be cited:
'After his death, this, though in my own judgment [it is] unlikely, is however said to have happened, that [his] heart, having been wrenched away from the bones already burned up, was found to be so enwrapped with much blood and membranes that it could not be laid bare except by great force, moreover having been uncovered it retained its shape, except that, having been consumed and dried up by the fire itself, it seemed to have hollows of emptiness: and this was reported by those who asserted that it was not [merely] their opinion, but that they had both seen and handled it and pierced it with a dagger to see whether it had been so petrified and hard that it was not burned by fire.
'Suetonius relates concerning Germanicus that when he was cremated his heart remained uninjured between the bones, because he had been killed by poison: for the nature of the heart is thought to be such that having been infected with poison it cannot be consumed by fire. But was it the poison of heresy in this man, or do we say truly that he had heart disease? for the hearts of persons who are affected by that do not burn either. That therefore may have been what seized him on January 28 [Feb. 25?] when he fell almost senseless to the ground, especially since he himself had said that the illness that had gripped him at that time was neither new nor unexpected.'
The fact that Cranmer's heart would not burn suggests pericardial

considerably his fear of death. Then, while he awaited his martyrdom, he was suddenly taken out of prison and lodged, more as a guest than as a prisoner, in the deanery of Christchurch. This seems to have been done by the Spanish friars upon their own initiative: who, after he had enjoyed a few days of liberty, came to him with a long Latin recantation categorically stating his acceptance of Roman doctrine, and told him that if he would but 'set his name in two words to this little leaf of paper' his life would be spared. In a moment of very human weakness he consented, and signed his name to this, his first recantation proper. It is possible that the friars had acted in all good faith, and did not know that the Queen and Pole had determined irrevocably on Cranmer's death. They instantly gave an English translation to an obscure firm of printers, who circulated it in London, probably without license: but the Council were furious at this unexpected move, and ordered all the copies to be recalled and burned. This deepened the general suspicion, recorded by the Venetian Ambassador, that the document was a forgery. But the real motive was that Pole was determined not to be ensnared into an act of clemency. He could not spare Cranmer's life: but he determined to humiliate him still further, and so drew up a longer and far more abject recantation, which Cranmer (who had been taken back to his cell in Bocardo) was made not only to sign, but actually to copy out in his own handwriting, without being told that it could not save him from the stake. This was done on March 18: and, having received it, the Council ordered the preparations for his burning to go forward. On March 21 he was taken out from the prison to meet his end, although he had not even yet received the formal announcement of it. He was taken to St Mary's, and there

effusion, while the adhesions mentioned confirm the theory of heart disease.

made to stand before the multitude, while Dr Cole preached against him for two hours, and then called upon him to read to the people the last confession of his errors, which he had been made to write during the last day of his imprisonment. With the tears streaming down his face, 'the very image and shape of perfect sorrow,' he drew forth the paper, and began to read it to the people. After a prayer for God's forgiveness on his errors, the most beautiful that he ever wrote, he exhorted the people to contempt of this world, to obedience to the King and Queen, to brotherly love, and to charity towards the poor. 'And now,' he read, 'I come to the great thing that so much troubleth my conscience more than anything that ever I did or said in my whole life': but at this point, instead of reading what was written in his manuscript, renouncing the books he had written against the Mass and declaring his belief in the Real and Substantial Presence of Our Lord under the forms of bread and wine, to the confusion of his adversaries he openly renounced and refused

as things written with my hand contrary to the truth which I thought in my heart, and written for fear of death, and to save my life, if it might be, ... all such bills and papers which I have written or signed with my hand since my degradation; wherein I have written many things untrue. And forasmuch as my hand offended, writing contrary to my heart, my hand shall first be punished therefore: for, may I come to the fire, it shall first be burned.

And as for the pope, I refuse him as Christ's enemy and antichrist, with all his false doctrine.

And as for the sacrament, I believe as I have taught in my book against the bishop of Winchester; the which my book teacheth so true a doctrine of the sacrament, that it shall stand at the last day before the judgment of God, where the papistical doctrine contrary thereto shall be ashamed to shew her face.

The last words were drowned in the general uproar, Cole shouting from the pulpit, 'Stop the heretic's mouth, and take him away!': the friars rushed at him, and dragged him from his platform, and hurried him to the place of martyrdom. On the way the friar Juan de Villa Garcia remonstrated with him, imploring him not to die in great desperation: 'Actually,' he cried, 'if [the Pope] would spare you your head, you would willingly confess him head [of the Church]': to which Cranmer, after some interval, replied with perfect honesty, 'If he had thus saved my life, I would have submitted to his laws.' But he had been saved from that surrender by Pole's implacable hostility: and, being bound to the stake, he stretched out his right hand into the flames, and endured his torment with great fortitude: and so died, and was numbered among Christ's martyrs.

As his struggle had been great, so his victory was the greater: his strength was ennobled by his weakness: in his last hour he stood as the Samson Agonistes of the English Reformation. By the sacrifice of his life, he secured the triumph of his policy. Nor was his heroism in the hour of death mere desperation, nor inconsistent with the whole tenour of his life. It must be admitted that his compliance in the matter of the Divorce, at the very outset of his Primacy, was discreditable in him. But against that must be set the persistent courage and tenacity of purpose, with which, though without that imprudence that would have lost him all he sought, he admonished, exhorted, persuaded and cajoled his royal master in the latter years of Henry's reign, at a time when syphilitic psychasthenia, complete mental, moral and physical degeneration[1], had made him the terror of all the other members of his Council. In the reign of Edward VI, he worked with a statesmanship rare among contemporary Reformers for the unity not only of

[1] MacLaurin, *Mere Mortals*, p. 66.

the Church of England, but of all the forces of Protestantism in Europe, and when hard pressed by the coalition of his enemies, though of a naturally timid disposition, he continued to resist Northumberland at grave peril of his life: and by his death he damned the Marian Counter-Reformation, and lit, more signally than even Latimer and Ridley, a candle that should never be put out.

But another Epilogue may be found in a page of Bullinger's *Diarium* for 1553:

6. Iulii moritur in Anglia Grynenici [i.e. Grenovici, at Greenwich] sereniss. et christianiss. rex Eduardus 6. Declaratur Ioanna ducis Suffolciae filia regina, quam mox deiecit Maria soror Eduardi ex Hispana matre. Opprimitur et capitur dux Northumbriae Ioan. Dudlaeus; una cum multis truncantur.

11. Augusti finio epist. Pauli ad Titum; 18. eiusdem ordior primam ad Corinth.

29. Augusti finio Nahum prophetam; Sept. 5. ordior Abacuk.

Septembris prima primum peregre proficiscitur Heinricus filius meus; quod nobis felix et faustum velit dominus Deus.

7. Novemb. finio prophetam Abacuk; ordior eiusdem mensis 14. Saphoniam.

Illo ipso tempore finio iiii libros meos scriptos de gratia Dei iustificante nos propter Christum per solam fidem absque operibus bonis etc., ad sereniss. christianum regem Danorum, Gothorum etc.; impressi sunt hi libri circa finem 53. et principium 54.

Dises jar was an früchten und win gut und fruchtbar. Im herbst schankt man guten win, den Kopf umb j Krüzer. Des wins ward ouch vil; der Müt kernen umb 15 und 16 Bz.

BIBLIOGRAPHY

ONLY the more important of the books consulted are mentioned in this list, which does not include either the collections of letters mentioned in the Preface or such indispensable works of reference as the *Dictionary of National Biography*, *Allgemeine Deutsche Biographie*, *Acts of the Privy Council* (ed. J. R. Dasent: vols II.–IV., New Series, 1870–2), *Calendar of State Papers* (*Domestic Series*) 1547–80 (ed. R. Lemon: 1856), Rymer's *Foedera* (tom. XV., 2nd edtn, 1728), Cooper's *Athenae Cantabrigienses* (ed. G. J. Gray: 1913), and Wood's *Athenae Oxonienses* and *Fasti Oxonienses* (2nd edtn, 1721). Other books, pamphlets, or articles will be found mentioned in the footnotes.

Any historian who attempts to write a history of this period cannot but be under a great obligation to Canon Dixon's monumental *History of the Church of England*: but for a short outline of the English Reformation I should be inclined to recommend above all others Canon G. G. Perry's *History of the Reformation in England* in the 'Epochs of Church History' Series.

GUSTAV ANRICH. *Martin Bucer.* 1914.
CARL BENRATH. *Bernardino Ochino von Siena. Ein Beitrag zur Geschichte der Reformation.* 1875. (Translation by HELEN ZIMMERN: *Bernardino Ochino of Siena: a contribution towards the history of the Reformation.* 1876.)
MARTIN BUCER. *Verantwortūg M. Butzers. . . .* 1523.
—— *Scripta Anglicana fere omnia.* (Ed. CONRAD HUBERT.) 1577.
HEINRICH BULLINGER. *Diarium* (*Annales Vitae*) 1504–74. (Ed. EMIL EGLI.) 1904.
J. SOUTHERNDEN BURN. *The History of the French, Walloon, Dutch, and other foreign Protestant refugees in England from the time of Henry VIII to the Revocation of the Edict of Nantes.* 1846.
BURNET. *History of the Reformation of the Church of England.* (Ed. N. POCOCK.) 7 vols. 1865.
CAMDEN SOCIETY. *Trevelyan Papers prior to* A.D. 1558. (Ed. J. P. COLLIER.) 1857.

304 BIBLIOGRAPHY

CAMDEN SOCIETY. *Wriothesley's Chronicle of England during the reigns of the Tudors.* (Ed. W. D. HAMILTON.) 2 vols. 1875, 1877.
—— *The Diary of Henry Machyn, Citizen of London.* (Ed. J. G. NICHOLS.) 1848.
—— *The Chronicle of Queen Jane and Queen Mary.* (Ed. J. G. NICHOLS.) 1850.
—— *Chronicle of the Grey Friars of London.* (Ed. J. G. NICHOLS.) 1852.
—— *Narratives of the Reformation chiefly from the MSS. of John Foxe the Martyrologist: with two contemporary biographies of Archbishop Cranmer.* (Ed. J. G. NICHOLS.) 1859.
—— *Troubles connected with the Prayer Book of 1549.* (Ed. N. POCOCK.) 1884.
E. CARDWELL. *The Two Liturgies of Edward VI compared.* 2nd edtn. 1841.
—— *Synodalia.* 2 vols. 1842.
—— *Documentary Annals of the Reformed Church of England,* vol. I. 2 vols. 1844.
(ALAN COPE?). *Bishop Cranmers Recantacyons.* (Ed. Lord HOUGHTON and JAMES GAIRDNER.) Philobiblon Society, Msc. vol. XV.
Archbishop CRANMER *on the True and Catholic Doctrine and Use of the Lord's Supper.* (Ed. C. H. H. WRIGHT: Preface by Dean WACE.) 1907.
HERMANN DALTON. *Johannes à Lasco. Beitrag zur Reformationsgeschichte Polens, Deutschlands, und Englands.* 1881. (Translation of the first half of this book by H. J. EVANS: *John à Lasco: his earlier life and labours.* 1886.)
R. W. DIXON. *History of the Church of England from the Abolition of the Roman Jurisdiction.* 2nd edtn, revised. 6 vols. 1893.
HASTINGS EELLS. *The attitude of Martin Bucer towards the Bigamy of Philip of Hesse.* Yale Hist. Publ. Msc. vol. XII. 1924.
H. A. L. FISHER. *The Political History of England.* (Vol. v. 1485–1547.) 1906.
FOX. *Actes and Monuments.* (Edtn, 1583.)
FULLER. *The Church History of Britain.* (Ed. J. G. NICHOLS.) Vol. II. 1868.
GASQUET and BISHOP. *Edward VI and the Book of Common Prayer.* 1890.
C. HARDWICK. *A History of the Articles of Religion.* 2nd edtn. 1859.
C. HEIN. *Die Sakramentslehre des Johannes a Lasco.* 1904.
HENRY BRADSHAW SOCIETY. *Cranmer's Liturgical Projects.* (Ed. J. WICKHAM LEGG.) 1915.
—— *The Order of the Communion,* 1548. (Ed. H. A. WILSON.) 1907.
JOHN HOOPER. *A Declaration of Christe and of his offyce.* 1547.
—— *An Answer unto my lord of wynthesters booke.* 1547.
H. JENKYNS (ed.). *The remains of Thomas Cranmer.* 1833.

GEORG KLINGENBURG. *Das Verhältnis Calvins zu Butzer.* 1912.
A. KUYPER (ed.). *Joannis a Lasco Opera tam edita quam inedita.* 1866.
JOHN LAMB (ed.). *A Collection of Letters, Statutes, and other documents, from the MS. Library of Corpus Christi College, illustrative of the History of the University of Cambridge during the period of the Reformation, from* A.D. *M.D., to* A.D. *MDLXXII.* 1838.
JOHN À LASCO. *Compendium doctrinae de vera unicaque Dei et Christi Ecclesia in qua Peregrinorum Ecclesia Londini instituta est.* 1551.
—— *Brevis et dilucida de Sacramentis Ecclesiae Christi tractatio.* 1552.
P. LORIMER. *John Knox and the Church of England.* 1875.
S. R. MAITLAND. *The Reformation in England.* 1906.
PETER MARTYR. *Loci Communes D.˙P. M. Vermilii.* (Ed. H. MASSONIUS.) 1583. (Translation by A. MARTEN: *The Common Places of Peter Martyr.* 1583.)
—— *Tractatio de sacramento Eucharistiae habita in Universitate Oxoniensi....Ad hēc Disputatio de eodem sacramento.* 1549. (Translation of the *Tractatio* by N. UDAL: *A discourse or traictise of Peter Martyr Vermill concernynge the Sacrament of the Lordes Supper.* 1550?.)
'RODERYCK MORS' (HENRY BRINKLOW). *The Complaynt of Roderyck Mors.* (Ed. J. M. COOPER.) Early English Text Society. 1874.
H. C. G. MOULE (ed.). *Bishop Ridley on the Lord's Supper.* 1895.
J. B. MULLINGER. *The University of Cambridge from the earliest times to the decline of the Platonist Movement.* Vol. II. 1873.
PARKER SOCIETY. JOHN BRADFORD: *Writings.* (Ed. A. TOWNSEND.) 2 vols. 1848, 1853.
—— Archbishop CRANMER: *On the Lord's Supper,* and *Remains and Letters.* (Ed. J. E. COX.) 1844, 1846.
—— JOHN HOOPER: *Early Writings.* (Ed. S. CARR.) *Later Writings.* (Ed. C. NEVINSON.) 1843, 1852.
—— LATIMER: *Works* and *Remains.* (Ed. G. E. CORRIE.) 1844, 1845.
—— NICHOLAS RIDLEY: *Works.* (Ed. H. CHRISTMAS.) 1841.
CARL PESTALOZZI. *Heinrich Bullinger. Leben und ausgewählte Schriften.* 1857.
FREDRIK PIJPER. *Jan Utenhove. ˘Zijn Lèven en zijne Werken.* 1883.
A. F. POLLARD. *England under Protector Somerset.* 1910.
—— *The Political History of England* (Vol. VI.1547–1603.) 1910.
—— *Thomas Cranmêr and the English Reformation* (1489–1556). Heroes of the Reformation Series. 1904.
THE PRAYER BOOK. *The First Prayer Book of King Edward VI,* 1549, and *The Second Prayer Book of King Edward VI,* 1552. (Ed. W. B.) Reprinted from copies in the British Museum. (Ancient and Modern Library of Theological Literature.)
—— *Liturgies of Edward VI.* (Ed. J. KETTLEY.) Parker Society. 1844.
—— See CARDWELL.

306   BIBLIOGRAPHY

FRANCIS PROCTER. *A History of the Book of Common Prayer with a Rationale of its Offices.* 11th edtn, revised. 1874.
PROCTER and FRERE. *A New History of the Book of Common Prayer on the basis of the former work by F. Procter.* By W. H. FRERE. 1901.
Baron F. DE SCHICKLER. *Les Églises du Refuge en Angleterre.* Vols. I. and III. 1892.
STRYPE (Oxford edtn). *Annals.* 8 vols. 1824.
—— *Cheke.* 1 vol. 1821.
—— *Cranmer.* 2 vols. 1840.
—— *Memorials.* 6 vols. 1822.
—— *Parker.* 3 vols. 1821.
JAN UTENHOVE. *Simplex et fidelis narratio de instituta ac demum dissipata Belgarum, aliorumq̄ peregrinorum in Anglia, Ecclesia.* 1560.
(WILLIAM WHITTINGHAM). *A Brieff discours off the troubles begonne at Franckford in Germany Anno Domini* 1554...*Abowte the Booke off off* [sic] *common prayer and Ceremonies....* 1575.
M. YOUNG. *Life and Times of Aonio Paleario.* 2 vols. 1860.
ZWINGLI. *Eyn kurtze klare sũm und erklärung des christenen gloubēs.* (Ed. LEO JUDA.) 1535?
—— *Ulrich Zwingli: eine Auswahl aus seinem Schriften.* (Ed. G. FINSLER, W. KOHLER, A. RÜEGG.) 1918.

INDEX

DATE DUE

AUG 1 2			
APR 2 8 2008			
MAY 0 2 2008			
GAYLORD			PRINTED IN U.S.A.